THE LITTLE PEARSON HANDBOOK

FOURTH EDITION

LESTER FAIGLEY
University of Texas at Austin

DR MICHAEL CAREY
University of the Sunshine Coast

GABRIELLA MUNOZ

Pearson Australia
707 Collins Street
Melbourne VIC 3008

www.pearson.com.au

Authorised adaptation from the United States edition, entitled THE LITTLE PENGUIN HANDBOOK, 4th Edition by FAIGLEY, LESTER, published by Pearson Education, Inc, Copyright © 2015.

Fourth adaptation edition published by Pearson Australia Group Pty Ltd, Copyright © 2018.

Senior Portfolio Manager: Stephen Heasley
Development Editor: Catherine du Peloux Menage
Project Manager: Bronwyn Smith
Production Manager: Abhishek Agarwal, iEnergizer Aptara®, Ltd
Rights and Permissions Editors: Elizabeth McShane and Claire Gibson
Lead Editor/Copy Editor: Dina Cloete
Proofreader: iEnergizer Aptara®, Ltd
Indexer: iEnergizer Aptara®, Ltd
Cover photographs: top left Cromagnon/Shutterstock; top right luckybusiness/123RF; bottom left Dean Drobot/Shutterstock; bottom right Robert Kneschke/Shutterstock
Typeset by iEnergizer Aptara®, Ltd

Printed in Malaysia (CTP VVP)

1 2 3 4 5 22

National Library of Australia
Cataloguing-in-Publication Data

Creator: Faigley, Lester, author.
Title: The little Pearson handbook / Lester Faigley, Gabriella Munoz, Michael Carey.
Edition: 4th edition.
ISBN: 9781488616846 (paperback)
Notes: Includes index.
Subjects: English language--Rhetoric--Handbooks, manuals, etc.
English language--Grammar--Handbooks, manuals, etc.
English language--Australia.
Other Creators/Contributors:
Munoz, Gabriella, author.
Carey, Michael, author.

Pearson Australia Group Pty Ltd ABN 40 004 245 943

Preface

Students learn best when they can find the information that they need in a handbook without being overwhelmed by detail. Many thousands of students have become better writers with the help of *The Little Pearson Handbook*.

The Little Pearson Handbook 4th Australasian edition has been updated and continues to offer student-friendly features and includes coverage of the most current Harvard, APA, MLA and CMS citation, documentation and style guidelines. The book has been reviewed by a panel of experienced university lecturers. Dr Michael Carey, Senior Lecturer in Education (TESOL) at the University of the Sunshine Coast and Gabriella Munoz, an experienced professional writer have further adapted and updated the book specifically for the Australasian context. This ensures that the handbook reflects the needs of Australasian students.

In this adaptation, Australian English is used alongside many recent Australian examples and cultural references. Updated references to Australian books and journals are featured throughout.

What's new in this edition?

- Expanded treatment of note taking, quoting, summarising and paraphrasing sources help students integrate sources more effectively and avoid plagiarism (Chapters 12 and 13).
- MLA, APA, CMS and Harvard documentation citation examples now include e-books and social media (Twitter and Facebook) referencing information to reflect current usage, as well as providing the latest style updates (Chapters 14–17).
- The chapter on MLA style has been updated and now covers the changes to the works-cited list as well as information on the changes to the in-text citation style in the 8th edition.
- More grammar, usage and punctuation details are given in Parts 5 and 6 to help students build their knowledge and skills to write in formal academic English.
- New **At a glance** sections at the beginning of each chapter provide a quick visual preview of the contents.

With more visuals and sample documents than other essential handbooks, this handy full-colour reference gives students just what they need to know about the writing and research processes.

The Little Pearson Handbook 4th Australasian edition will help students:

- understand complicated academic writing processes step by step
- learn by seeing examples of writing
- quickly find answers to common writing questions
- learn concepts explained in clear, accessible language.

The publishers wish to thank the following reviewers who provided invaluable feedback for the second, third and fourth editions:

Angela Shetler, University of Sydney
Lyn Gannon, Griffith University
Dr Ruth Bacchus, Charles Sturt University
Associate Professor Fiona Bogossian, University of Queensland
Dr Helen Boon, James Cook University
Dr Glenda Cain, University of Notre Dame
Waveney Croft, QUT
Jillian Downing, University of Tasmania
Morris Gland, Deakin University
Dr Marcus Harmes, University of Southern Queensland
Lindy Isdale, Central Queensland University
Dr Sue Lovall, Griffith University
Dr Christopher Klopper, Griffith University
Daryl Nation, Monash University
Dr Lucy Neave, Australian National University
Associate Professor Alison Owens, CQ University
Associate Professor Simon Pyke, University of Adelaide
Dr Donna Satterthwait, University of Tasmania
Associate Professor Fay Sudweeks, Murdoch University
Dr Anne Thwaite, Edith Cowan University
Dr Ben Wadham, Flinders University

Contents

PART 1 Composing

PART 2 Planning Research and Finding Sources

PART 3 Incorporating and Documenting Sources

PART 4 Effective Style and Language

PART 5 Understanding Grammar

PART 1 Composing

1 Think as a Writer

AT A *GLANCE*

- Understand the process of communication (see 1a below)
- Learn how to get readers to take you seriously (see 1c)

1a Think About the Process of Communication

Whether you are writing a paper for a science course, designing your website, sending emails or preparing slides for a sales presentation, you are participating in the complex process of communication. This involves the interaction of three essential elements: the writer or speaker, the audience and the subject. These three elements form the rhetorical situation, which is often represented by a triangle.

Speaker, subject (what you are trying to communicate) and audience are necessary for an act of communication to occur. These three elements interact with each other. Speakers make adjustments to their message depending on the audience. (Think of how you talk to small children.) Just as speakers adjust to audiences, audiences continually adjust to speakers.

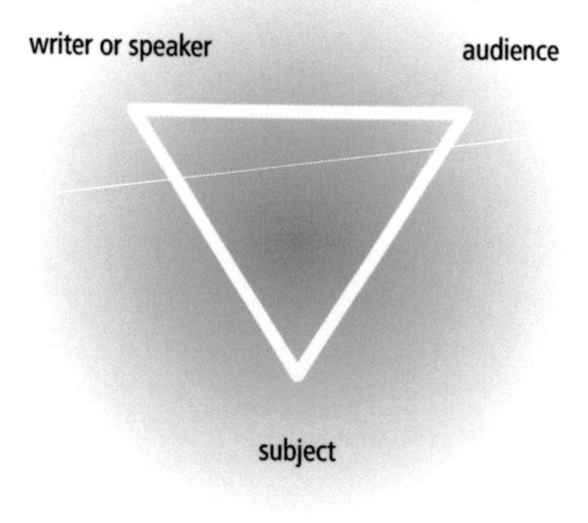

The rhetorical triangle

1b Think About Your Audience

In academic writing, you often produce content for readers you know directly, including your classmates, lecturers and tutors. In the workplace, you may not always know who is going to read your reports or memos. Ask yourself who will read your writing and what kind of information you need to provide to engage them.

SMARTER WRITING

Understand your audience

- Who is most likely to read what you write?
- How much does your audience know about the subject? Are there any key terms or concepts that you will need to explain?
- How interested is your audience likely to be? If they lack interest in your subject, what can you do to engage them?
- What are audience members' attitudes likely to be towards your subject? If they hold attitudes different from yours, how can you get them to consider your views?
- What would motivate your audience to want to read what you write?

1c Think About Your Credibility

Some writers already have credibility with their audience because of who they are—perhaps they are an expert in their field or have published extensively. Most writers, however, have to convince their readers to keep reading by demonstrating knowledge of their subject and concern about their readers' needs.

SMARTER WRITING

Build your credibility

- How can you convince your audience that you are knowledgeable about your subject? Do you need to do research?
- How can you convince your audience that you have their interests in mind?
- What strategies will enhance your credibility? Should you cite experts on your subject? Can you acknowledge opposing positions, indicating that you have taken a balanced view?
- Do the appearance, accuracy and clarity of your writing give you credibility?

2 Read, View and Write with a Critical Eye

AT A *GLANCE*

- Know how to read with a critical eye (see 2a below)
- Analyse visual texts (see 2b)
- Discover how to write with a critical eye (see 2c)

2a Become a Critical Reader

To become a more effective reader, you need a set of strategies while you read. These strategies help you to engage with material through analysis and reflection.

Preview

No subject is ever completely new; it is likely that many people have written and talked about the subject before. Begin by asking the following questions:

- Who wrote this material?
- Where did it first appear? In a book, journal, newspaper or online?
- What is the topic or issue?
- Where does the writer stand on the topic or issue?
- What else has been written about the topic or issue?
- Why was it written?

Summarise

Summarising means using your own words to explain the main ideas of the material you read, so make sure you understand what is at issue. Take your time to read, circle any terms or references that you don't understand and look them up. Ask yourself these questions before writing your summary:

- What is the writer's main claim or question?
- If there doesn't appear to be a specific claim, what is the main focus?
- What are the key ideas or concepts that the writer considers?
- What are the key terms? How does the writer define those terms?

Respond

As you read, write down your thoughts. Ask yourself these questions:

- Do I agree or disagree with the writer's claims? Why, or why not?
- To what points made by the writer should I respond?
- Which ideas might be developed or interpreted differently?
- What do I need to look up to further my understanding?
- How does this help me in my research?

Analyse

On your second or third reading, analyse the structure (the way in which the parts of the material have been organised) using the following questions:

- How is the piece of writing organised?
- What does the writer assume the reader knows and believes?
- Where is the evidence? Can you think of contradictory evidence?
- Does the writer acknowledge opposing views? Does the writer deal fairly with opposing views?
- What kinds of sources are cited? Are they documented? Are the sources credible (that is, are they from a peer-reviewed journal, government or non-government website or an esteemed organisation)?
- How does the writer represent herself or himself? If the author refers to studies, are the methodologies valid and reliable? Has protocol been followed in research (i.e. ethics approvals and so on)?

2b Become a Critical Viewer

Like critical reading, critical viewing requires you to reflect in depth on what you see. Think of an image as a piece of writing that needs to be read to be fully understood. However, learning how to read and understand an image isn't easy because you have to investigate who the creator is, the subject of the image and its history. If it is a moving image, such as a video or film, you will need to find out about the director, writer, producers and actors to fully understand the context in which it was made. Use the following strategies.

Preview

Critical viewing requires thinking about the context first.

- Who created this image?
- What or who is the subject of the image? If it's a public figure, how does their background affect the image?
- Why was it created?
- Where and when did it first appear?
- What media and techniques did the creator use?
- What has been written about the creator or the image?

Respond

Make notes as you view the image with these questions in mind:

- What was my first impression of the image and its subject?
- After thinking more about the image and perhaps reading about it, how has that first impression changed or expanded?

Analyse

The following analytical questions apply primarily to still images.

- How is the image composed or framed?
- Where do my eyes go first?
- How does the image appeal to or confront the values of the audience?
- Was it intended to serve a purpose besides art or entertainment?

The Department of Public Works commissioned the photograph on page 7 in 1932 to document the construction of the Sydney Harbour Bridge. In it we can see more than 40 men posing for the photographer. They were about to start painting the bridge. Their faces are filled with pride as they look out over the coastal city. Most of them are smiling, looking directly at the camera and expressing a sense of mateship, as if they knew this iconic structure would become part of Australia's history.

Another approach to critical viewing is to analyse the content as well as the social context in which the image was taken. The interwar period (1919–1939) changed the world order. Europe's political landscape changed, the United States became a world leader, and women continued their fight for equal rights. Western culture reached one of its peaks during the 1920s and during the 1930s financial markets survived one of

Photograph by the New South Wales Department of Public Works, Sydney
Collection: Museum of Applied Arts & Sciences

their worst crises. The men in 'Harbour Bridge painters on central arch' reflect this historical moment. They have hope. They have jobs and they believe living standards will get better. Their work helped to revitalise the local economy in the midst of the Great Depression, connected Sydney's CBD with the Northern suburbs and provided Australia with one of its quintessential sights.

This photograph remains relevant in today's political climate, and can be contrasted with other iconic images captured during the construction of Chicago's high-rises or San Francisco's Golden Gate Bridge.

2c Become a Critical Thinker and Writer

Now that you have learned how to read words and images with a critical eye, you can use similar strategies to develop your critical thinking skills. By thinking about the context of the material and asking questions about the speaker, subject and audience to come up with your own ideas, you are engaging in the critical thinking process.

Analysing what you are reading or viewing and reflecting on the process of communication will help you to learn how to apply similar techniques in your own communication. You will become a more critical writer as you consider your role as speaker and how you need to adjust your subject to appeal to an audience. Use the following strategies.

Preview

- What is my topic or issue?
- What is my argument or claim for this topic or issue?
- What is my purpose with this piece of writing?
- Who is my audience?

Respond

As you write, think about the topic or issue you are addressing and ask yourself these questions:

- Am I clearly responding to the assignment question?
- Am I responding fully to the arguments or claims made in the materials or sources that I have read and referenced?
- Am I acknowledging opposing views in a balanced, objective way?

Analyse

Just as you have analysed other writers' texts and images, you need to apply the same strategies to engage critically with your own writing. After you have written a draft, set aside time to analyse and reflect with the help of these questions:

- Is my writing organised in a logical way?
- Is my position or thesis statement clearly stated?
- Have I used clear topic sentences to guide the reader?
- Have I supported my writing with evidence? Are my sources credible? Have I documented all my sources?
- Have I used language that is appropriate for my purpose and audience?

For tips on revising, editing and proofreading, see Chapter 4.

3 Plan and Draft

AT A *GLANCE*

- Write a working thesis (see 3b)
- Plan a strategy (see 3c)
- Learn how to write introductions and conclusions (see 3d)

3a Find a Topic and Establish Goals

Lecturers may give you a list of essay questions to choose from, a set assignment or let you come up with your own topic. Whatever the scenario, assignments will contain key words such as *analyse*, *compare and contrast*, *define*, *evaluate* or *discuss*. These words tell you what to do.

- **Analyse:** Break something down into its component parts and determine its essential features.
- **Argue:** Present a logical argument, supporting citations, or evidence for and/or against a proposition.
- **Compare:** Examine how two or more things are similar.
- **Contrast:** Examine how two or more things are different.
- **Cite:** Quote or refer to a book, author, lecture or paper as an authority, proof or example.
- **Define:** Make a claim about how something should be defined.
- **Describe:** Carefully observe, select details and use your own words to give a written account of a situation or topic.
- **Evaluate:** Argue that something is good, bad, best or worst, according to criteria that you set out and define clearly.
- **Propose:** Identify a particular problem and explain why the solution you suggest is the best one.
- **Discuss:** Describe and interpret a perspective through critical examination of all issues relating to the subject. Identify the pros and cons.
- **Report:** Present all the information you have gathered and then make your own assessment.
- **Justify:** Show adequate grounds for decisions or conclusions.

3b Write a Working Thesis

Once you have identified your subject, you need to find a specific focus. This is key to writing a strong essay. If your topic is too broad, you will encounter many problems at the writing stage and your research won't be as effective as it should.

Use questions to focus a broad topic

Childhood obesity might be a current and interesting research topic, but it is too broad. Ask questions that will break a big topic into smaller ones.

- Why are there more obese children today than in past generations?
- How has the food industry contributed to obesity?
- What changes in our culture have contributed to obesity?
- What strategies are effective for preventing childhood obesity?

Consider other angles to expand a narrow topic

Sometimes a topic can become too narrow or limiting. Sugar consumption may be one contributing factor leading to obesity in children, but a narrow focus such as this overlooks other factors that together lead to childhood obesity.

- Why do some children who consume a lot of sugar in the form of lollies and soft drinks maintain a healthy weight?
- Children have always eaten lollies. Why are there more obese children today than in past generations?
- Even when parents limit their child's consumption of sugar, some children still gain weight. Why?

Turn your topic into a thesis or position statement

Your thesis or position statement tells the audience your main idea or claim. Much of the writing that you will do at university and in your career will have an explicit idea or claim, usually stated near the beginning. Your thesis or position statement should be closely tied to your purpose—to reflect on your own experience, to explain some aspect of your topic or to argue for a position or course of action.

A reflective thesis

Watching a group of obese 7-year-old children struggle during gym class has taught me that childhood obesity has long-lasting psychological effects.

An informative thesis

Rates of childhood obesity have continued to increase over the past decade despite increasing awareness of its detrimental effects.

A persuasive thesis

Parents must encourage healthy eating and exercise habits in order to reverse the growing trend towards obesity in children.

Determine Your Organisation

Working outlines

A working outline is an initial sketch of how you will arrange the main sections of your essay or report. Jotting down the main points and a few subpoints before you begin can help you identify potential research and be a great help in your writing.

Formal outlines

A formal outline typically begins with the thesis or position statement, which anchors the entire outline. Each numbered or lettered item clearly supports the thesis, and the relationship between the items is clear from the outline hierarchy. Roman numerals indicate the highest level; next come capital letters, then Arabic numbers and finally lower-case letters. The rule to remember when deciding whether you need to use the next level down is that each level must have at least two items: a '1' needs a '2'; an 'a' needs a 'b'. Formal outlines can be helpful because they force you to look carefully at your organisation and determine if your argument is logical, well supported with evidence and balanced.

Discipline-specific organisation

In the social sciences, research reports typically follow a specific organisation, with an abstract that gives a brief summary of the contents followed by four main sections and a list of references. This organisation allows other researchers to identify information quickly.

1. **Introduction:** identifies the problem, reviews previous research and states the hypothesis that was tested.
2. **Methods section:** describes how the participants were selected and how the experiment was conducted.
3. **Results section:** reports the findings of the study and often includes tables and figures that provide statistical results and tests of statistical significance.
4. **Discussion section:** interprets the findings and often refers to previous research.

For more information on how writing is organised in various disciplines, see Chapter 6.

SMARTER STUDYING

Essay introductions

An essay introduction may need one or more paragraphs depending on the word count of the essay. Its purpose is to establish the content and direction of the essay's argument or discussion for the reader. The format for an essay introduction is expected to include most of the following components:

General lead-in statement

The general lead-in statement usually appears first in your introductory paragraph. It is a restatement of the assignment question and an opportunity to provide some background information on the main concept to be discussed. It is also an opportunity to indicate a broader understanding of the literature and how the focus of the discussion is situated in the discipline. For example, let's look at the question:

'What do we mean by the curriculum and what do teachers need to know in order to engage effectively with curriculum requirements?'

For this question, the lead-in statement may look something like this:

Marsh (2010) states that curriculum is more than the syllabus content prescribed by an education authority; it also encompasses 'what an

(continued on next page)

(continued)

> *individual learner experiences as a result of schooling' (p. 67). This suggests that an effective and authentic learning environment requires the teacher to engage with both the formal and the hidden curriculum.*

Note: If possible, avoid literally restating the assignment question. Although this may not detract from your mark, it is unlikely to add to it either. Remember, if every student submits the same introductory statement, there is little to differentiate a pass mark from a credit, a distinction and a high distinction.

Also, note how the writer refers to the formal and the hidden curriculum. This evidence of wider reading indicates to the audience that the writer has an understanding of the full scope of the curriculum and establishes credibility.

Overview

The overview of points to be discussed throughout the essay must be relevant to your essay's thesis or position statement. The points should be listed in the order that they will be presented throughout the essay, usually opening with the strongest or most relevant point. For example, following on from the general lead-in statement above, an overview of the points to be discussed in the essay may look like this:

> *While a deep knowledge of the syllabus material has been established as a fundamental requisite, it is of equal importance for teachers to acquire classroom management skills. This means that it is also essential to develop relationships with students and the community; an understanding of different learning styles; and a teaching philosophy and style informed by the literature, reflective strategies and student-focused classroom practices.*

Note: If a point is not referred to in your overview, it should not be discussed in your essay. An overview assists you in keeping the line of discussion relevant, so if you find yourself writing about a point that is not listed in your overview, review it and decide whether your argument is straying from the topic, or whether you have found a point that needs to be included in your overview.

Thesis or position statement

The thesis or position statement is a declaration of the writer's viewpoint/argument/perspective in relation to the essay question.

(continued on next page)

In other words, it is your short answer to the essay question. It is very important that the writer situates the thesis statement in the literature of the discipline by supporting it throughout the body of discussion with credible evidence. For example, a thesis or position statement for the essay question referred to above may look like this:

> *It is vital that a teacher exhibits all of these attributes in order to engage effectively with the requirements of the wider curriculum.*

Note: The body of discussion will elaborate upon these attributes of an effective teacher identified in the overview and why they are crucial to effective engagement with the curriculum. Of course, this must involve reference to credible sources through in-text referencing.

Definitions

Definitions may be in a separate paragraph if necessary. For the essay question above, it would be appropriate to define 'curriculum requirements':

> *According to the consultation paper, 'Defining mandatory outcomes in the K–6 curriculum' (Board of Studies NSW, 2004), the curriculum requires that 'Courses of study are to be based on and taught in accordance with the K–6 syllabuses developed by the Board'. However, the Board of Studies NSW refers to areas of schooling outside the formal Key Learning Areas (KLAs) as also forming a part of the curriculum by stating: 'The total activities of students in any year are not limited to those related to Board syllabuses. Schools and school authorities may provide "additional activities"' (2004). Implicit in this statement is the expectation that teachers and schools will manage the needs of their school community, including those that fall outside of the standard curriculum.*

Where do you think this definition should go in the introduction?

Statement of limitations

Although not always required, a statement of limitations can be important if answering an essay question that covers a broad subject area. This statement is simply a sentence that specifies the parameters or the scope of the essay. A limiting statement for the above essay question would probably refer to the fact that the essay deals specifically with the Australian education system in New South Wales.

Write Effective Introductions and Conclusions

Effective beginning paragraphs capture the reader's interest and set the tone for the piece. Think of them as a hook—a juicy sentence that will pique the reader's interest.

Start beginning paragraphs with a bang

Try beginning with one of the following strategies to get your reader's attention.

A concisely stated thesis

If property prices continue to increase across Australia's capital cities, most people under the age of 35 won't be able to buy property and will need to rent throughout their lifetime and possibly face homelessness.

Imagery

Beds, couches and old toys are piled outside a five-bedroom house near Canberra where families that cannot pay rent seek temporarily refuge. When you step inside, you can smell the desperation. When and where will these families find a new home?

A problem

Economists worry about Australia's property boom because it seems to be copying the same model that created the US housing bubble and led to the global financial crisis of 2008. An Australian financial crisis would see an increase in the number of homeless families in the country.

Conclude with strength

Use the ending paragraph to touch on your key points, but don't merely summarise. Leave your readers with something that will inspire them to continue to think about what you have written.

Issue a call to action

Urging our leaders to create a new housing policy is a step we need to take to protect the more than 105,000 homeless people in Australia, as well as the families who have been evicted because they cannot afford rent or couldn't find a place to stay after their lease expired.

Make recommendations

The state governments of New South Wales and Victoria ought to implement rent-control programs that take into consideration the number of people who live on the premises and the weekly payments they can afford. Such programs would guarantee familes have a place to live in major cities like Sydney and Melbourne.

Speculate about the future

Unless the six states agree to redesign planning laws and make sure there are enough affordable housing spaces across the nation, the number of homeless families may double within the next five years.

Write Effective Paragraphs

In an academic essay, the body of paragraphs should follow the sequence of key points outlined in your introduction (See Smarter Studying, page 13). Effective paragraphs examine these key points in the context of their relevance to the thesis or position statement. To achieve this, the paragraphs themselves should adhere to a structure. The Point-Explanation-Evidence-Link (PEEL) paragraph structure is a useful model to apply.

Let's take a closer look at a paragraph formatted according to the PEEL structure. The paragraph below could be included in the body of discussion in response to the following question:

'What do we mean by the curriculum and what do teachers need to know in order to engage effectively with curriculum requirements?'

Point

The first sentence is a topic sentence, stating the key point that will be discussed in that paragraph. The key point must be included in the introductory paragraph's overview. The key point in this example is that teachers need to be thoroughly knowledgeable about the subject matter they are teaching:

According to Shulman (as cited in Marsh, 2010), a deep knowledge of the formal curriculum content is one of the fundamental components to successful teaching practice.

Explanation

The next few sentences are a demonstration of your understanding of this key point by explaining and elaborating upon elemental aspects. For example, this may include basic assumptions or principles, underlying theories or models. It may be necessary to include an in-text reference. In this example, the explanatory sentences provide background information on the elements of the curriculum and its context of NSW:

In the context of the NSW curriculum, this means teachers should acquire a thorough understanding of the subject matter referred to in the Board of Studies NSW syllabus documents. The K–6 syllabus documents and supporting materials are organised according to Key Learning Areas (KLAs) and these include: English; Mathematics; Science & Technology; Human Society & Its Environment; Personal Development, Health & Physical Education; and Creative Arts (Board of Studies NSW, 2012). Although these documents do not include background information for all units of work, they do provide a framework for teachers to research the topics and related content.

Evidence

The discussion of a key point must be supported by evidence from credible sources. This may include such things as examples, definitions, data, facts, statistics, references to case studies, findings and recommendations from reports and curriculum documents. All evidence must be referenced in the text. In this example, these sentences summarise the structure and content of the syllabus documents. They connect the need for teachers to be thoroughly knowledgeable across the subject matter of syllabus units to Marsh's perception of successful teaching and achieving learning outcomes:

Teachers are expected to integrate the curriculum expectations or learning outcomes with their knowledge of the subject matter and produce a program of instruction to be implemented in their classroom (Marsh, 2010). A program of instruction includes activities that facilitate student learning, in addition to assessments that gauge the effectiveness of the lessons and the skills and knowledge attained by the students.

Link

The purpose of concluding sentences is twofold. First, they link your discussion of this key point to your thesis or position statement in the introductory paragraph. In other words, they establish the relevance, to your argument, of the evidence presented. Second, they can provide a link to the following paragraph, introducing either the next key point or another supporting paragraph for the key point at hand. In this example, the first two linking sentences connect the key point to the thesis or position statement in the introduction (which in this case is 'It is vital that a teacher exhibits all of these attributes in order to engage effectively with the requirements of the wider curriculum'). The last linking sentence provides a verbal bridge to the paragraph that follows by suggesting there are other points that play a significant role in effectively teaching the curriculum:

> *Therefore, in order to achieve the prescribed outcomes attributed to each KLA, it is essential for primary teachers to actively engage with the K–6 syllabus. Furthermore, they should be guided by these documents in expanding their knowledge of the subject matter and apply this knowledge to their teaching/learning activities. However, it must be established that although fundamental to successful teaching practice, deep knowledge of the subject matter alone is not sufficient to engage effectively with the wider curriculum.*

3f Focus Your Paragraphs

Often writers will begin a paragraph with one idea, then other ideas occur to them while they are writing and are included. When paragraphs go in different directions, they confuse readers. When you revise your paragraphs, check for focus. Ensure you keep the discussion to one idea per paragraph. Sometimes, particularly when you are writing essays with a word requirement of more than 1000 words, you may need to split the discussion of a key point into several paragraphs. To do this effectively, identify the subpoints that make up the discussion of a key point and write a paragraph for each. Remember that it's not about the length of the paragraph, but about its content. Aim for short, concise, clear paragraphs that leave your readers wanting more.

4 Revise, Edit and Proofread

AT A *GLANCE*

- Use strategies for rewriting (see 4b)
- Edit for specific goals (see 4c)
- Get some useful proofreading tips (see 4d)

Don't think that just because you have finished writing your assignment, your work is done. Experienced writers evaluate their material several times before submitting it. To ensure your assignment shines, revise, edit and proofread it more than once.

4a How to Evaluate Your Draft

Use the following questions to make sure your assignment meets all the requirements.

- Does your paper or project meet the assignment requirements?
- Does your writing have a clear focus that reflects your position?
- Are your main points adequately developed?
- Can you make your writing clearer by rearranging sections or key points?
- Do you consider your readers' knowledge and points of view?
- Do you conclude emphatically?

When you finish answering these questions, make a list of your goals for the revision.

4b Learn Strategies for Rewriting

1. **Keep your audience in mind**. Reread each paragraph's opening sentence and ask yourself whether the language is strong and engaging enough to keep your reader interested. Make sure each

paragraph communicates clear ideas and evaluate whether you need to split the longer ones in two or more to ensure clarity.

2. **Sharpen your focus wherever possible**. Revise your thesis or position statement and supporting paragraphs as needed. Check to see that your focus remains consistent throughout the essay.
3. **Check that key terms are adequately defined**. What are your key terms? Are they defined precisely enough to be meaningful and appropriate for the context of your discussion?
4. **Develop where necessary**. Key points and claims may need more explanation and supporting evidence.
5. **Check links between paragraphs**. Underline the first and last sentences of each paragraph in your paper. Do these sentences together make a logical argument?
6. **Consider your title**. Be as specific as you can in your title, and, if possible, suggest your stance. The 'title:subtitle' format is common in academic writing, particularly in the humanities. For example: 'The Subaltern Revolution: A Marxist Reading of Bangladesh's Microcredit System'.
7. **Consider your introduction**. In the introduction you want to get off to a fast start and convince your reader to keep reading.
8. **Consider your conclusion**. Try to leave your reader with something interesting and provocative.

4c Edit for Specific Goals

1. **Check the connections between sentences**. If you need to signal a relationship between one sentence and the next, use a transitional word or phrase (words like *for example, furthermore, however, in contrast, next, similarly, therefore, hence*).
2. **Check the flow of your sentences**. If you notice that a sentence is hard to read or doesn't sound right when you read it aloud, rephrase it.
3. **Eliminate wordiness**. See how many words you can take out without losing the main meaning of your sentences (see Chapter 19).

4. **Use active verbs**. Any time you can use a verb other than a form of *be* (*is*, *are*, *was*, *were*) or a verb ending in *–ing*, take advantage of the opportunity to make your style more lively (see Section 18b).
5. **Use specific and inclusive language**. As you read, stay alert for any vague words or phrases. Check to make sure that you have used inclusive language throughout (see Chapter 21).

4d Proofread Carefully

1. **Know what your spelling and grammar checker can and can't do**. Spelling and grammar checkers don't catch words that are used incorrectly (e.g. 'to much' should be 'too much'), missing endings (e.g. 'three dog' should be 'three dogs') and other similar errors.
2. **Check for grammar and mechanics**. Nothing hurts your credibility with readers more than a text with numerous errors. Set your dictionary default to English (Australia) or English (UK) to minimise inconsistencies and errors.

4e Review the Writing of Others

Your lecturer may ask you to review your classmates' drafts.

1. **Begin with the big picture**. Evaluate your classmate's draft using the questions in Section 4a about whether the project meets the assignment requirements and so on.
2. **Call attention to local problems last**. After you have checked for global problems, such as clarity, help your classmate by identifying local problems: sentence construction, word choice and errors.
3. **Write a letter to the writer**. Summarise your comments for your classmate, focusing on global problems first.

SMARTER WRITING

Proofread like a pro

When you proofread your assignment, you are examining it to find and correct mistakes. Take your time and read each word and sentence more than once to ensure there are no errors that may take points off your final mark. Answer these questions when you are proofreading.

- Does every sentence make sense? Does every sentence have a subject and a predicate?
- Is my spelling consistent (i.e. is everything written in Australian English)? Am I sure there are no typographical errors?
- Are there any grammatical problems? Have I corrected them?
- Are my citations consistent throughout the paper (same referencing style)?
- Have I clearly identified any direct quotes? Have I clearly attributed any ideas I paraphrased?
- Have I checked the names of all the authors cited in my assignment? Are their names spelled correctly?
- Have I made sure that the figures, tables and other visual information are identified correctly?

For tips on grammar, see Part 5.

5 Write Arguments

AT A *GLANCE*

- Find an arguable topic (see 5b)
- Write a position argument (see 5c)
- Write a proposal argument (see 5e)

Write Position Arguments and Proposal Arguments

How you develop a written argument depends on your goals. You may want to convince your readers to change their way of thinking about an issue or perhaps get them to consider the issue from your perspective. Or you may want your readers to take some course of action based on your argument. These two kinds of arguments can be characterised as **position** and **proposal arguments**.

5b Find an Arguable Topic and Make a Claim

Position arguments often take two forms—definition arguments and rebuttal arguments.

Definition arguments. People argue about definitions (for example, is graffiti vandalism or art?) because of the consequences of some things being defined in a certain way. If you can get your audience to accept your definition, then usually your argument will be successful.

Definition arguments take the form shown here:

> Something is (or is not) ______________ because it has (or does not have) Criteria A, Criteria B and Criteria C (or more).

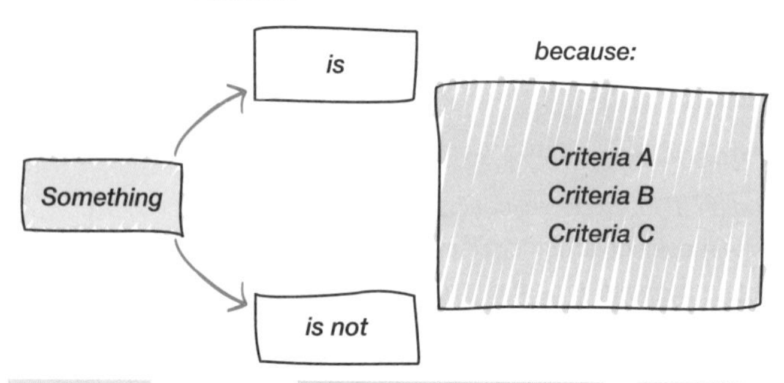

Graffiti is art because it is a means of self-expression, it shows an understanding of design principles and it stimulates both the senses and the mind.

Rebuttal arguments. Rebuttal arguments take the opposite position. You can challenge the criteria a writer uses to make a definition or you can challenge the evidence that supports the claim if it is incomplete or wrong. Sometimes you can find counterevidence. Often when you rebut an argument, you identify one or more fallacies in that argument.

Rebuttal arguments take this form:

The opposing argument has serious shortcomings that undermine the claim

flawed reason 1
flawed reason 2

The great white shark gained a false reputation as a 'man eater' from the 1975 movie Jaws, but in fact shark attacks on humans are rare and most bites have been 'test bites', which is common shark behaviour towards unfamiliar objects.

Supporting claims with reasons

The difference between a slogan, such as *Oppose candidate X*, and an arguable claim, such as *Oppose candidate X because they will not lower taxes or improve schools*, is the presence of a reason linked to the claim. A reason is typically offered in a **because clause**, a statement that begins with the word *because* and provides a supporting reason for the claim. The word *because* signals a **link** between the reason and the claim.

Organise and Write a Position Argument

Before you write

Think about your readers

- What do your readers already know about the subject?
- What is their attitude towards the subject? If it is different from your position, how can you address the difference?
- What are the chances of changing the opinions and beliefs of your readers? If your readers are unlikely to be persuaded, can you get them to at least acknowledge that your position is reasonable?
- Are there any sensitive issues you should be aware of in relation to your argument?

Write an introduction

Engage your readers quickly

- Get your readers' attention with an example of what is at stake.
- Define the subject or issue.
- State your thesis to announce your position.

3 Organise and write the body of your paper

Develop reasons

- Can you argue from a definition? Is ______ a ______?

  EXAMPLES

  Is design art or craft?

  Are zoos guilty of cruelty to animals?
- Can you compare and contrast? Is ______ like or unlike ______?
- Can you argue that something is good (better, bad, worse)?
- Can you argue that something caused (or may cause) something else?
- Can you refute objections to your position?

Support reasons with evidence

- Can you support your reasons by going to a site and making first-hand observations?
- Can you find facts, statistics or statements from authorities to support your reasons?

Consider opposing views

- Acknowledge other stakeholders for the issue, and consider their positions.
- Explain why your position is preferable.
- Make counterarguments if necessary.

4 Write a conclusion

End with more than a summary

- First, summarise key points and how they are relevant to the position you have established throughout the essay.
- You can then reinforce what is at stake or give an example that gets at the heart of the issue.

5 Revise, revise, revise

Evaluate your draft

- Make sure your position argument meets the assignment requirements.
- Can you sharpen your thesis statement to make your position argument clearer?
- Can you add other reasons to strengthen your argument?
- Can you supply additional evidence?
- When you have finished revising, edit and proofread carefully.

5d Make a Proposal

Every day we hear and read arguments that encourage us to take action. We even make these arguments ourselves: we should eat better; we should sleep more; we should achieve a better work–life balance. Convincing others to take action for change is always hard. Other people may not see the problem that you see or may not think it is important. Nevertheless, most people aren't satisfied with doing nothing when they think that what is at stake is important.

In a proposal argument, you present a course of action in response to a recognisable problem. The proposal says what can be done to improve the situation or to change it altogether.

1. You define the problem.
2. You propose a solution or solutions.
   and
3. You explain why the solution is feasible and why it will work.

Proposal arguments take the form shown here.

SOMEONE should (or should not) do SOMETHING because ______

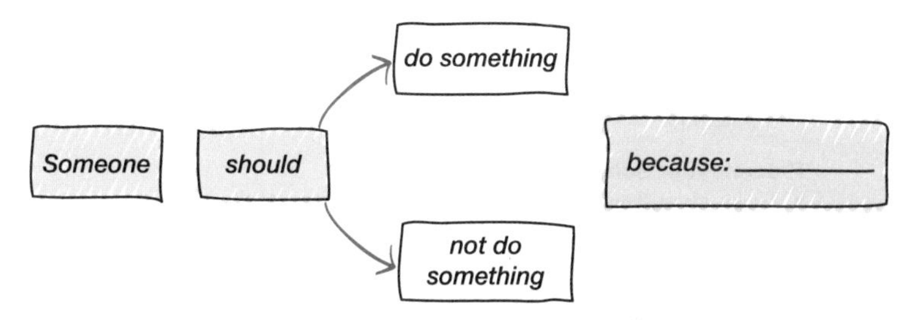

The Simply Healthy@Schools Sleep Program should be implemented in all schools because more than one-third of children don't get enough sleep at night. The program would help children increase their productivity and have better learning outcomes.

Organise and Write a Proposal Argument

1 Before you write

Think about your readers

- How much are your readers affected by the problem you are addressing?
- Do your readers agree that the problem you are addressing is important?
- If your readers are unaware of the problem, how can you use evidence to convince them that solving the problem is important?

2 Write an introduction

Identify the problem

- Do background research on what has been written about the problem and what solutions have been attempted.
- Summarise the problem for your readers and identify whose interests are at stake.
- Describe what is likely to happen if the problem isn't addressed.

3 Organise and write the body of your paper

Describe other solutions that have been proposed or attempted

- Explain why other solutions don't solve the problem or are unrealistic.

Present your solution

- Make clear the goals of your solution. Some solutions do not completely solve the problem.
- Describe the steps of your proposal in detail.
- Describe the positive consequences (or how negative consequences might be avoided) as a result of your proposal.

Argue that your solution can be done

- Your proposal is a good idea only if it can be put into practice, so you need to explain how it is feasible.
- If your proposal requires money, explain where the money will come from.
- If your proposal requires people to change their present behaviour, explain how they can be convinced to change.

4 Write a conclusion

End with a call to action

- Think about shared community values (such as fairness, justice or clean air and water) that you might raise with your readers.
- Put your readers in the position that, if they agree with you, they will take action.
- Explain exactly what they need to do.

5 Revise, revise, revise

Evaluate your draft

- Make sure your proposal argument meets the requirements of the assignment.
- Can you better explain the problem or provide more evidence about it?
- Can you add more evidence that your proposal will solve the problem?
- Do you explain why your solution is better than other possible solutions?
- When you have finished revising, edit and proofread carefully.

You can read an example proposal in Section 16h.

6 Write in Academic Genres

AT A *GLANCE*

- Write an observation (see 6a below)
- Write a critical analysis (see 6b)
- Write a case study (see 6c)
- Write a scientific report (see 6d)
- Write an essay exam (see 6e)

6a Write an Observation

Observations are common in the natural sciences and in social science disciplines such as psychology, sociology and education. They begin as notes taken first-hand by the writer. Observations should include as many relevant and specific details as possible.

Elements of an observation

Title	Include a precise title.
Description and context	Be specific about what or whom you are observing. How did you limit your site or subject? What background information do readers need?
Record of observations	Report what you observed in some logical order: chronologically, from most obvious features to least obvious, or in some other pattern.
Conclusion or summary	Give your readers a framework in which to understand your observations. What conclusions can you draw from them? What questions are left unanswered?

What you need to do

- Carry a notebook and make extensive field notes. Provide as much information as possible about the activities you observe.
- Record in your notebook exactly when you arrived and left, where you were and exactly what you saw and heard.
- Analyse your observations before you write about them. Identify patterns, and organise your report according to those patterns. Situate your analysis in the literature of the discipline.

Sample observation

Animal Activity in Kambah Pool
from 15 April to 22 April 2016

Kambah Pool is a popular swimming spot on the shores of the Murrumbidgee River in Canberra. Situated along the Murrumbidgee River Corridor, the natural swimming area is both a wildlife habitat and a busy hub of human activity; it offers sandy beaches, hiking trails, picnic tables and public toilets.

My first observation was on 15 April from 1.45 pm to 4 pm on a warm sunny day with an air temperature of 23 °C. I used a mask and snorkel to observe below the water. It was remarkable how oblivious people and wildlife were of each other. While from 40 to 55 people splashed on the surface, many fish (mostly Murray cod with two large spiny freshwater crayfish on the bottom) swam below them, and large numbers of yabbies crept along the rocky portion of the pool's bottom. Eight small Macquarie turtles alternately swam at the surface and dived below near the dam at the deep end. Twelve endangered trout cod (*Maccullochella macquariensis*), ranging in colour from bright orange to paler yellow, were active by the larger spring at the centre of the pool.

Specific times, weather conditions, numbers of individual species and behaviours are recorded.

At the times when humans are not present or nearly absent, animal activity noticeably increases. From the side of the pool on 16 April (clear, 22 °C) from 5.25 pm until closing at 6 pm, I observed two platypi coming up for air while feeding on small yabbies and freshwater mussels. Nine ducks (seven freckled ducks and two mallards) landed on the pool at 5.40 pm and remained when I left. (Freckled ducks migrate to the area in large numbers in the winter; the mallards are probably domesticated ducks.) A pair of blue-winged shovelers (male and female) were also on the cliff above the shallow end.

Write a Critical Analysis

The goal of a critical analysis is to understand how a particular act of writing or speaking influenced particular people at a particular time. Writing a critical analysis (also called a 'textual analysis') is frequently assigned in university.

Elements of a critical analysis

Introduction	Begin your analysis by giving the necessary background.
The context	Explain the relationship between the piece of writing or speaking and the larger cultural and historical circumstances in which it was produced.
The text	Describe how the writer or speaker builds credibility (*ethos*), appeals to the values and emotions of the audience (*pathos*) and uses intellectual reasoning (*logos*). Look at how the organisation and style support the author's purpose.
Conclusion	Draw implications from your analysis.

What you need to do

- **Examine the author.** What was the author's purpose: to change beliefs? to inspire action? to amuse?
- **Examine the audience.** Who was the intended audience? What were their attitudes and beliefs?
- **Examine the larger context.** Why did this text appear at this particular time? What else was going on in society?
- **Examine the kind of text.** A speech? An essay? A letter? An advertisement? An editorial? What are the expectations or conventions of this kind of text?
- **Examine the content.** What is the author's main idea or claim? How is the idea or claim supported?
- **Examine the language and style.** Is the style formal or informal? Does the author use humour? What metaphors or other figurative language are used?

Sample page from a critical analysis

On 9 August 2016, Australians were required to complete the national census for the Australian Bureau of Statistics (ABS). For the first time, Australians were given the option to complete the census online, or by the

(continued)

traditional method of a paper form. Also, for the first time, Australians were required to include their name and address on the form—an issue that caused some dissent from the public and some Federal government senators. Speculation also circulated that the whole online process could crash if the expected peak online traffic of up to 200 online form submissions per second proved too much for the system.

As predicted by some, the online submission process began to crash for users only hours after opening and was immediately shut down. The incident has received much media coverage fuelled by several recent embarrassing incidents experienced by the returned Malcolm Turnbull Coalition government.

An online article on the fallout of this incident, reported by ABC political reporters Anna Henderson, Stephanie Anderson and Francis Keany presented a balanced argument by presenting the views of those responsible: Prime Minister Malcolm Turnbull, the ABS and the software contractor IBM, but also the views of the Labor opposition party leader, Bill Shorten. However, the quotes from these players which were selected to exemplify these views could be seen as excessively emotive, divisive and blaming in tone. For example, the article reported that Labor had criticised the Prime Minister for distancing his Government from blame, with Opposition Leader Bill Shorten describing the unfolding events as 'one of the biggest shambles in government'. Conversely, Mr Turnbull deflected the blame from his party by stating the problems were 'predictable' and the ABS-contracted service provider IBM should have been prepared.

The introduction establishes the necessary background.

The context is established by describing the cultural and political circumstances.

The online article is critiqued for the balance of argument (partial or impartial) and the way that the writers selected quotes from the main players in the story to exemplify their views.

6c Write a Case Study

Case studies are used in a wide range of fields, such as nursing, psychology, business and anthropology. Case studies are narrow in focus, providing a rich, detailed portrait of a specific event or subject.

Elements of a case study

Introduction	Explain the purpose of your study and how or why you selected your subject. Use language appropriate to your discipline, and specify the boundaries of your study.
Methodology	Explain the theories or formal process that guided your observations and analysis during the study.
Observations	Describe the 'case' of the subject under study by writing a narrative, utilising interviews, research and other data to provide as much detail and specificity as possible.
Discussion	Explain how the variables in your case might interact. Don't generalise from your case to a larger context; stay within the limits of what you have observed.
Conclusion	What does all this information add up to? What is implied, suggested or proven by your observations? Situate your analysis in the literature of the discipline. What new questions arise?
References	Using the appropriate format, cite all of the outside sources you have used. (See Chapter 14 for Harvard Documentation and Chapter 15 for APA Documentation.)

What you need to do

- Understand the specific elements of your assignment. Ask your lecturer about what your case study should include.
- Use careful observation and precise, detailed description to provide a complex picture with a narrow focus.
- Write your observations in the form of a narrative, placing yourself in the background (avoid using *I* or *me*).
- Analyse your findings and interpret their possible meanings, but draw your conclusions from the observed facts.

Sample case study

Some disciplines require title pages. See Section 15g for an example of an APA title page.

Young children and screen time

Introduction

Young children are exposed to a range of digital devices (e.g., computers, mobile phones, TV) from birth and their use of digital media is rapidly increasing (Livingstone, 2014). The constant evolution of digital technology impacts upon the types of digital experiences pre-schoolers engage

(continued)

in at home which in turn shapes early development in potentially positive and negative ways (Karuppiah, 2015). This has led to increased concerns about screen time which are reflected in Australian Government policy screen time guidelines for pre-schooler use of screen-based digital devices (Australian Government, 2014). Government policy restricts children under two to no screen time and 2 to 5 year olds to less than an hour per day (Australian Government, 2014). The present study aims to provide a current snapshot of the home digital environment in a sample of Australian families to firstly determine which digital devices are currently most popular among pre-schoolers and to measure child screen time.

The introduction identifies both the problem and the particular subject of the case study.

Discussion

The present study showed that TVs and tablets in this sample of Australian families were the most popular digital devices used by pre-schoolers. The average daily time pre-schoolers in the present study spent watching TV was less (80 mins/day) than the mean time reported in an Australian National report of 2 to 5 year olds (Sweetser et al., 2012; 120 mins/day). More households had mobile computers compared with traditional desktop computers with over 80% of families owning one or more tablets, perhaps reflecting a shifting home preference to mobile computers. Children's average TV screen time alone (80 mins) exceeded the National daily screen time recommendation (Australian Government, 2014). In contrast, parents reported that children only spent 20 minutes on tablets which is less than UK pre-schoolers who use tablets on average for 79 mins per day (Marsh et al., 2015).

Conclusion

National screen time policies exist to discourage parents from allowing pre-schoolers to be physically inactive for extended periods of time. However, these recommendations do not differentiate between types of digital devices or directly takes into account individual family circumstances. A one-size-fits-all screen time guideline may not be the

(continued on next page)

The conclusion sums up what has been observed. Many case studies don't give definitive answers but rather raise further questions to explore.

best way to address screen time concerns. In order to provide a stronger rationale for these guidelines, policy recommendations should be presented in a more flexible way that takes into account different digital devices and the purpose of digital activities. Furthermore, providing family-based strategies such as helping parents create a mindful approach to digital technology may assist in positively shaping pre-schoolers' early development.

6d Write a Scientific Report

Scientific reports follow a strict structure, enabling specialists in a given field to quickly assess the experimental methods and findings in any report. Check with your lecturer about the specific elements required for your scientific report.

Elements of a scientific report

Title	State exactly what was tested, using language specific to the field.
Abstract	Briefly state the questions and the findings in the report.
Introduction	Give the full context of the problem, defining the hypothesis being tested.
Methods	Describe the materials used as well as the method of investigation. Your methods and procedure sections should be specific enough to allow another researcher to replicate your experiment.
Procedure	Step by step, narrate exactly what you did and what happened. In most fields, you will use the passive voice.
Results	State the outcomes you obtained, providing carefully labelled charts and graphics as needed.
Discussion	State why you think you got the results you did, using your results to explain. If there were anomalies in your data, note them as well.
Conclusion	Briefly, what was learned from this experiment? What still needs to be investigated?
References	Using the appropriate format, cite all of the outside sources you have used. (See Chapter 14 for science lab reports and Chapter 15 for psychology scientific reports.)

What you need to do

- Understand the question you are researching or the hypothesis you are testing and the process you will use before you begin. If you need clarification, ask your lecturer.
- Take thorough notes at each step of the process. You may be asked to keep a notebook with a specific format for recording data. Review your notes before you begin drafting your report.
- Don't get ahead of yourself. Keep the methods, procedure, discussion and conclusion sections separate. Remember that other scientists will look at specific sections of your report expecting to find certain kinds of information. If that information isn't where they expect it to be, your report won't make sense.
- Write your abstract last. Writing all the other sections of the report first will give you a much clearer picture of your findings.

Sample scientific report

Wave interference in visible light using the double-slit method

Abstract

Filtered light was projected through one slit in a piece of cardboard, producing a single bar of light, brightest in the centre and shaded darker towards the edges, on the wall behind the cardboard. When a second slit was added to the cardboard, the projected image changed to alternating bands of bright light and darkness. The conclusion reached is that wavelength patterns in the light cancelled or reinforced one another as they reached the wall, increasing or decreasing the observed light. These results are consistent with the wave theory of light.

6e Write an Essay Exam

Lecturers use essay exams to test your understanding of course concepts and to assess your ability to analyse ideas independently. To demonstrate these skills, you must write an essay that responds directly and fully to the question being asked. References to the literature on the subject are not required in an exam, unless it is an open-book exam.

Elements of an essay exam

Introduction	Briefly restate the question, summarising the answer you will provide.
Body	Each paragraph should address a major element of the question.
Paragraphs	Order them so the reader can tell how you are responding to the question.
Conclusion	*Briefly* restate your answer to the question, not the question itself.

What you need to do

- Make sure you understand the question and what is required. Respond with the kinds of information and analysis the question asks you to provide.
- Plan your response before you begin writing, using an outline, list or diagram. Note how much time you have to write your response and plan accordingly.
- Address each element of the question and provide supporting evidence.
- Relate the point of each paragraph clearly to the larger argument.
- Save a few minutes to proofread and add information where needed.

Sample exam essay

HIS 312: Australian History Describe the political and cultural variables that contributed to the forced removal of Aboriginal and Torres Strait Islander children from their families and communities, establishing the Stolen Generations.

Amy Zhao began her response to the essay question by jotting down ideas for each of the two categories mentioned. Her outline also served as a map for the structure of her essay.

political	cultural
white Australia policies	racist ideologies of inferiority
assimilation legislation	lack of knowledge or respect for Indigenous culture

A combination of cultural and political variables brought about the separation of Aboriginal and Torres Strait Islander children from their families and the establishment of the Stolen Generations. Most important among these variables were the racist ideologies, limited cultural awareness and legislative policies that dominated the period.

Amy uses the key terms from the question to indicate where she is addressing that element of the question.

Racist ideologies have been present in Australia since its colonisation by the British and subsequent claiming of land rights. Beginning with official policies in the early 1900s, the decision to forcibly remove Indigenous children from their families and place them in non-Indigenous family homes and institutions was viewed by the dominant white society as a positive step that would improve the lives of such children. White Australians established such homes and institutions with the goal of assimilating a race of people whom they viewed as inferior. Such racist ideologies were supported by political motivations for power and limited knowledge or respect of Aboriginal and Torres Strait Islander culture, and ultimately led to the Stolen Generations.

Credit

7 Write for Online Courses

AT A *GLANCE*

- Use courseware (see 7a below)
- Keep track of online coursework (see 7b)
- Participate in online course discussions (see 7c)

7a Use Courseware

Whatever course management system your discipline uses, take advantage early in the semester of tutorials and help documents that guide you in how to email, post to a discussion or submit an assignment for your course. After the course begins, you will want to be comfortable with these features. Even if you will not be face-to-face with your lecturer, you'll need to know when to ask for help.

7b Keep Track of Online Coursework

Plan your time

Online courses require self-discipline and strong organisation to keep your work on track. At the beginning of the term, use the course syllabus or online course schedule to create your own detailed schedule to be sure you keep up with reading and assignments. Some students choose to use a traditional planner; others do well using an online calendar or other reminders. The important thing is to stay on top of due dates.

Then, stick to the schedule you have outlined. Know the course policy for late assignments, written work and participation. The sooner you start the work for the course, the better. As in any other class, keeping up with reading and due dates is essential. Many students who take online courses report that it is especially important not to fall behind. Without the reminders that face-to-face interaction in the classroom can provide, it is up to you to remember what you should be working on and when.

Stay organised

Hard-drive failure or Internet service interruptions tend to happen when it is least convenient. As in any course, be sure you back up files as a regular part of your routine. Technical problems will not excuse you from online work. Plan to have alternative ways to access the Internet, email and your course materials if your usual means of access is down.

Staying connected also means keeping up with communication from your lecturer and participating in required discussion forums or other online activities. Regardless of whether your class meets only online or both online and face-to-face, success in online courses comes when you participate fully in the community and discussions.

7c Participate in Online Course Discussions

Your lecturer is likely to give specific instructions about how often you are required to participate in online discussion forums and may also specify the number and kinds of posts you must make. If you aren't sure about discussion requirements, ask your lecturer. Once the class has begun, read earlier posts carefully as you choose how to make a point in a class discussion.

When you are posting the first entry in a discussion thread, give your post a clear, specific subject line that lets readers know what you are writing about before they open it. For new or response posts, offer the context (the assignment or reading name), the date and name of a previous post or other background information.

Discussion post assignment

Discussion #2: Visual signs

Think of some clothing or style that is popular among your friends: tattoos, baseball caps, piercings, jewellery, runners and so on. Interview a friend who wears the item and photograph him or her, focusing on the item. Upload the photo to the discussion board.
Write a post of 250–400 words about the significance of the item and what it says about the generation that values it.

Discussion post

Thread: Expressing your personality through clothing: bright and bold
Author: Lindsey Rodriguez
Posted date: Thursday, 6 October 2016, 4.54.31 pm AEST
Edited date: Thursday, 6 October 2016, 4.58.23 pm AEST

Clear subject line repeats assignment language.

Clothing is one of the many ways people can visually display their personality. From basics like dresses, pants or skirts to accessories like scarves, hats or jewellery, people can pick and choose what suits their style. For some, the emphasis will be on functionality. For others, clothing is a way to make a statement about who you are, even before you say anything.

Photograph responds to assignment and shows details described in post.

For example, wearing bright, colourful patterns is a way to call attention to your clothing choice. While some patterns might be subtle and muted in tones, there is nothing subtle about layering a striped blue jacket

(continued)

over a fluorescent T-shirt and pairing it with a blue lace skirt and ripped pink stockings. This is one example of the type of outfit that Annie Wang wears every day. If you were to visit her flat and leaf through her wardrobe, you would not be able to find a single piece of black, white or grey clothing. For Annie, colourful patterns are an expression of her inner self, and she sees that self as loud, bright and cheerful.

Annie's sense of fashion is unlike anything I've seen before. She seems to effortlessly put together outfits that clash in a way that works. When I first met her, she was standing in the queue for coffee on campus, and she was wearing a striped neon yellow dress over teal lace tights, with bright red flats to top it off. But as outrageous as her fashion sense seemed to me at first glance, it was also obvious how comfortable Annie was with her choices. She laughed boisterously, gesturing wildly as she described a night out to her friend. I would find out later that Annie was an art student, and she viewed her childhood experimentations with clothing as her first attempts at artistic expression. Clothing was more than a functional necessity—it was a statement. Like many of her classmates, Annie expresses herself through her fashion choices. For her, that means matching her outfits to her mood for the day, choosing from an overstuffed wardrobe of colour and pattern.

Post relates results of interview.

As fashion continues to evolve and trends come and go, people will always find a way to express themselves through their clothing. For Annie and her generation, bold patterns and bright colours are one way to express their youth, creativity and individualism as they experiment with their identity and style.

Post length is appropriate to assignment.

7d Observe Netiquette

In online courses, your discussion posts, wiki entries and other written work speak for and create an impression of you. Your lecturer and classmates will rely on your comments and conversations in writing to relate to you and assess your ideas. Follow commonsense rules of netiquette.

- **Remember your classmates are people like you.** Address them by name, if possible, and sign your post with your name. Don't say things online that you would not say to a classmate face-to-face.
- **Be aware of tone.** Sarcasm and attempts at humour often come off badly when you are having a discussion online. Also, writing in all capital letters equates to shouting in online discussions. Therefore, only use capital letters for normal grammar and punctuation purposes.
- **Be a forgiving reader.** You don't need to point out every minor error. If you feel strongly about a mistake, send the writer a private email rather than communicating with the entire class.
- **Keep the discussion civil.** A reply like 'what a stupid idea' can lead to a flame war with name-calling, and the possibility of exploring an issue ends.
- **Don't spam your classmates.** Refrain from sending off-topic messages to everyone. Your classmates have enough to sort through without having to deal with frivolous messages.
- **Make yourself credible.** Check for punctuation, grammar and spelling errors before you post.

Photo credit

PART 2 Planning Research and Finding Sources

Research Map: Conducting Research

University research writing requires that you:

- find a topic
- determine your goals
- ask questions about your topic
- find out what has been written about your topic
- evaluate what has been written about your topic, and
- make a contribution to the discussion about that topic.

Here are the steps in planning research and finding sources.

1 Plan the research project

First, analyse what you are being asked to do; go to Section 8a.

Ask a question about a topic that interests you and narrow that topic; go to 8b.

Determine what kinds of research you will need; go to 8c.

Conduct field research if it is appropriate for your project. See strategies for

- **CONDUCTING INTERVIEWS:** go to 11b.
- **ADMINISTERING SURVEYS:** go to 11c.
- **MAKING OBSERVATIONS:** go to 11d.

2 Draft a working thesis

Draft a working thesis; go to 8d.

Create a working bibliography; go to 8e.

3 Find and track sources

Consult a research librarian if possible, and determine where and how to start looking.

Find sources online and in print:

- For sources in **DATABASES**, go to 9b.
- For sources on the **WEB**, go to 9c.
- For **VISUAL SOURCES**, go to 9d.
- For **PRINT SOURCES**, go to 9e.

Keep track of sources; go to 9f.

4 Evaluate sources

Decide which sources are going to be useful for your project. For each source you'll need to determine the:

- **RELEVANCE** to your research question; go to 10a.

Evaluate the different types of sources you are using:

- **DATABASE** and **PRINT SOURCES:** go to 10b.
- **WEB SOURCES:** go to 10c.

8 Plan Your Research

AT A *GLANCE*

- Analyse your assigment (see 8a below)
- Find and narrow a topic (see 8b)
- Draft a working thesis (see 8d)

8a Analyse the Research Task

If you have an assignment that requires research, look closely at what you are being asked to do.

Look for words that signal what is expected

- An *analysis* or *examination* asks you to look at an issue in detail, explaining its history, the people and places affected, and what is at stake.
- A *review of scholarship* requires you to summarise what key scholars and researchers have written about the issue.
- An *evaluation* requires you to make critical judgments.
- An *argument* requires you to assemble evidence in support of a claim you make.

Identify your potential readers

- How familiar are your readers with your subject?
- What background information will you need to supply?
- If your subject is controversial, what opinions or beliefs are your readers likely to hold?
- If some readers are likely to disagree with you, how can you convince them?

Assess the project's length, scope and requirements

- What kind of research are you being asked to do?
- What is the length of the project?

- What kinds and number of sources or field research are required?
- Which documentation style—such as Harvard (see Chapter 14) or APA (see Chapter 15)—is required?

8b Find and Narrow Your Topic

Begin by doing one or more of the following:

- **Visit 'Research by Subject' on your library's website.** Clicking on a subject such as 'Australian Literature' will take you to a list of online resources. Often you can find an email link to a reference librarian who can assist you. If there is no email address, go to the library and ask for help.
- **Look for topics in your courses.** Browse your course notes and readings. Are there any topics you might want to explore in greater depth?
- **Browse public libraries and other online resources. Visiting your State Library,** Trove (trove.nla.gov.au) or the Library of Congress Virtual Reference Shelf (www.loc.gov/rr/askalib/virtualref.html) may help you identify sites, periodicals, maps and images relevant to your topic.
- **Consult a specialised encyclopedia.** Specialised encyclopedias focus on a single area of knowledge, go into some depth about a subject and often include bibliographies. Check if your library database page has a link to the Gale Virtual Reference Library, which offers entries from many specialised encyclopedias and reference sources.
- **Look for topics as you read.** When you read actively, you ask questions and respond to ideas in the text. Review all your notes, you may find a potential topic there.

It can be tricky to find a balance between what you want to say about a topic and the amount of space you have to say it in. Usually your lecturer or tutor will suggest a length for your project, which should help you decide how to limit your topic. If you suspect your topic is becoming unmanageable and the project may be too long, look for ways to narrow your focus.

Off track	A five-page paper on Australian musical films
On track	A five-page paper exploring race and culture in the Australian musical films *Bran Nue Dae* and *The Sapphires*
Off track	A ten-page paper on accounting fraud
On track	A ten-page paper examining how a new law would help prevent corporate accounting fraud

8c Determine What Kind of Research You Need

When you begin your research, you will have to make a few educated guesses about where to look. Ask these questions before you start:

- How much information do you need? The assignment may specify a minimum number of sources you should consult.
- Are particular types of sources required? If so, do you understand why those sources are required and where to find them?
- How current should the information be? Some assignments require you to use the most up-to-date information you can locate.

Secondary research

Most people who do research rely partly or exclusively on the work of others as sources of information. Research based on the work of others is called **secondary research**. Chapters 9 and 10 explain in detail how to find and evaluate database, Web and print sources.

Primary research

Much of the research done at a university creates new information through **primary research:** experiments; data-gathering surveys and interviews; detailed observations and the examination of historical documents. Chapter 11 explains how to plan and conduct three types of field research: interviews (11b), surveys (11c) and observations (11d).

8d Draft a Working Thesis

If you ask a focused and interesting research question, your answer will be your **working thesis.** This working thesis will be the focus of the remainder of your research and ultimately of your research project.

Ask questions about your topic

When you have a topic that is interesting to you, manageable in scope and possible to research using sources or doing field research, then your next task is to ask researchable questions.

Explore a definition

- While many (most) people think X is a Y, can X be better thought of as a Z?

  Most people think of deer as harmless animals that are benign to the environment, but their overpopulation devastates young trees in forests, leading to loss of habitat for birds and other species that depend on those trees.

Evaluate a person, activity or thing

- Can you argue that a person, activity or thing is either good, better or best (or bad, worse or worst) within its class?

  Netflix remains the most relevant streaming service in the world because of its original content and the way it is redefining television.

Examine why something happened

- Can you argue that, while there were obvious causes of Y, Y would not have occurred had it not been for X?

  University students are called irresponsible when they run up high credit card debts that they cannot pay off, but these debts would not have occurred if credit card companies did not aggressively market cards and offer high lines of credit to students with no income.

- Can you argue for an alternative cause rather than the one many people assume?

  ANZAC Day may be seen by many as simply the anniversary of the first major military action of Australian and New Zealand Army Corps in Gallipoli during World War I, but in fact the day of remembrance has come to signify a national identity rooted in the service and sacrifice of our veterans.

Counter-objections to a position

- Can the reverse or opposite of an opposing claim be argued?

  New medications that relieve pain are welcomed by runners and other athletes, but these drugs also mask signals that our bodies send us, increasing the risk of serious injury.

Propose a solution to a problem

- Can you propose a solution to a local problem?

  Our local council must make sure that new urban developments include green areas and are properly serviced by public transport, to avoid traffic congestion and guarantee people's well-being.

Turn your answers into a working thesis

Topic	Reading disorders
Researchable question	Why do some people learn to read top-to-bottom Chinese characters more easily than left-to-right alphabetic writing?
Working thesis	The direction of text flow may be an important factor in how an individual learns to read.

8e Create a Working Bibliography

When you begin to collect sources, get full bibliographic information for everything you might want to use in your project: articles, books, websites and other materials. Decide which documentation style you will use. If your lecturer does not specify a style, ask them. (The major documentation styles—Harvard, APA, MLA and CMS—are dealt with in detail in Chapters 14–17.) Consider installing a program such as Endnote on your computer. You can maintain a reference library easily by entering the requirement elements manually or by directly exporting from a database. Speak with a university librarian for advice regarding the most suitable program for you.

In general, as you research and develop a working bibliography, the rule of thumb is to write down more information rather than less. You can always delete unnecessary information when the time comes to format your citations according to your chosen documentation style.

SMARTER WRITING

Know when to stop researching and start writing

With so many resources readily available, it is easy to spend a lot of time reading background information that you will not need for your project. You may also feel the need to review as many papers as you can on the subject to demonstrate that your research has been extensive. However, it is important to be efficient when it comes to university work, and give yourself enough time to write a compelling essay that reflects your hard work. Bear in mind that your markers will not give you a higher mark just because you have a long bibliography. Your mark will only be affected by the quality of your argument. Answer these questions to know when to stop researching and start writing:

- Can you answer your working thesis?
- Do you have enough information to offer a solution? Does your solution makes sense?
- Do you have enough evidence to back your claims?
- Have you identified the key discussions and scholarship on your topic?

If the answer is yes to all of them, it is time to start writing.

9 Find Sources

AT A *GLANCE*

- Find sources in databases (see 9b)
- Find sources on the Web (see 9c)
- Keep track of sources (see 9f)

9a Develop Strategies for Finding Sources

Libraries still contain many resources not available on the Web. Even more importantly, libraries have professional research librarians who can help you locate sources quickly.

Learn the art of effective keyword searches

Keyword searches take you to the sources you need. Start with your working thesis and generate a list of possible keywords to facilitate your search.

First, think of keyword combinations that make your search **more specific.** For example, a search for sources related to youth voter participation might focus more specifically on young adults *and*:

voter registration
historical participation rates, or
voter turnout.

Also, think about **more general** ways to describe what you are doing—what synonyms can you think of for your existing terms? Instead of relying on 'young adult', try keywords such as:

under 30
Millennials, and
university students.

Use a thesaurus to find synonyms for your keywords.

SMARTER WRITING

Find the right kinds of sources

Type of source	Type of information	How to find them
Scholarly books	Extensive and in-depth coverage of nearly any subject	Library catalogue
Scholarly journals	Reports of new knowledge and research findings by experts	Online library databases
Trade journals	Reports of information pertaining to specific industries, professions and products	Online library databases
Popular magazines	Reports of summaries of current news, sports, fashion and entertainment subjects	Online library databases and through Web searches
Newspapers	Recent and current information; foreign newspapers are useful for international perspectives	Online library databases and through Web searches
Government publications	Government-collected statistics, studies and reports; especially good for science and medicine	Library catalogue and local, state and federal government websites
Videos, audio files, documentaries, maps	Information varies widely	Library catalogue, Web and online library databases

9b Find Sources in Databases

Sources found through library databases have already been filtered for you by trained librarians. They will include some common sources such as popular magazines and newspapers, and will give you access to many journals, abstracts, studies, e-books and other writing produced by specialists whose work has been peer-reviewed. Databases are a great tool because most of the time you'll find all the information that you need there, which makes your research more time efficient.

How to use databases

Your library has a list of databases and indexes by subject. If you can't find this list on your library's website, ask a reference librarian for help. Follow these steps to find articles:

1. Select a database appropriate to your subject. (For example, if you are researching breast cancer, you might start with *Health Reference Centre*, *MEDLINE*, *PsycINFO* or *PubMed*.)
2. Search the database using your list of keywords. (You could start with *breast cancer* and then combine *breast cancer* with other terms, such as treatments, to narrow your search.)
3. Once you have chosen an article and identified the complete citation, make a PDF, print or email it to yourself (look for the email link after you click on the item you want). Saving the full text is better than cutting and pasting because you might lose track of which words are yours, leading to unintentional plagiarism. If you are using a program such as EndNote, add the reference to your library.
4. If the full text is not available, check the online library catalogue to see if your library has the journal. When you cannot find a journal, book or paper, ask a librarian. Most libraries have agreements with other institutions that may have the text you are looking for. Don't forget to check your local or state library as well.

SMARTER WRITING

Know the advantages of database versus Web sources

	Library database sources	Web sources
Speed	✓ Users can find information quickly	✓ Users can find information quickly
Accessibility	✓ Available 24/7	✓ Available 24/7
Organisation	✓ Materials are organised for efficient search and retrieval	Users must look in many different places for information
Consistency and quality	✓ Librarians review and select resources	Anyone can claim to be an 'expert', regardless of qualifications
Comprehensiveness	✓ Collected sources represent a wide and representative body of knowledge	No guarantee that the full breadth of an issue will be represented
Permanence	✓ Materials remain available for many years	Materials can disappear or change in an instant
Free of overt bias	✓ Even sources with a definite agenda are required to meet certain standards of documentation and intellectual rigour	Sources are often a soapbox for organisations or individuals with particular agendas and little knowledge or experience
Free of commercial slant	✓ Because libraries pay for their collections, sources are largely commercial-free	Sources are often motivated primarily by the desire to sell you something

Common databases

Academic OneFile	Indexes, periodicals from the arts, humanities, science, social sciences and general news, with full-text articles and images
Academic Search Premier and **Complete**	Provide full-text articles for thousands of scholarly publications
ArticleFirst	Indexes journals in business, humanities, medicine, science and social sciences
Business Search Premier	Provides full-text articles in all business disciplines
EBSCOhost Research Databases	Gateway to a large collection of EBSCO databases, including *Academic Search Premier* and *Complete*, *Business Source Premier* and *Complete*, *ERIC* and *Medline*
Google Books	Allows you to search within books and gives you snippets surrounding search terms for copyrighted books; many books out of copyright have the full text; available for everyone
Google Scholar	Searches scholarly literature according to criteria of relevance; available for everyone
General OneFile	Contains millions of full-text articles about a wide range of academic and general-interest topics
JSTOR	Provides scanned copies of scholarly journals
LexisNexis Academic	Provides the full text of a wide range of newspapers, magazines, government and legal documents, and company profiles from around the world
ProQuest Databases	Like EBSCOhost, ProQuest is a gateway to a large collection of databases with over 100 billion pages, including the best archives of doctoral dissertations and historical newspapers

Other useful databases are accessible through the National Library of Australia (www.nla.gov.au), the state libraries (www.sl.nsw.gov.au, www.sl.vic.gov.au, etc.) and the Australian Bureau of Statistics (www.abs.gov.au).

9c Find Sources on the Web

The Web offers you some resources for current topics that would be difficult or impossible to find in a library. The key to success is knowing where you are most likely to find current and accurate information about the particular question you are researching and knowing how to access that information.

Use search engines wisely

Search engines designed for the Web work in ways similar to library databases and your library's online catalogue, but with one major difference: databases typically do some screening of the items they list, whereas search engines potentially take you to everything on the Web—billions of pages in all.

Most search engines offer you the option of an advanced search, which gives you the opportunity to limit search results. The advanced searches on *Google* and *Yahoo!* give you the options of using a string of words to search for sites that contain all the words, the exact phrase or any of the words, or that do not contain certain terms. They also allow you to specify the site, the date range, the file format and the domain. For example, if you want to limit a search for *breast cancer* to Australian government websites such as the Department of Health and Ageing, you can specify the domain as **.gov.au.**

Find online government sources

The federal government has made many of its publications available on the Web. Often the most current and most reliable statistics are government statistics. Among the more important government resources are the following:

- **Australian Bureau of Statistics** (www.abs.gov.au). Source for official Australian government statistics on a wide range of economic and social matters.

- **Australian Department of Foreign Affairs and Trade** (www.dfat.gov.au). Source for information on other countries and regions, including details of their history, government, political conditions, economy and foreign relations.
- **Australian Institute of Health and Welfare** (www.aihw.gov.au). Resource for information on Australia's health and welfare.
- **National Library of Australia** (www.nla.gov.au). Many of the resources of the largest library in Australia are available here.
- **Australian Commonwealth Government** (www.australia.gov.au). The place to start when you are not sure where to look for government information.
- **Australian Department of Industry, Innovation and Science** (www.industry.gov.au) The who's who of Australian science and a good place to find the latest Australian science news.

Find online reference sources

Your library's website may have a link to **reference sites**, either on the main page or under another heading such as **research tools**.

Reference sites are usually organised by subject, and you can find resources under the subject heading:

- **Business information** (links to business databases and sites such as Hoover's that profile companies)
- **Dictionaries** (including the *Macquarie Dictionary* and various subject dictionaries and language dictionaries)
- **Encyclopedias** (including *Britannica Online* and others)
- **Reference books** (commonly used books such as atlases, almanacs, biographies, handbooks and histories)

Search interactive media

Several search engines have been developed for interactive media. Facebook and Twitter also have search engines for their sites.

SMARTER WRITING

Know the limitations of Wikipedia

Wikipedia is a valuable resource for popular culture topics that are not covered in traditional encyclopedias. You can find out how many Guinness world records Shane Crawford has set, the modified rules of women's Australian Rules football, the most recent inductees into the Rock and Roll Hall of Fame, and the all-time highest-grossing films.

Nevertheless, many lecturers and the scholarly community in general do not consider Wikipedia a reliable source of information for a research project. This is not because the information may be incorrect but because Wikipedia and other wikis change constantly. The underlying idea of documenting sources is that readers can consult the same sources that you consulted. To be on the safe side, treat Wikipedia as you would a blog. Consult more reliable sources to confirm what you find on Wikipedia, and cite those sources to establish your credibility.

Discussion list search engines

- **Google Groups** (groups.google.com). Archives discussion forums dating back to 1981.
- **Yahoo! Groups** (groups.yahoo.com). A directory of groups by subject.

Blog search engines

- **Google Blog Search** (blogsearch.google.com). Searches blogs in several languages besides English.
- **IceRocket** (blogs.icerocket.com). Searches blogs, Myspace and Twitter.
- **Wordpress Blog search** (en.search.wordpress.com). Searches in more than 3 million blogs created with this platform.

9d Find Multimedia Sources

Massive collections of images, audio files (including podcasts), videos, maps, charts and other resources are now available on the Web.

Find images

The major search engines for images include the following:

- **Bing Images** (www.bing.com/images)
- **Google Image Search** (images.google.com)
- **Picsearch** (www.picsearch.com)
- **Yahoo! Image Search** (images.search.yahoo.com)

Libraries and museums also offer large collections of images.

Find videos

- **Bing Videos** (www.bing.com/videos)
- **Google Videos** (video.google.com)
- **Ted** (ted.com)
- **Yahoo! Video Search** (video.search.yahoo.com)
- **YouTube** (www.youtube.com)
- **Vimeo** (vimeo.com)

Find podcasts

- **iTunes Podcast Resources** (www.apple.com)
- **PodcastDirectory.com** (www.podcastdirectory.com)

Find charts, graphs and maps

You can find statistical data represented in charts and graphs on many statistical and geographical websites.

- **Australian Bureau of Statistics** (www.abs.gov.au)
- **Google Earth** (earth.google.com)
- **National Geographic Map Machine** (www.nationalgeographic.com)

Respect copyright

Although images, videos and other multimedia files are easy to download from the Web, it does not mean that everything is available for you to use legally. Look for the creator's copyright notice or creative commons licence and suggested credit line. These will tell you if you can reproduce the multimedia file. If you aren't sure, contact the creator via email or through their social media channels and ask for permission.

 Find Print Sources

No matter how current the topic you are researching, you will probably find information in print sources that is simply not available online. Print sources have other advantages as well:

- Books are shelved according to subject, allowing easy browsing.
- Books often have bibliographies, directing you to other research on the subject.
- You can search for books in multiple ways: author, title, subject or call number.
- The majority of print sources have been evaluated by scholars, editors and publishers, who decided whether they merited publication.

Find books

The floors of your library where books are shelved are referred to as 'the stacks'. The call number will enable you to find the item in the stacks. You will need to consult the locations guide for your library, which gives the level and section where an item is shelved.

Find journal articles

Like books, scholarly journals provide in-depth examinations of subjects. The articles in scholarly journals are written by experts, and they usually contain lists of references that can guide you to other research on a subject.

Some lecturers frown on using popular magazines, but these journals can be valuable for researching current opinion on a particular topic. Some widely known magazines, such as *Popular Science,* have been around for more than 100 years and can be used as primary sources for historical research. Databases increasingly contain the full text of articles, allowing you to read and save the contents onto your computer.

 Keep Track of Sources

As you begin to collect your sources, make sure you get full bibliographic information for everything you might want to use in your project.

Decide which documentation style you will use. (The major documentation styles—Harvard, APA, MLA and CMS—are dealt with in detail in Chapters 14–17.)

Locate elements of a citation in database sources

For any source you find on a database, MLA style requires you to provide the full print information, the name of the database in italics and the URL or DOI. The 8th edition of the MLA Handbook provides an easy-to-follow template that tells you what information to include and in which order (see Chapter 16).

Author(s)	McGuirk, Rod
Title of article	"Australian Carbon Tax on its Way Out"
Publication information	
Name of periodical	*Great Falls Tribune* [Great Falls, Mont]
Date of publication (and edition for newspapers)	7 July 2014
Section and page number	A5
Database information	
Name of database	*ProQuest*
Date you accessed the site	28 Apr. 2015

The citation would appear as follows in an MLA-style works-cited list (see Section 16e):

> McGuirk, Rod. "Australian Carbon Tax on its Way Out." *Great Falls Tribune,* 7 July 2014, p. A5. *ProQuest,* search.proquest.com.ezproxy/central/docview/1543308176/88E19EE85776468APQ/.

APA style no longer requires listing the names of common databases or listing the date of access, unless the content is likely to change (see Section 15e). If you name the database, do not list the URL.

> McGuirk, R. (2014, July 07). Australian carbon tax on its way out. *Great Falls Tribune*, p. A5. Retrieved from ProQuest database.

The citation would appear as follows in the Harvard-style references list:

McGuirk, R 2014, 'Australian carbon tax on its way out', *Great Falls Tribune*, 7 July, p. A5, viewed 28 April 2015 from ProQuest database.

Locate elements of a citation in Web sources

As you conduct your online research, make sure you collect the necessary bibliographic information for everything you might want to use as a source. Because of the potential volatility of Web sources (they can and do disappear overnight), their citations require extra information. You'll arrange this information in different ways depending on the citation format you use.

Collect the following information about a website. The example below is an article in a magazine published on the Web.

Author(s), if available (if not, use the associated institution or organisation)	McDonald, Jody
Title of article	For the Love of Birds
Publication information	
Name of site or online journal	*Overland.org.au*
Sponsoring organisation if available	Overland
Date of publication (for an article) or of site's last update	2 September 2016
Date you accessed the site	15 October 2016
URL	https://overland.org.au/2016/09/for-the-love-of-birds/

An MLA-style works-cited entry for this article would look like this:

McDonald, Jody. "For the Love of Birds." *Overland.org.au*. 2 Sept. 2016, overland.org.au/2016/09/for-the-love-of-birds/.

In an APA-style references list, the citation would look like this:

McDonald, J. (2016, September 02). For the Love of Birds. *Overland.org.au*. Retrieved from https://overland.org.au/2016/09/for-the-love-of-birds/

In a Harvard-style references list, the citation would look like this:

> McDonald, J 2016, 'For the Love of Birds', *Overland.org.au*, 2 September, viewed 15 October 2016, https://overland.org.au/2016/09/for-the-love-of-birds/

You will find more examples of how to cite Web sources in MLA style in Section 16f, in APA style in Section 15e and in Harvard style in Section 14g.

Locate elements of a citation in print sources

For books, you will need at minimum the following information, which can typically be found on the front and back of the title page.

Author(s)	Graham Brown and Karon Hepner
Title of the book	*The Waiter's Handbook*
Publication information	
Edition	4th
Place of publication	Sydney
Name of publisher	Pearson Australia
Date of publication	2012
Medium of publication	Print

Here's how the book would be cited in an MLA-style works-cited list.

> Brown, Graham, and Karon Hepner. *The Waiter's Handbook*. 4th ed, Pearson Australia, 2012.

Here's the APA-style citation for the same book:

> Brown, G. & Hepner, K. (2012). *The waiter's handbook*, (4th ed.). Sydney, NSW: Pearson Australia.

Here's the Harvard-style citation for the same book:

> Brown, G & Hepner, K 2012, *The waiter's handbook*, 4th edn, Pearson Australia, Sydney.

You will also need the page numbers if you are quoting directly or referring to a specific passage, and the title and author of the individual chapter if your source is an edited book with contributions by several people.

For journals you will need the following:

Author(s)	Diplock, Jane
Title of article	"The Global Financial Architecture: Twenty-first Century Solutions"
Publication information	
Name of journal	*Australian Accounting Review*
Volume number (and issue number if paginated by issue)	19(3)
Date of publication (and edition for newspapers)	2012
Page numbers of the article	155–60
Medium of publication	Print
Document Object Identifier (DOI), if available, for APA and MLA	10.1080/02773940903413407

An entry in an MLA-style works-cited list would look like this:

Diplock, Jane. "The Global Financial Architecture: Twenty-first Century Solutions." *Australian Accounting Review*, vol. 19, no. 3, 2012, pp. 155–60, 10.1080/02773940903413407

And in APA style, it would look like this:

Diplock, J. (2012). The global financial architecture: Twenty-first century solutions. *Australian Accounting Review, 19*(3), 155–160. doi:10.1080/02773940903413407

And in Harvard style, like this:

Diplock, J 2012, 'The global financial architecture: twenty-first century solutions', *Australian Accounting Review*, vol. 3, no. 19, pp. 155–60, doi: 10.1080/02773940903413407

10 Evaluate Sources

AT A *GLANCE*

- Importance and relevance of sources (see 10a below)
- How to evaluate database and print sources (see 10b)
- Evaluate Web sources (see 10c)

10a Determine the Relevance of Sources

Use these guidelines to determine the importance and relevance of your sources to your research question.

- Do you need to consult primary or secondary sources, or both?
- Does a source you have found address your research question?
- Does a source support or disagree with your thesis? (Include work that challenges your views. Representing opposing views accurately enhances credibility.)
- Does a source add significant information?
- Is the source current? (For most topics, find the most up-to-date information.)
- What indications of possible bias do you note in the source?

10b Evaluate Database and Print Sources

Books are expensive to print and distribute, so publishers generally protect their investment by providing some level of editorial oversight. Printed and online materials in your library undergo another review by professional librarians who select them to include in their collections. Library database collections, which your library pays to access, are also screened, which eliminates many poor-quality sources.

However, this initial screening doesn't free you from the responsibility of evaluating the quality of the sources. Many printed and database sources contain their share of inaccurate, misleading and biased information. Also, all sources carry the risk of being outdated when you are looking for current information.

SMARTER WRITING

Checklist for evaluating database and print sources

In your research, apply the criteria librarians have developed for evaluating sources.

1. **Source.** Who published the book or article? Enter the publisher's name on Google or another search engine to learn about the publisher. Scholarly books and articles in peer-reviewed journals are generally more reliable than popular magazines and books, which may emphasise the sensational or entertaining at the expense of accuracy and comprehensiveness.
2. **Author.** Who wrote the book or article? What are the author's qualifications? Enter the name on a search engine to learn more about the author. Does the author represent an organisation?
3. **Timeliness.** How current is the source? If your topic is a fast-developing subject like treating ADHD, currency is crucial. Even historical topics are subject to controversy or revision.
4. **Evidence.** Where does the evidence come from—facts, interviews, observations, surveys or experiments? Is the evidence adequate to support the author's claims?
5. **Biases.** Can you detect particular biases on the part of the author? How do the author's biases affect the interpretation offered?
6. **Advertising.** For print sources, is advertising a prominent part of the journal or newspaper? How might the ads affect the credibility or the biases of the information that gets printed?

10c Evaluate Web Sources

Nearly every large company and political and advocacy organisation has a website. Readers expect these sites to represent the company or the point of view of the organisation. Many sites on the Web, however, are not so clearly labelled.

SMARTER WRITING

Checklist for evaluating Web sources

Use these criteria for evaluating websites:

1. **Source.** What organisation sponsors the website? Look for the site's owner at the top or bottom of the home page or in the Web address. Enter the owner's name on Google or another search engine to learn about the organisation. If a website doesn't indicate ownership, you have to make a judgment about who put it up and why.
2. **Author.** Is the author identified? (Look for an 'About Us' link if you see no author listed.) Enter the name in a search engine to learn more about the author. Websites often give no information about their authors other than an email address or Twitter handle, and sometimes not even that. That makes it difficult or impossible to determine the author's qualifications. Be cautious about information on anonymous sites.
3. **Purpose.** Is the website trying to sell you something? Many websites are infomercials that might contain useful information, but they are no more trustworthy than other forms of advertising. Is the purpose to entertain? To inform? To persuade?
4. **Timeliness.** When was the website last updated? Look for a date on the home page. Many Web pages do not list when they were last updated, thus you cannot determine their currency.
5. **Evidence.** Are sources of information listed? Factual information should be supported by indicating where the information came from—reliable websites will list and link to their sources.
6. **Biases.** Does the website offer a balanced point of view? Many websites conceal their attitude with a reasonable tone and seemingly factual evidence such as statistics. Citations and bibliographies do not ensure that a site is reliable. Look carefully at the links and sources cited, and peruse the 'About Us' link if one is available.

11 Plan Field Research

AT A *GLANCE*

- Prepare your interview (see 11b)
- Design and administer surveys (see 11c)
- How to make detailed observations (see 11d)

11a Know What You Can Obtain from Field Research

Even though much of the research you do for university courses will be secondary research conducted at a computer or in the library, some topics do call for primary research, requiring you to gather information on your own. Field research of this kind can be vital for exploring local issues. It is also used extensively in professions that you may be joining after university.

Be aware that the ethics of conducting field research require you to inform people about the purpose of your paper or project. If you are uncertain about the ethics of doing field research, talk to your lecturer.

The three most common types of field research that can be conducted at university are **interviews, surveys** and **observations**.

- **Interviews.** Interviewing experts on your research topic can help build your knowledge base. You can also use interviews to discover what the people most affected by a particular issue are thinking and feeling.
- **Surveys.** Small surveys can often provide insight on local issues.
- **Observations.** Local observations can also be a valuable source of data. For example, if you are researching why a particular office on your campus doesn't operate efficiently, you might observe what happens when students enter and how they are handled by the staff.

11b Conduct Interviews

Before you contact anyone to ask for an interview, think carefully about your goals; knowing what you want to find out through your interviews will help you determine which people you need to interview and what questions you need to ask.

- Decide what you want or need to know and who can best provide that information for you.
- Schedule each interview in advance and let the person know why you are conducting the interview.
- Plan your questions in advance. Write down a few questions and have a few more in mind. Listen carefully so you can follow up on key points.
- Come prepared with a notebook and pen for taking notes and jotting down short quotations. Record the date, time, place and subject of the interview. If you want to record the interview, ask for permission in advance.
- When you are finished, thank your subject and ask his or her permission to get in touch again if you have additional questions.
- When you are ready to incorporate the interview into a paper or project, think about what you want to highlight about the interview and which direct quotations to include.
- Sometimes people may not have time for a face-to-face interview, but might answer questions via email. In that case, prepare your questions as if you were having a face-to-face interview. Add an open-ended question such as 'Is there anything else you would like to add?' at the end to let your interviewees expand on any particular issues. Give them a deadline so that they know when they have to reply. Follow up if necessary.

11c Design and Administer Surveys

Use surveys to find out what groups of people think (or are willing to admit they think) about a topic. Surveys need to be carefully designed.

- Write a few specific questions. To make sure your questions are clear, test them on friends or classmates before you conduct the survey.
- Include one or two open-ended questions, such as 'What do you like about X?' or 'What don't you like about X?' Open-ended questions can be difficult to interpret, but sometimes they turn up information you didn't anticipate.
- Decide which people you need to survey and how many people to include. If you want to claim that the results of your survey represent the views of international students, your method of selecting

respondents should give all students an equal chance of being selected. Don't select only your friends.

- Decide how you will contact participants in your survey. If you are going to mail or email your survey, include a statement about what the survey is for and a deadline for returning it. You may need to get permission to conduct a survey in a public place. Don't forget about free online survey software, such as SurveyMonkey (surveymonkey.com), which can save time.
- Think about how you will interpret your survey. Multiple-choice formats make data easy to tabulate, but often they miss key information. Open-ended questions will require you to figure out a way to analyse responses.
- When writing about the results, be sure to include information about who participated in the survey, how the participants were selected and when and how the survey was administered.

11d Make Observations

Observing what goes on in a place can be an effective research tool. Your observations can inform a controversy or topic by providing a vivid picture of real-world activity.

- Choose a place where you can observe with the least intrusion. The less people wonder about what you are doing, the better.
- Carry a notebook and write extensive field notes. Get down as much information as you can, and don't worry about analysing it until later.
- Record the date, exactly where you were, exactly when you arrived and left, and important details such as the number of people present.
- Write on one side of your notebook so you can use the facing page to note key observations and analyse your data later.

At some point you have to interpret the data. When you analyse your observations, think about what constitutes normal and unusual activities for this place. What can you determine about the purposes of these activities?

PART 3 Incorporating and Documenting Sources

12 Understand and Avoid Plagiarism

AT A *GLANCE*

- Types of plagiarism (see 12a below)
- Understand how to quote sources correctly (see 12c)
- Differences between summarising and paraphrasing (see 12d)

12a What is Plagiarism?

Plagiarism means claiming credit for someone else's intellectual work, no matter whether it's to make money or to get a better grade. Intentional or not, plagiarism has dire consequences. A number of famous people have had their reputations tarnished by accusations of plagiarism, and several journalists have lost their jobs and careers for copying the work of other writers and passing it off as their own.

Deliberate plagiarism

If you buy a paper on the Web, copy someone else's paper word for word, or take an article off the Web and turn it in as yours, it's plain stealing, and people who take that risk should know that the punishment will be severe—usually failure for the course and sometimes expulsion. Deliberate plagiarism is easy for your lecturers to spot because they recognise shifts in style, and it is easy for them to use search engines to find the sources of work stolen from the Web.

Patch plagiarism

Some students view the Internet as a big free buffet where they can grab anything, paste it in a file, and submit it as their own work. Other students intend to submit work that is their own, but they commit patch plagiarism because they aren't careful in taking notes to distinguish the words of others from their own words.

What you are required to acknowledge

The following sources should be acknowledged with an in-text citation and an entry in the list of references (Harvard and APA styles), the list of works cited (MLA style) or the bibliography (CMS style).

- **Quotations.** Short quotations should be enclosed within quotation marks, and long quotations should be indented as a block quotation. See Section 13b for how to integrate quotations with signal phrases.
- **Summaries and paraphrases.** Summaries represent the author's argument in miniature as accurately as possible. Paraphrases restate the author's argument in your own words and your own sentence structure.
- **Facts that are not common knowledge.** For facts that are not easily found in general reference works, cite the source.
- **Ideas that are not common knowledge.** The sources of theories, analyses, statements of opinion and arguable claims should be cited.
- **Statistics, research findings, examples, graphs, charts and illustrations.** As a reader, you should be sceptical about statistics and research findings when the source is not mentioned. When a writer does not cite the sources of statistics and research findings, there is no way of knowing how reliable the sources are or whether the writer is making up the statistics.

When in doubt, always document the source.

What you are not required to acknowledge

Common sense governs issues of academic plagiarism. The standards of documentation are very strict, but there are two cases in which you do not need to cite your source. You do not have to document the following:

- **Facts available from many sources.** For example, many reference sources report that the death toll from the sinking of the *Titanic* on 15 April 1912 was around 1500.
- **Results of your own field research.** If you take a survey and report the results, you don't have to cite yourself. However, you still need to cite individual interviews.

COMMON ERRORS

Plagiarism in academic writing

If you find any of the following problems in your academic writing, you may be guilty of plagiarising someone else's work. Because plagiarism is usually inadvertent, it is especially important that you understand what constitutes using sources responsibly. Avoid these pitfalls.

- **Missing attribution.** Make sure the author of a quotation has been identified. Include a lead-in or signal phrase that provides attribution to the source, and identify the author in the citation.
- **Missing quotation marks.** You must put quotation marks around words quoted directly from a source.
- **Inadequate citation.** Give a page number to show where in the source the quotation appears or where a paraphrase or summary is drawn from.
- **Paraphrase relies too heavily on the source.** Be careful that the wording or sentence structure of a paraphrase does not follow the source too closely.
- **Distortion of meaning.** Don't allow your paraphrase or summary to distort the meaning of the source, and don't take a quotation out of context, resulting in a change of meaning.
- **Missing reference entry.** The references page or works-cited page must include all the sources cited in the project.
- **Inadequate citation of images.** A figure or photo must appear with a caption and a citation to indicate the source of the image. If material includes a summary of data from a visual source, an attribution or citation must be given for the graphic being summarised.

12b Avoid Plagiarism When Taking Notes

The best way to avoid unintentional plagiarism is to take care to distinguish source words from your own words. Create a folder for your research project and clearly label the files.

- **Create a working bibliography and make separate files for content notes.** Create a file for each source. If you work on paper, use a separate page for each source. Write down all the information you need for a list of references or a list of works cited in your working bibliography.

- **If you copy anything from a source when taking notes, place those words in quotation marks and note the page number(s) where those words appear.** If you copy words from an online source, take special care to note the source. You could easily copy online material and later not be able to find where it came from. When in doubt, do an online search of the sentence or paragraph in question to locate the original source.
- **Print out the entire source so you can refer to it later.** Having photocopies or complete printed files allows you to double-check later that you haven't used words from the source by mistake and that any words you quote are accurate.

12c Avoid Plagiarism When Quoting Sources

Most people who get into plagiarism trouble lift words from a source and use them without quotation marks or forget to identify block quotations (see page 87). Where the line is drawn is easiest to illustrate with an example. In the following passage, Danah Boyd and Kate Crawford discuss the opposing ways in which Big Data—what they define as 'very large data sets and the tools and procedures used to manipulate and analyze them' and 'a computational turn in thought and research' (p. 665)—has been perceived.

> Like other socio-technical phenomena, Big Data triggers both utopian and dystopian rhetoric. On one hand, Big Data is seen as a powerful tool to address various societal ills, offering the potential of new insights into areas as diverse as cancer research, terrorism, and climate change. On the other, Big Data is seen as a troubling manifestation of Big Brother, enabling invasions of privacy, decreased civil freedoms, and increased state and corporate control. As with all socio-technical phenomena, the currents of hope and fear often obscure the more nuanced and subtle shifts that are underway.
>
> —Danah Boyd and Kate Crawford, 'Critical questions for big data: Provocations for a cultural, technological, and scholarly phenomenon' (*Information, Communication & Society*, 15.5, 2012), pp. 663–664.

If you were writing a paper that concerned the use of Big Data analysis in social research and arguments for and against it, you might refer to Boyd and Crawford's work on the discourses surrounding this techno-cultural shift. Your options are to paraphrase the source or to quote it directly.

If you quote directly, you must place quotation marks around all words you take from the original:

> Two scholars from Microsoft Research argue that dystopian discourses surrounding Big Data denounce 'invasions of privacy, decreased civil freedoms, and increased state and corporate control' (Boyd & Crawford 2012, p. 664).

Notice that the quotation is introduced and not just dropped in. This example follows Harvard style, where the citation goes outside the quotation marks but before the final full stop. In Harvard style, source references are made according to the author's last name, which refers you to the full citation in the references list. Following the author's name is the year of publication and the page number where the quotation can be located.

If the author's name appears in the sentence, cite the year of publication and the page number in parentheses directly after his or her name:

> According to Boyd and Crawford (2012, p. 664) Big Data is seen by enthusiasts as having 'the potential of new insights into areas as diverse as cancer research, terrorism, and climate change'.

If you want to quote material that is already quoted in your source, use double quotation marks for that material:

> Boyd and Crawford (2012, p. 665) discuss the extent to which Big Data is transforming human thought: 'Just as Ford changed the way we made cars—and then transformed work itself—Big Data has emerged a system of knowledge that is already changing the objects of knowledge, while also having the power to inform how we understand human networks and community. "Change the instruments, and you will change the entire social theory that goes with them", Latour (2009) reminds us (p. 9)'.

Avoid Plagiarism When Summarising and Paraphrasing

In many cases you will want to include the ideas and facts from a source, but the exact words from the source are not especially important. It is in theses cases when you will need to either paraphrase or summarise.

Summarising

A summary states the major idea of an entire source or part of a source in a paragraph or sentence. The key is to put the summary in your own words. If you use words from the source, you have to put these within quotation marks.

Plagarised summary

Boyd and Crawford (2012, p. 664) argue in 'Critical questions for big data: Provocations for a cultural, technological, and scholarly phenomenon' that Big Data is seen almost as a Big Brother figure that **enables invasions of privacy, decreased civil freedoms, and increased state and corporate control.**

Most of the words of this example are lifted directly from the original.

Acceptable summary

Although Big Data can be perceived as a tool to control citizens because it provides access to private information, Boyd and Crawford (2012, p. 664) also suggest that it can be used to gain insight into areas such as environmental and medical sciences, which may further our understanding of our planet and the human body.

Paraphrasing

When you paraphrase, you represent the idea of the source in your own words at about the same length of the original, but you still need to include the reference to the source of the idea. The following paraphrase is an example of patch plagiarism.

Plagiarised paraphrase

Danah Boyd and Kate Crawford (2012, pp. 663–664) argue that there is **both utopian and dystopian rhetoric** triggered by Big Data. Supporters of Big Data see it **as a powerful tool to address various societal ills, offering the potential of new insights into** many different domains such as **cancer research, terrorism, and climate change**. Opponents of Big Data think it is **a troubling manifestation of Big Brother, enabling invasions of privacy, decreased civil freedoms, and increased state and corporate control.**

Even though the source is listed, this paraphrase is unacceptable. Too many of the words in the original are used directly here, including much or all of entire phrases. When a string of words is lifted from a source and inserted without quotation marks, the passage is plagiarised. Changing a few words in a sentence is not paraphrase. Likewise, it is unacceptable to keep the structure of the sentence and change a few words.

A true paraphrase represents an entire rewriting of the idea from the source.

Acceptable paraphrase

Danah Boyd and Kate Crawford (2012, p. 664) argue that Big Data has both supporters and detractors. Those who see in it a favourable light identify potential benefits in areas such as medicine, environmental sciences and analysis of terrorist activities. Those who think that Big Data is a menace argue that it will allow states and corporations to control citizens. They also contend that privacy and civil freedoms are at risk.

Even though there are a few words from the original in this paragraph, such as *corporations* and *civil freedoms*, these sentences are original in structure and wording while accurately conveying the meaning of the source.

Paraphrasing is not synonym of editing someone else's words to make them sound our own. Paraphrasing is a craft that allows to use our critical reading and thinking skills to make someone else's ideas our own. The exercise helps us come up with our own conclusions and with new ideas that ought to enrich the discussion on a particular topic.

SMARTER WRITING

Turnitin and online submissions

Most universities have adopted online platforms through which students can submit their assignments and then receive their marks and feedback. The most popular platform is Turnitin, which also produces a similarity report that provides a percentage number that indicates how much of your work is copied verbatim from an external source. When you submit an assignment, the system compares it with journals and books in databases, as well as with thousands of assignments previously submitted through Turnitin. Lecturers can decide whether to show students this similarity report or to keep it hidden. A high similarity percentage can alert your lecturers or tutors to a potential problem. They will then examine your assignment more closely to identify any instances of plagiarism. If your marker makes the similarity report visible and you get a high percentage number (over 40%), proofread your assignment to make sure you have cited your sources properly. You can also consider turning some direct quotes into paraphrased sentences or summaries.

Credit

Page 79. Boyd D and Crawford K 2012, 'Critical questions for big data: Provocations for a cultural, technological, and scholarly phenomenon', *Information, Communication & Society*, vol. 15, no. 5, pp. 662–669. Reprinted by permission of Taylor and Francis Ltd.

13 Use Sources Effectively

AT A *GLANCE*

- Use quotations effectively (see 13a below)
- Choose the best signal phrases for your paper (see 13b)
- Learn all about block quotations (13b)

13a Quoting and Paraphrasing

Use sources to support what you say; don't allow them to say it for you. Next to plagiarism, the worst mistake you can make with sources is to string together a series of long quotations. This leaves your readers wondering whether you have anything to say.

When to quote and when to paraphrase

The general rule in deciding when to include direct quotations and when to paraphrase lies in the importance of the original wording.

- If you want to refer to an idea or a fact and the original wording is not critical, make the point in your own words and cite the source.
- Save direct quotations for language that is memorable or conveys the character of the source.

SMARTER WRITING

Use quotations effectively

Quotations are a frequent problem in research papers. Review every quotation to ensure that each is used effectively and correctly.

- **Limit the use of long quotations.** If you have more than one block quotation on a page, check to see if some can be paraphrased or summarised.
- **Check that each quotation supports your main points rather than making major points for you.** A common mistake is to drop in quotations without introducing them or indicating their significance.

(continued on next page)

(continued)

- **Check that each quotation is introduced and attributed.** Each quotation should be introduced and its author or title named.
- **Check for verbs that signal a quotation**: Smith *claims*, Jones *argues*, Brown *states*. Use a signal verb that suggests how you are using a source. If you write 'McNeil contends', your reader is alerted that you are likely to disagree with your source.
- **Check that each quotation is properly formatted and punctuated.** Prose quotations longer than thirty words (Harvard), forty words (APA) or four lines (MLA) should be indented as a block quotation without quotation marks. Shorter quotations should be enclosed within quotation marks.
- **Check that you cite the source for each quotation.** You must cite the sources of all direct quotations, paraphrases and summaries.
- **Check the accuracy of each quotation.** Be careful not to misquote. Compare what is in your paper with the original source. If you need to add words to make a quotation grammatical, make sure the added words are in square brackets to indicate a change from the original. Use ellipses to indicate omitted words.
- **Read your paper aloud.** Each quotation should flow smoothly when you read your paper aloud. Put a tick beside rough spots so you can revise them later.

13b Integrate Quotations

All sources should be well integrated into your paper. Introduce quotations by attributing them in your text:

> Although most immigrants seek to establish themselves in coastal cities, those who have settled in regional and rural areas of the country over the last few years have helped relieve some of the labour shortages in regional and rural Australia and reduce 'the trend to population decline in many non-coastal regional and rural cities and towns, helping to regenerate non-metropolitan Australia' (Collins 2013).

The preceding quotation is used correctly, but it loses the impact of the source. Compare it with the following:

> Although most immigrants seek to establish themselves in coastal cities, those who have settled in regional and rural Australia over the last few years are regenerating non-metropolitan areas of the country by providing enough labour and reducing 'the trend to population decline in many non-costal regional and rural cities and towns' (Collins 2013).

Use signal phrases

Signal verbs often indicate your stance towards a quotation. Introducing a quotation with 'X says' or 'X believes' tells your readers nothing. Find a verb that suggests how you are using the source. For example, if you write 'X affirms', your reader is alerted that you may agree with the source. Be precise.

Signal phrases that report information or a claim

X argues that …
X claims that …
X observes that …
As X puts it, …
X reports that …
As X sums it up, …

Signal phrases when you agree with the source

X affirms that …
X has the insight that …
X points out insightfully that …
X theorises that …
X verifies that …

Signal phrases when you disagree with the source

X contends that …
X denies that …
X disputes that …
X overlooks that …
X refutes that …
X rejects that …

Signal phrases in the sciences

Signal phrases in the sciences often use the past tense, especially for interpretations and commentary:

X described ...

X found ...

X has suggested ...

Introduce block quotations

Long direct quotations, called **block quotations**, are indented from the margin instead of being placed in quotation marks. In Harvard style, a quotation longer than thirty words should begin on a new line and be indented. Single spacing and a smaller type font than the rest of the text are used. In APA style, a quotation of forty words or longer is indented five spaces. In MLA style, a quotation longer than four lines should be indented ten spaces. In both APA and MLA styles, long quotations are double-spaced. You still need to integrate a block quotation into the text of your project by mentioning who wrote or said it. Don't forget:

- no quotation marks appear around block quotations
- words quoted in the original retain quotation marks
- the page number citation appears after the full stop at the end of the block quotation.

It is a good idea to include at least one or two sentences following the quotation to describe its significance to your thesis.

Double-check quotations

You should double-check all quotations you use to be sure they are accurate and that all words belonging to the original are set off with quotation marks or placed in a block quotation. If you wish to leave out words from a quotation, indicate the omitted words with an ellipsis (...) (see Section 34e), but make sure you don't alter the meaning of the original quote to suit your argument.

14 Harvard Documentation

AT A *GLANCE*

- Know the elements of Harvard Documentation (see 14a)
- Citing sources in Harvard style (see 14b)
- Creating the reference list (see 14c to 14h)
- View sample pages from a research paper with Harvard documentation (see 14i)

Different disciplines use different styles of documentation. If you are unsure about which documentation style to use, ask your lecturer or tutor. It is very important that you check the assignment guide for your Department or School, as some details may vary from the guidelines in this chapter. You may be penalised for not adhering to the requirements. Whichever style you adopt, ensure you apply its conventions consistently throughout your work.

- **Harvard** referencing is a generic author–date style used across various disciplines (see this chapter) and commonly used in Australia.
- **APA** (American Psychological Association) is followed in the social sciences and education (see Chapter 15) and uses author–date style.
- **MLA** (Modern Language Association) is the preferred style in the humanities and fine arts (see Chapter 16) and uses author–page style.
- **CMS** (*Chicago Manual of Style*) offers flexibility in documentation style and the option of using note documentation (see Chapter 17).

Research writing requires you to document the sources of all of your information that is not common knowledge. Harvard style enables authors and readers to immediately identify the original source of the information provided and its year of publication (and, if necessary, the page number) through in-text citations that follow an author–date method.

Harvard Documentation Map

1 Collect the right information

For every source you need to have:

- the name of the author or authors
- the full title, and
- complete publication information.

For instructions, go to the illustrated examples in Section 14d of the three major source types:

- **PRINTED ARTICLE**
- **PRINTED BOOK**
- **WEB PUBLICATION**

For other kinds of sources, such as visual and multimedia sources, see Section 14h.

2 Cite sources in two places

Remember, this is a two-part process. To create citations:

(a) in **the body of your paper**, go to 14b

(b) in a **reference list at the end of your paper**, go to 14c.

If you have questions that the examples in this chapter do not address, consult the *Style manual: for authors, editors and printers*, 6th edition, which Harvard style is based on.

3 Find the right model citations

You'll find **illustrated examples of sources** in Section 14d:

- **JOURNALS, MAGAZINES, NEWSPAPERS AND DOCUMENTS**, go to 14e.
- **BOOKS** or parts of a book, go to 14f.
- **ONLINE**, go to 14g.
- **VISUAL AND MULTIMEDIA**, go to 14h.

4 Format your paper

You will find a **sample research paper in Harvard style** and instructions on formatting the body of your paper and your reference list in Section 14i.

A note about footnotes

Harvard style does not use footnotes for documentation. Use in-text citations instead (see Section 14b). The only use of footnotes in Harvard style is for providing additional information.

14a The Elements of Harvard Documentation

Titles are normally written with minimal capitalisation. However, the titles of periodicals (journals, magazines and newspapers) are written with maximal capitalisation.

Page numbers are used for direct quotations, including figures and tables, or when the information used is taken from specific pages. If including page numbers, put a comma after the year and use the abbreviations *p.* (page) and *pp.* (pages) followed by a space before the number(s). If page numbers are consecutive, they are listed as shown:

Gallagher 2013, p. 100
Gallagher 2013, pp. 100–29 (for pages 100–129)
Gallagher 2013, pp. 343–79 (for pages 343–379)

If direct quotations are used, they must be copied exactly as they were written in the original, enclosed in single quotation marks and incorporated fluently into your writing. There is a full stop after the citation if it is at the end of the sentence.

When the author's name is mentioned in the sentence, the in-text citation must include the page number and is written as follows:

Mobbs (2013, p. 228) explains that in 34 years' time we will need about 0.01 hectare per human to feed an estimated global population of 8 billion, and that 'the increase in the global population will be entirely in developing countries'.

If the author's name is not mentioned in the sentence, the in-text citation is written like this:

An environmental consultant explains that in 34 years' time we will need about 0.01 hectare per human to feed an estimated global population of 8 billion, and that 'the increase in the global population will be entirely in developing countries' (Mobbs 2013, p. 228).

At the end of the work, a reference list giving further details of all sources cited in-text is included so that readers can refer to the original source. The corresponding entry in the reference list would be:

Mobbs, M 2013, *Sustainable food*, UNSW Press, Sydney

See page 121 for a sample reference list.

14b Citing Sources in a Harvard-Style Project

Jennifer Nguyen is writing an essay on the role of the Special Broadcasting Service (SBS) in Australian media and its effects on the public. You can see the complete paper in Section 14i.

How to quote and cite a source in the text of a Harvard-style paper

Jennifer searched for an article on the *Informit* database using the search terms 'SBS' and 'multicultural'. She found the article below, saved it and printed a copy.

Simple Search | Advanced Search | Browse Publications

searching APAFT CHANGE DATABASES

Search

Limit Search: This issue · This Publication · Anywhere CLEAR SEARCH

BACK TO TABLE OF CONTENTS

Image of Publication

Peer Reviewed

Citation only

More information about this publication

The Special Broadcasting Service and the future of multiculturalism: An insight into contemporary challenges and future directions

Communication, Politics & Culture
Volume 46 Issue 1 (2013)

Roose, Joshua M; Akbarzadeh, Shahram

Abstract: In the past decade multiculturalism across Western nations has come under sustained critique and attack from its political opponents. It has been asserted that multiculturalism leads to the creation of ghettos and segregated communities, which undermine liberal democratic values and heighten the risk of attraction to extremist violence, particularly in regard to Muslim communities. The ferocity of these attacks has led many scholars to claim that multiculturalism is 'in retreat'. But such claims have rarely been tested as they relate to publicly funded government agencies and institutions. These are key sites governing the daily practice and representation of multiculturalism that impact on populations in everyday life. In the Australian context, the Special Broadcasting Service (SBS) is a pivotal example of a multicultural institution, with its programming and community engagement widely considered among the world's best practice in promoting pluralism and respect between cultures. In more recent times, however, a series of controversial episodes on the network's flagship 'ideas forum', the Insight television program, have led to anger in Australian Muslim communities, and a boycott by a variety of community leaders, academics and activists. This study reveals a notable shift away from the core values of multiculturalism in the SBS and Australian society.

Institutional users Login to access article

To cite this article: Roose, Joshua M and Akbarzadeh, Shahram. The Special Broadcasting Service and the future of multiculturalism: An insight into contemporary challenges and future directions [online]. Communication, Politics & Culture, Vol. 46, No. 1, 2013: [93]-116. Availability: <http://search.informit.com.au/documentSummary;dn=533117757274226;res=IELAPA> ISSN: 1836-0645. [cited 14 Jun 17].

Personal Author:	**Roose, Joshua M; Akbarzadeh, Shahram;**
Source:	Communication, Politics & Culture, Vol. 46, No. 1, 2013: [93]-116
DOI:	
Document Type:	Journal Article
ISSN:	1836-0645
Subject:	**Mass media and culture; Political science; Muslims--Ethnic identity; National security; Multiculturalism; Special Broadcasting Service (Australia);**
Identifier:	Insight (television program)
Peer Reviewed:	Yes

Database: APAFT

Our products | Help and FAQ | News | Disclaimer | Privacy | Trial | Case Studies | Contact us

To support her argument that SBS has greatly influenced how multiculturalism is perceived by the Australian public, she wanted to quote from an article by Joshua M. Roose and Shahram Akbarzadeh that discussed the role of the *Insight* program and some of the challenges it has faced.

Jennifer can (a) mention the authors in the text of her paper with a signal phrase or (b) place the authors' names inside parentheses following the paraphrase (see pages 85–87). In both cases she must include the page number where she found the quote inside the parentheses.

Author's name in signal phrase

> In both cases, the moderator, journalist Jenny Brockie, didn't seem to be able to guide the comments of audience and guests, which in turn created tension among its viewers and the Muslim community in Australia. As Roose & Akbarzadeh (2013, p. 104) explain 'the impact of SBS representation on Australian Muslim communities was corrosive, undermining trust that many Muslims had placed in the network to provide non-polemical representation of Islam and Muslims'

OR

Author's name in parenthetical citation

> In both cases, the moderator, journalist Jenny Brockie, didn't seem to be able to guide the comments of the audience and guests, which in turn created tension among its viewers and the Muslim community in Australia. 'The impact of SBS representations on Australian Muslims communities was corrosive, undermining trust that many Muslims had placed in the network to provide a non-polemical representation of Islam and Muslims' (Roose & Akbarzadeh 2013, p. 104).

If Jennifer opts to include a quotation that is thirty words or longer, she must begin the quote on a new line and use indenting and single spacing.

Include in-text citations for summaries and paraphrases

In another paragraph, Jennifer summarised another argument and gave the page number from that source.

> For example, the documentary *Go back to where you came from* was broadcasted in June 2011. The three-part documentary was filmed like a reality television show. It worked almost like an experiment that allowed us to see if negative attitudes towards asylum seekers change when their journeys are depicted on-screen and the audience recognises itself in those journeys (Cover 2013, p. 411).

14c Creating the Reference List

Jennifer is ready to create an entry for the reference list at the end of her paper. She asked herself a series of questions to create an entry for this source in her reference list.

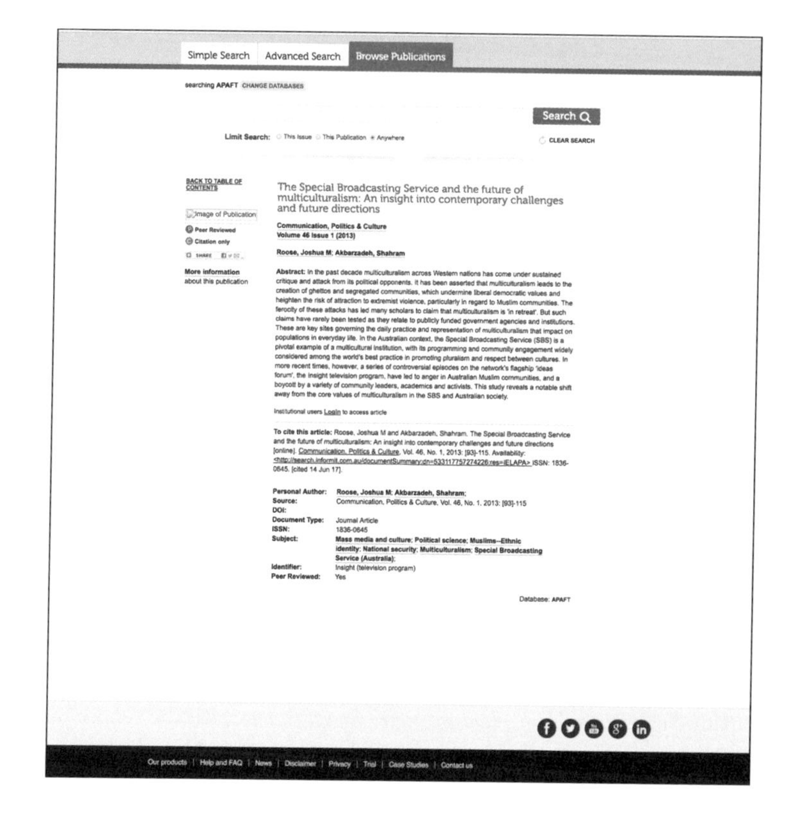

1. What information do I need to pull from this screenshot?

For a source like this article from an online database, she needs to know five things: (1) what type of source it is; (2) the author; (3) the title; (4) the publication information; and (5) information about the online database.

2. I know this is from my library's online database, but that could be one of several different types of sources. What kind of source is this?

Jennifer selected journals for the source type in her *Informit* search; thus she knew that her source type would be a journal article.

3. Now how do I find the author's name?

Look for a bold heading that says something like 'AUTHOR' or 'BYLINE'. If more than one author is listed, take note of all names listed.

4. What is the title of my source?

If the title is not immediately evident, look for a heading that says 'TITLE' or 'HEADLINE'.

5. Where do I find the publication information?

The name and the date of the journal are usually listed at the top of the page, but are sometimes found at the bottom. In this case, the issue number is listed beside 'ISSUE' and the page numbers are listed beside 'PAGINATION'.

6. Where do I find the name of the database?

For databases distributed by RMIT Publishing, you have to look for the name of the database. RMIT Publishing is the vendor that sells access to many databases such as *Academic Search Complete. Informit* is the vendor that distributes access to databases of research from Australia, New Zealand and the Asia-Pacific region.

Jennifer listed the information.

AUTHORS	*Roose, Joshua M & Akbarzadeh, S*
TITLE OF ARTICLE	*'The Special Broadcasting Service and the future of multiculturalism: an INSIGHT into contemporary challenges and future directions'*
PUBLICATION INFORMATION	
Name of journal	*COMMUNICATION, POLITICS & CULTURE*
Date of publication	*2013*
Volume and page numbers	*Vol. 46, 93–115*
DATABASE INFORMATION	
Name of database	*Informit*
Date the site was accessed	*15 Nov. 2016*

Then she used the instructions on page 96 to format her citation.

Nguyen 10

References

Roose, JM & Akbarzadeh, S 2013, 'The Special Broadcasting Service and the Future of Multiculturalism: an *Insight* into contemporary challenges and future directions', *Communication, Politics & Culture*, vol. 46, pp. 93–115.

14d Illustrated Examples in Harvard Style

Printed article

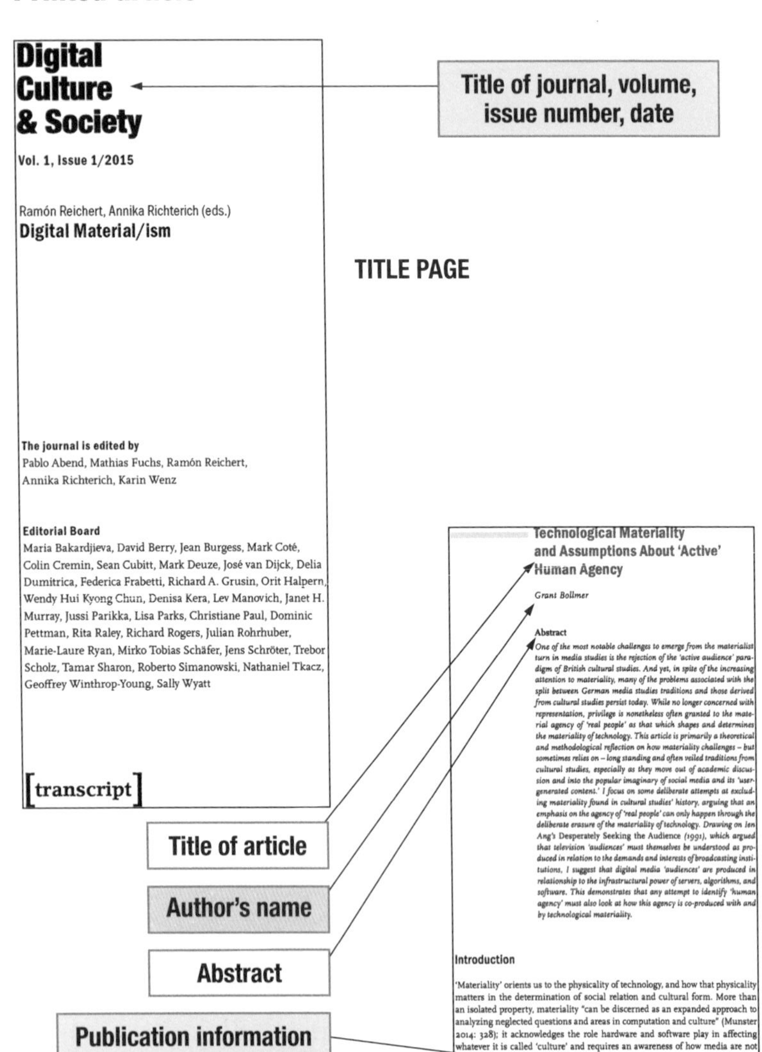

Digital Culture & Society

Vol. 1, Issue 1/2015

Ramón Reichert, Annika Richterich (eds.)

Digital Material/ism

The journal is edited by
Pablo Abend, Mathias Fuchs, Ramón Reichert, Annika Richterich, Karin Wenz

Editorial Board
Maria Bakardjieva, David Berry, Jean Burgess, Mark Coté, Colin Cremin, Sean Cubitt, Mark Deuze, José van Dijck, Delia Dumitrica, Federica Frabetti, Richard A. Grusin, Orit Halpern, Wendy Hui Kyong Chun, Denisa Kera, Lev Manovich, Janet H. Murray, Jussi Parikka, Lisa Parks, Christiane Paul, Dominic Pettman, Rita Raley, Richard Rogers, Julian Rohrhuber, Marie-Laure Ryan, Mirko Tobias Schäfer, Jens Schröter, Trebor Scholz, Tamar Sharon, Roberto Simanowski, Nathaniel Tkacz, Geoffrey Winthrop-Young, Sally Wyatt

[transcript]

Technological Materiality and Assumptions About 'Active' Human Agency

Grant Bollmer

Abstract

One of the most notable challenges to emerge from the materialist turn in media studies is the rejection of the 'active audience' paradigm of British cultural studies. And yet, in spite of the increasing attention to materiality, many of the problems associated with the split between German media studies traditions and those derived from cultural studies persist today. While no longer concerned with representation, privilege is nonetheless often granted to the material agency of 'real people' as that which shapes and determines the materiality of technology. This article is primarily a theoretical and methodological reflection on how materiality challenges – but sometimes relies on – long standing and often veiled traditions from cultural studies, especially as they move out of academic discussion and into the popular imaginary of social media and its 'user-generated content.' I focus on some deliberate attempts at excluding materiality found in cultural studies' history, arguing that an emphasis on the agency of 'real people' can only happen through the deliberate erasure of the materiality of technology. Drawing on Ien Ang's Desperately Seeking the Audience *(1991), which argued that television 'audiences' must themselves be understood as produced in relation to the demands and interests of broadcasting institutions, I suggest that digital media 'audiences' are produced in relationship to the infrastructural power of servers, algorithms, and software. This demonstrates that any attempt to identify 'human agency' must also look at how this agency is co-produced with and by technological materiality.*

Introduction

'Materiality' orients us to the physicality of technology, and how that physicality matters in the determination of social relation and cultural form. More than an isolated property, materiality "can be discerned as an expanded approach to analyzing neglected questions and areas in computation and culture" (Munster 2014: 328); it acknowledges the role hardware and software play in affecting whatever it is called 'culture' and requires an awareness of how media are not transparent channels used by human beings for communication with other

DOI 10.14361/dcs-2015-0107
DCS | Digital Culture and Society | Vol. 1, Issue 1 | © transcript 2015

Bollmer, G 2015, 'Technological materiality and assumptions about "active" human agency', *Digital Culture and Society*, vol. 1, no. 1, pp. 95–110.

Author's name

The author's surname comes first, followed by a comma and the author's initial. If there are two or more initials, there is no space between them.

Two authors' names are joined by an ampersand. There is no comma between the first author's initial and the ampersand.

Year of publication

The year in which the article was published follows the author's initial, without a comma.

Title of article

The title of the article is enclosed in single quotation marks and written with minimal capitalisation. It is followed by a comma.

If the article title includes another title or words that are normally in italics, use italics or double quotation marks for that component of the title.

Publication information

Name of journal
The journal title is written in italics with maximal capitalisation. It is followed by a comma.

Volume, issue or other identifying information, and page numbers
The volume number and issue number are recorded using the abbreviations *vol.* and *no.*
In each case, there is a space between the abbreviation and the number.

If only a month or season is listed, rather than a volume and/or number, use the month or season in place of the volume and/or number.

For weekly or biweekly publications, include the day(s) and month of publication, with the day(s) preceding the month.

For page numbers, use the abbreviations *p.* or *pp.* and leave a space before the number. If an article continues to a non-consecutive page, provide both sets of numbers.

Printed book

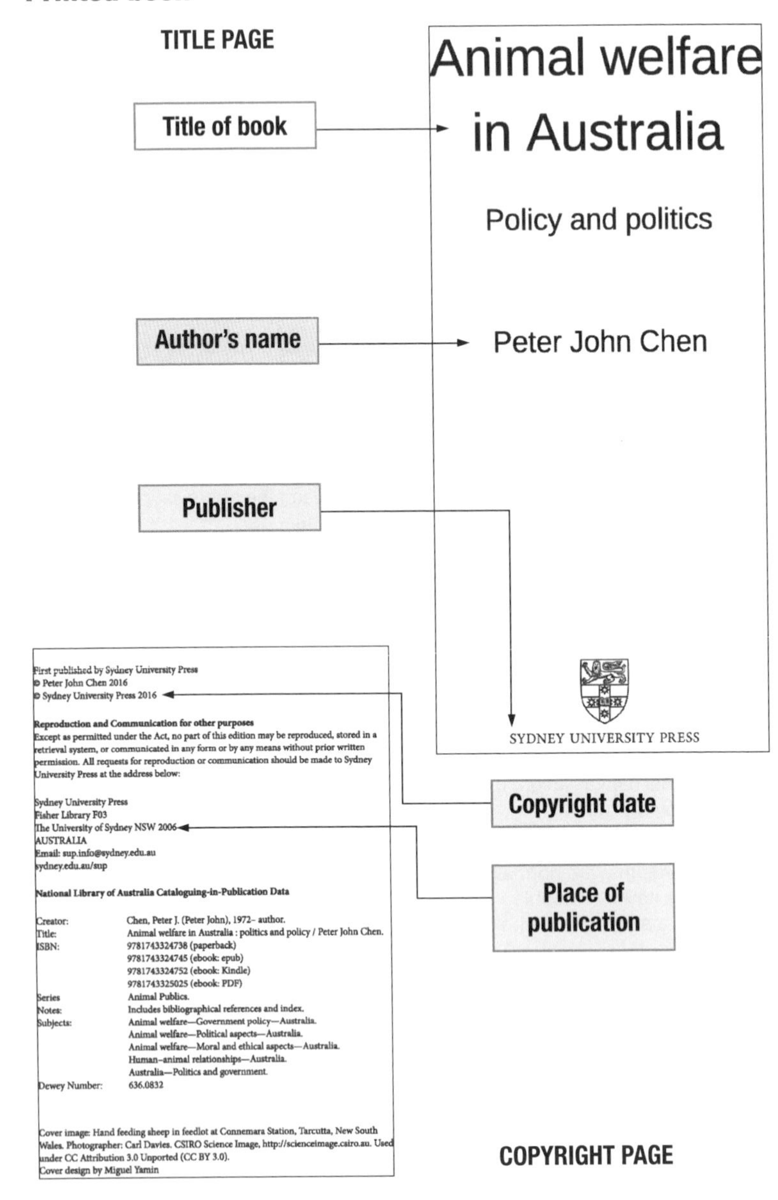

First published by Sydney University Press
© Peter John Chen 2016
© Sydney University Press 2016

Reproduction and Communication for other purposes
Except as permitted under the Act, no part of this edition may be reproduced, stored in a retrieval system, or communicated in any form or by any means without prior written permission. All requests for reproduction or communication should be made to Sydney University Press at the address below:

Sydney University Press
Fisher Library F03
The University of Sydney NSW 2006
AUSTRALIA
Email: sup.info@sydney.edu.au
sydney.edu.au/sup

National Library of Australia Cataloguing-in-Publication Data

Creator:	Chen, Peter J. (Peter John), 1972– author.
Title:	Animal welfare in Australia : politics and policy / Peter John Chen.
ISBN:	9781743324738 (paperback) 9781743324745 (ebook: epub) 9781743324752 (ebook: Kindle) 9781743325025 (ebook: PDF)
Series	Animal Publics.
Notes:	Includes bibliographical references and index.
Subjects:	Animal welfare—Government policy—Australia. Animal welfare—Political aspects—Australia. Animal welfare—Moral and ethical aspects—Australia. Human–animal relationships—Australia. Australia—Politics and government.
Dewey Number:	636.0832

Cover image: Hand feeding sheep in feedlot at Connemara Station, Tarcutta, New South Wales. Photographer: Carl Davies. CSIRO Science Image, http://scienceimage.csiro.au. Used under CC Attribution 3.0 Unported (CC BY 3.0).
Cover design by Miguel Yamin

Chen, PJ 2016, *Animal welfare in Australia: policy and politics*, Sydney University Press, NSW.

Author's or editor's name

The author's surname comes first, followed by a comma and the author's initial. If there are two or more initials, there is no space between them.

For edited books, put the abbreviation *(ed.)* between the initial and the date, without a comma.

Kavanagh, P (ed.) 1969.

Year of publication

The year the book was published follows the author's initial, without a comma.

If the year of publication is not known, write *n.d.* If it is only approximate, write *c.* and leave a space before the year.

Cooper, W 2013

Jones, J n.d.

Morris, Q c. 1987

Book title

Use the title as it is written on the title page. Write the title in italics, with only the first word of the title and any proper nouns beginning with capital letters. If the title includes a colon, the next word does not have a capital letter.

Publication information

Publisher
Cite the publisher's name in full unless the authoring body has a long name and is also the publisher, in which case the publisher's name may be abbreviated and explained in a list.

Place of publication
If two or more places are listed, cite only the first in the list. If a publisher's name makes the place of publication clear, the place may be omitted. Place names that are not well-known or that exist in more than one location may be clarified by adding the state or country.

Web publication

HOME PAGE

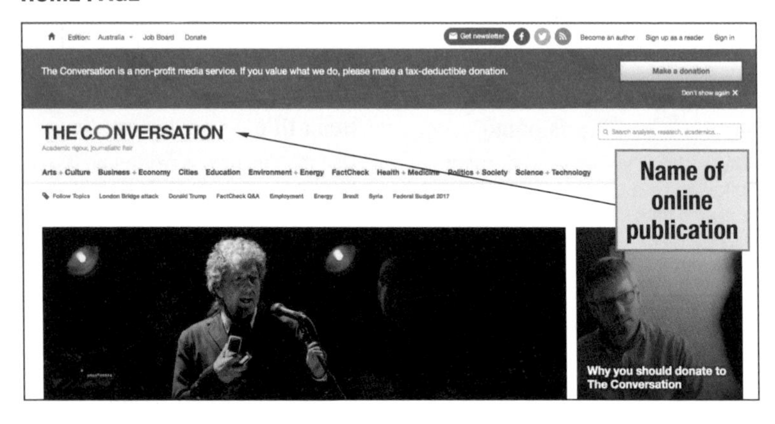

FIRST PAGE OF THE ARTICLE

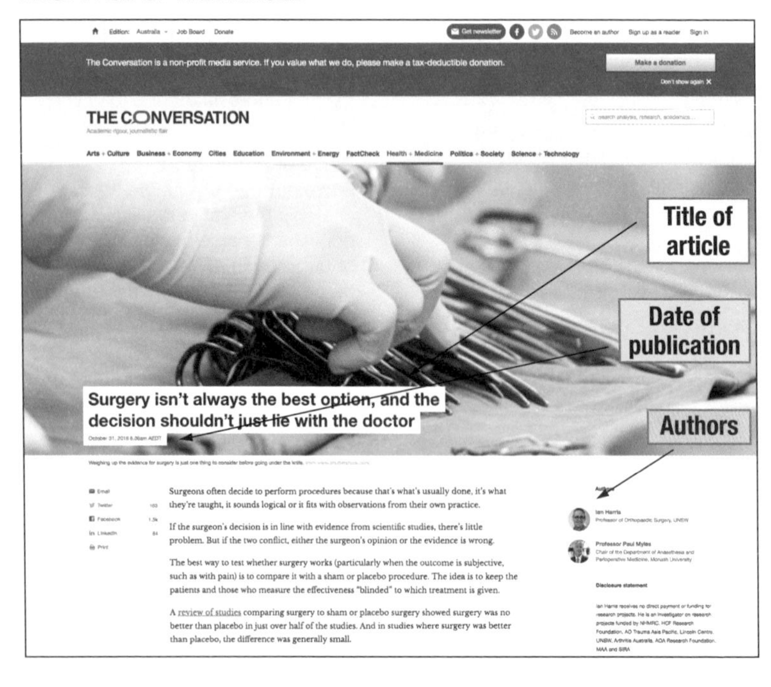

Harris, I & Myles, P 2016, 'Surgery isn't always the best option, and the decision shouldn't just lie with the doctor', *The Conversation*, 31 October, viewed 1 November 2016, <https://theconversation.com/surgery-isnt-always-the-best-option-and-the-decision-shouldnt-just-lie-with-the-doctor-64228>.

Author's name

The author may be an individual, a group or an organisation. List the author in the same way as for books and journals.

If there is no author, begin the reference with the title.

Dates

Two dates are required: the date the site was produced or revised, and the date it was viewed.

Title

If there is only one title, it is listed in the same way as a book.

On some websites, different pages have a title. In this case, the title is listed in the same way as the title of an article in a journal. The name of the site is treated like a book.

URL

Copy and paste the URL from your browser into your text. Enclose it in angle brackets and put a full stop after the end bracket.

CITING ONLINE SOURCES IN HARVARD STYLE

The elements required to cite online sources in a reference list are essentially the same as for other works, except that the date the source is viewed and the website details are required. If there is a document number or Digital Object Identifier (DOI), include it in the citation.

Journals, Magazines, Newspapers and Documents in the Harvard-Style Reference List

Index of reference entries

Journals and magazines

Newspapers

Documents

Sample reference list entries for journals and magazines

1. Article by one author

Tribe, J 2008, 'Tourism: a critical business', *Journal of Travel Research*, vol. 46, no. 3, pp. 245–55.

2. Article by two authors

Knight, WB & Deng, Y 2016, 'N/either here n/or there: culture, location, positionality, and art education', *Visual Arts Research*, vol. 42, no. 2, pp. 105–111.

3. Article by three authors

Olivier, J, Walter, SR & Grzebieta, RH 2013, 'Long term bicycle related head injury trends for New South Wales, Australia, following mandatory helmet legislation', *Accident Analysis & Prevention*, vol. 50, pp. 1128–34.

4. Article by four or more authors

Connaughton, D, Hanton, S, Jones, G & Wadey, R 2008, 'Mental toughness research: key issues in this area', *International Journal of Sport Psychology*, vol. 39, no. 3, pp. 192–204.

5. Article by an unknown author

'Report raises concerns over the regulation of online ads' 2009, *Marketing Week*, 17 December, p. 6.

6. Article in a journal paginated by volume

For some journals, page numbers continue consecutively through an entire volume from one issue to the next. In this case, only the volume number is required, not the issue number.

Jensen, L 2008, 'Locating Australian Asian Studies', *Journal of Australian Studies*, vol. 32, pp. 543–51.

7. **Article in a journal paginated by issue**

If each issue forming part of a volume is paginated separately, both the volume and issue numbers must be listed.

Mattes, R 2012, 'The "Born Frees": the prospects for generational change in post-*apartheid* South Africa', *Australian Journal of Political Science*, vol. 47, no. 1, pp. 133–53.

If an article continues to a non-consecutive page, provide both sets of page numbers.

Sharwood, A 2009, 'Under the radar', *Weekend Australian Magazine*, 24–25 October, pp. 14–18, 20.

8. **Review**

Roe, Jill 2016, review of *Minding her own business: colonial businesswomen in Sydney* by Catherine Bishop, *Australian Historical Studies*, vol. 47, pp. 495–6.

If the review has a title, include it after the year and enclose it in single quotation marks followed by a comma.

9. **Letter to the editor**

Mustoe, S 2009, 'Dragon fire', letter, *Australian Geographic*, January–March, p. 11.

10. **Editorial**

Rees, G 2009, 'Get set for Windows 7', editorial, *Australian PC User*, September, p. 8.

Sample reference list entries for newspapers

11. **Article by one author**

Viellaris, R 2010, 'Labour figures reveal jobless hotspots', *Courier-Mail*, 2–3 January, p. 3.

12. Article by two or three authors

Rood, D & Gregory, P 2010, 'Hoon drivers can expect tough new punishments', *The Age*, 20 January, p. 5.

13. Article by an unknown author

Provide the details in-text and list the source by the article title in the reference list.

(*Waikato Times*, 19 February 2016, p. 6)

. . . as reported in *Waikato Times* (19 February 2016, p. 6).

'Politics shape the world' 2016, *Waikato Times*, 19 February, p. 6.

14. Review

Bunbury, S 2014, 'Scandinavian edge to cop buddy genre', review of *The keeper of lost causes*, *The Age*, 17 July, p. 30.

15. Letter to the editor

Black, C 2014, 'A trail of wreckage', letter, *The Age*, 25 October, p. 32.

16. Editorial

If the author is not named, provide the details in-text and omit the source from the reference list.

(*Courier-Mail*, 30 December 2009, editorial, p. 62)

Sample reference list entries for documents

The publication details in government documents vary, so referencing conventions need to be considered according to the details available. If there is a catalogue number, this may be included after the title. Further information regarding in-text citations and reference list entries for various types of government publication can be obtained from Commonwealth of Australia 2002, *Style manual: for authors, editors and printers*, 6th edn, rev. Snooks & Co., John Wiley & Sons, Milton, Queensland, pp. 220–3.

17. Government document produced by a department, agency or branch with no specific author

For a document produced by a government department or agency, cite the department or agency as the author.

Department of Education, Science and Training 2005, *Teachers enhancing numeracy*, DEST, Canberra.

For a document prepared by a branch of a department or agency, cite the department or agency as the author and list the branch after the title.

18. Government document produced by a department, agency or branch with a specific author named

Cite the department, agency or branch as the author and list the individual author after the title.

Australian Bureau of Statistics 1997, *Youth, Australia: a social report*, report prepared by W McLennan, Cat. No. 4111.0, ABS, Canberra.

19. Pamphlet or brochure

'Parish Church radio play-day' 2009, *Jigsaw*, October, pp. 1–4.

20. Thesis or proceedings

Albarrán-Torres, CA 2014, 'Encoding chance: a technocultural analysis of digital gambling', PhD thesis, University of Sydney, Sydney.

14f Books in the Harvard-Style Reference List

Index of reference entries

Sample reference list entries for books

The reference list should be arranged alphabetically. If there are two or more entries beginning with the same name, single-author works should be listed before multi-author works. If an author whose name is listed alphabetically is also the editor, translator, reviser or compiler of other works listed, the edited, translated, revised or compiled work is placed after the single-author and/or multi-authors works.

Joyce, A 2013, . . .

Joyce, A & Parry, S 1987, . . .

Joyce, A (ed.) 2016, . . .

21. Book by one author

Schüll, ND 2012, *Addiction by design: machine gambling in Las Vegas*, Princeton University Press, Princeton.

22. Two or more books by the same author with different years of publication

List the books in chronological order.

Isaacs, B 2008, *Toward a new film aesthetic*, Bloomsbury Academic, London.

Isaacs, B 2013, *The orientation of future cinema: technology, aesthetics, spectacle*, Bloomsbury Academic, London.

23. Two or more books by the same author with the same year of publication

The identifying letters used to differentiate between the works in in-text citations are retained in the reference list.

Australian Bureau of Statistics 1992a, *Australia's environment: issues and facts*, ABS, Canberra.

Australian Bureau of Statistics 1992b, *Surviving statistics: a user's guide to the basics*, ABS, Canberra.

24. Book by two authors

Books by two authors are listed according to the first author named on the title page. The order of the authors as per the title page is retained.

Patterson, M & Macintyre, M 2014, *Managing modernity in the Western Pacific*, University of Queensland Press, Brisbane.

25. Book by three authors

Carabello, BA, Ballard, WL & Gazes, PC 1994, *Cardiology pearls*, Hanley & Belfus, Philadelphia.

26. Book by four or more authors

All authors must be listed in the reference list.

Khorram, S, Van der Wiele CF, Koch, FH, Nelson SAC, Potts, MD 2016, *Principles of applied remote sensing*, Springer International Publishing, New York.

27. Book by a group or organisation

If the group or organisation is referred to by an abbreviation in in-text citations, the abbreviation should be cross-referenced in the reference list.

AHTAC—*see* Australian Health Technology Advisory Committee.

The group or organisation should be listed in full in the appropriate place alphabetically, disregarding *A*, *An* or *The* at the beginning of the name of the group or organisation.

Australian Health Technology Advisory Committee 1994, *Treatment options for benign prostatic hyperplasia (BPH)*, Australian Government Publishing Service, Canberra.

28. Book by an unknown author

The title appears alphabetically in italics in the reference list, disregarding *A*, *An* or *The*.

Lobel, M 2002, . . .

The local agent's manual 2008, . . .

Lodder, C 1983, . . .

29. Book with an editor

If the focus is not on the author, highlight the role of the editor or editors by using (*ed.*) or (*eds*) between the initials and date. Note that *ed.* has a full stop but *eds* does not.

Chandler, J (ed.) 2016, *The best Australian science writing 2016*, NewSouth, Sydney.

Fisher, BAJ & Fisher, DR (eds) 2012, *Techniques of crime scene investigation*, CRC Press, Boca Raton, FL.

30. Second or subsequent edition of a book

If an edition other than the first is used, give the publication date of the relevant edition after the title of the work.

Slater, TF & Freedman RA 2014, *Investigating astronomy*, 2nd edn, W.H. Freeman & Co, New York.

31. Chapter in an edited book

Normally, the author is the focus of the reference for a chapter in an edited book, so the editor's role is indicated after the author.

Wilken, R 2016 'The de-gamification of Foursquare', in T Leaver & M Willson (eds), *Social, casual and mobile games: the changing gaming landscape*, Bloomsbury Academic, London.

14g Online Sources in the Harvard-Style Reference List

Index of reference entries

Sample reference list entries for online sources

32. Publication by a known author

Hawking, S 2008, *Into a black hole*, viewed 5 November 2016, <http://www.hawking.org.uk/into-a-black-hole.html >.

33. Publication by a group or organisation

Australian Marine Conservation Society 2010, *Seafood summit 2010: AMCS heads to peak meeting*, viewed 18 February 2010, <www.amcs.org.au/default2.asp?active_page_id=567>.

34. Article in an online scholarly journal

McGregor, M, Brown, B & Glöss, M 2015, 'Disrupting the cab: Uber, ridesharing and the taxi industry', *Journal of Peer Production*, no. 6, viewed 6 November 2016, <http://peerproduction.net/issues/issue-6-disruption-and-the-law/essays/disrupting-the-cab-uber-ridesharing-and-the-taxi-industry/ >.

35. Article in an online newspaper

Perkins, M 2008, 'Australians help find undersea volcanoes', *The Age*, 20 June, viewed 18 February 2010, <www.theage.com.au/national/australians-help-find-undersea-volcanoes-20080619-2tkg.html>.

36. Article in an online magazine

Case, A 2016, 'The lost art of leisure', *Womankind Magazine*, 27 May, viewed 8 November 2016, <http://www.womankindmag.com/articles/the-lost-art-of-leisure/>.

37. Online book

Lobato, R & Meese, J 2016, *Geoblocking and global video culture*, Institute of Network Cultures, viewed 8 November 2016, <http://networkcultures.org/blog/publication/no-18-geoblocking-and-global-video-culture/>.

38. Online government publication

Department of Health 2016, *National strategic framework for rural and remote health*, April, viewed 31 October 2016, <http://www.health.gov.au/internet/main/publishing.nsf/Content/national-strategic-framework-rural-remote-health>.

39. Media release

Australia Institute 2009, *Unpaid overtime a $72 billion gift to employers*, media release, The Australia Institute, Canberra, 18 November, viewed 17 January 2010, <https://www.tai.org.au/index.php?q=node%2F19&pubid=701&act=display>.

Sample reference list entries for unedited online sources

Unedited sources are not normally used in academic writing. Further information is available in Chapter 9.

40. Wiki entry

'Anzac Day' 2016, *Wikipedia*, viewed 7 November 2016, <https://en.wikipedia.org/wiki/Anzac_Day>.

41. Email communication

If the email is a personal communication, it may only be used after gaining the permission of the person being referred to and should be cited in-text but not included in the reference list. An individual's email address should not be cited without permission.

If the email is not a personal communication, the email address may be cited in the reference list.

Moore, K 2016, email, 20 April, <moorek@myemail.com.au>.

42. Online posting to a discussion list

With discussion list postings, the author's name may be an alias or only the first name may be given. Provide the author's name, author's identifying details such as email address if available, year of posting, title of posting, description of posting, day and month of posting, name of list owner, date of viewing and the URL.

Allyson 2010, 'Re: Progressive ESL Lesson Planning', online posting, 6 February, teachers.net, viewed 8 February 2010, <http://teachers.net/mentors/esl_language/topic5828/2.06.10.09.44.59.html>.

43. Personal home page

Kinghorn, B 2009, home page, viewed 8 February 2010, <www-personal.une.edu.au/~bkinghor/>.

44. Blog posting

As with discussion list postings, the author's name in a blog may be an alias or an email address, or only the first name may be given.

> Twilley, N 2015, 'Honey fences', *Edible Geography*, blog posting, 3 December, viewed 10 November 2016, <http://www.ediblegeography.com/honey-fences/>.

45. Social media (Facebook post)

> Turnbull, M 2016, Facebook update, 3 November, viewed 5 November 2016, <https://www.facebook.com/malcolmturnbull/posts/10154756860716579>.

14h Visual and Multimedia Sources in the Harvard-Style Reference List

Index of reference entries

Sample reference list entries for visual and multimedia sources

46. Cartoon

> Petty, B 2015, 'Mining Boom', cartoon, *The Age*, 5 January, p. 15.

47. Advertisement

Job Services Australia, advertisement, *The Monthly*, October 2009, p. 73.

48. Online map

'Tasmania' 2010, map, *Tasmania*, State of Tasmania, viewed 11 January 2010, <www.discovertasmania.com/__data/assets/pdf_file/ 0005/15845/Whole_Island_Map_TR.pdf>.

49. CD Rom

Department of Conservation and Land Management c. 1997, *Wild about Western Australia*, CD Rom, Department of Conservation and Land Management, Como, WA.

50. Podcast

Zukerman, W 2015, 'The female brain', *Science VS*, podcast radio program, ABC Radio, 9 June, <https://soundcloud.com/science-vs-season-1/the-female-brain>.

51. Online video clip

Braincraft, 'What a tooth reveals about autism', video, *YouTube*, 28 April 2016, viewed 5 November 2016, <https://www.youtube.com/watch?v=uq4kpIm40Aw>.

52. Film, video and DVD

Samson and Delilah 2009, DVD, Madman Entertainment, and starring Rowan McNamara and Marissa Gibson.

53. Television or radio program

Book Club 2011, television program, ABC, Sydney, 18 February 2015.

54. Lecture notes

Lecture notes are cited in-text and in the reference list. Include the following elements in the reference list: name of author(s) or the institution, year of publication, *title and subtitle of document*, presentation media, name of institution, location of institution.

Golding, D 2016, *Week 9: Fassbinder and German cinema,* PowerPoint slides, Swinburne University of Technology, Hawthorn.

14i Sample Pages from a Research Paper with Harvard Documentation

For further information on the Harvard referencing system, consult Commonwealth of Australia 2002, *Style manual: for authors, editors and printers*, 6th edn, rev. Snooks & Co., John Wiley & Sons, Milton, Queensland.

FORMATTING A COVER PAGE IN HARVARD STYLE

If a cover page is required for a research paper or assignment, include

- Assignment title (if appropriate, the student may choose a title)
- Assignment task (the wording of the set assignment)
- Length
- Course name and code
- Name of the institution
- Name of the lecturer/tutor
- Student name
- Student ID number
- Date due

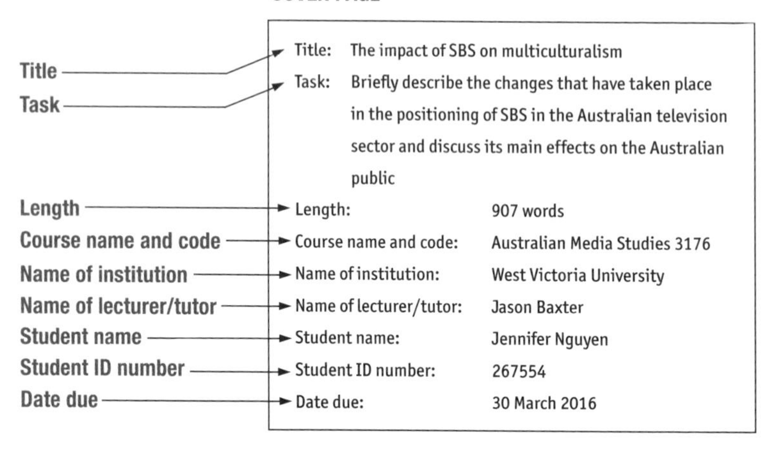

Style manual: for authors, editors and printers, 6th edition, on which Harvard referencing style is based, does not specify guidelines for formatting tertiary education research papers or assignments. Your institution or lecturer will normally provide specific guidelines regarding assignment components such as cover page, abstract and executive summary, and give guidance regarding layout.

Introduction

In line with Australia's recognition of itself as a multicultural society, the Special Broadcasting Service (SBS) was established initially as a radio service in 1975 and subsequently, in 1980, as a public service television broadcaster. SBS was not set up as merely a replica of other television stations but was established specifically to cater to an increasingly linguistically and culturally diverse population. Since that time, SBS has assumed a unique position in Australian television. It has profoundly influenced the delivery of news to the Australian viewing public in general, and through production choices such as subtitling, and the creation of original shows, among them the current affairs program *Insight* (1995–present), the documentary *Go back to where you came from* (2011) and the comedy *The family Law* (2016), it has played a pivotal role in building a broader Australian perspective on multiculturalism.

Initial consideration

An important task of SBS management since its inception has been to position the network in accordance with its Charter, namely 'to provide multilingual and multicultural . . . television services that inform, educate and entertain all Australians, and, in doing so, reflect the country's multicultural society'. However, what made SBS different from existing television services was that its audience was markedly different from that of other broadcasters. Whereas the audiences of the existing broadcasters could easily relate to US, British and local content on linguistic and cultural levels, SBS had to pioneer the provision of content relevant to a diverse audience with varying language and cultural backgrounds.

As SBS established itself, its differences were noted in the wider Australian society and SBS soon became familiar even to those who had never watched it. One reason for this was the repeated references to SBS on commercial television, particularly in comedy segments in the late 1980s. At that time, SBS was perceived as a channel for ethnic minorities and, as Hawkins and Ang (2007, p. 3) note, there was an underlying 'cultural anxiety, a sense of uncertainty and unease about *foreignness*'. SBS posed a potential threat to the sense of national identity of some sectors of the Australian population and, for those adhering to the predominantly Anglo-Saxon mindset of the time, the way to deal with this was to laugh about it.

Mainstream acceptance

SBS has clearly moved in the Australian psyche. By the late 1990s, it had become popular with older, well-educated, middle-class viewers but has more recently attracted a younger audience, albeit through the screening of programs which do not claim to be multicultural

(Flew & Harrington 2010). In addition, SBS has recognised that 'many younger culturally and linguistically diverse Australians do not participate in, or are frustrated by, long-standing forms of community representation or cultural identity' (Brown 2008, p. 6) and has produced programs that challenge cultural stereotypes and give voice to various groups within Australian society.

For example, the documentary *Go back to where you came from* was broadcasted in June 2011. The three-part documentary was filmed like a reality television show. It worked almost like an experiment that allowed viewers to see if negative attitudes towards asylum seekers change when the asylum seekers' journeys are relived on-screen (Cover 2013, p. 411).

The six Australian participants, three men and three women, embarked on a reversed 25-day journey that started on a boat and took them to Africa and the Middle East. They experimented the pain, hunger, fear and uncertainty that asylum seekers have endured during their journeys in the hope to reach Australian shores.

According to Trendfinder, *Go back to where you came from* became the number one topic on Twitter worldwide (AdNews 2011) and made headlines internationally. This secured two more series for the show, which aired in 2012 and 2015, and highlighted the fact that contemporary Australia still needs to work on its multicultural agenda.

Likewise, SBS's 2016 show, *The family Law*, based on Benjamin Law's best-selling memoir, gives voice to Asian immigrants. The show offers a portrait of multicultural suburbia that is rarely seen in commercial television.

However, not all of SBS's attempts have been successful. In 2010, *Insight* screened the episodes 'Banning the Burqa' (September) and 'Fear of Islam' (November). As Roose and Akbarzadeh explain, the first episode was screened at the time France and other countries, including Australia, were discussing laws to ban the burqa. The second tried to generate a discussion around the Islamic and Western values and their incompatibility when it comes to issues such as the Sharia law (2013, p. 103).

In both cases, the moderator, journalist Jenny Brockie, didn't seem to be able to guide the comments of the audience and guests, which in turn created tension among its viewers and the Muslim community in Australia. 'The impact of SBS representations on Australian Muslims communities was corrosive, undermining trust that many Muslims had placed in the network to provide a non-polemical representation of Islam and Muslims' (Roose & Akbarzadeh 2013, p. 104).

As Meagher (2009, p. 20) states, 'there is an issue in that Australia today seems to have a less clearly articulated multicultural policy or agenda' than it did in the past. SBS is now viewed as a part of mainstream Australian television but it still has a long way to go when it comes to its portrayal of minorities. SBS needs to find a balance between commercialism and quality debate to avoid polemics against minorities.

News

A major impact of SBS has been the opening of Australia to the world through its news broadcasts. SBS realised early on that very few items from international news feeds sent to Australia were being used by other channels. This gave SBS the opportunity to develop a niche by using the items not taken up by the other channels to create an international news program which contrasted markedly with the standard news format comprising local, state, national and perhaps, finally, international news.

The contribution of SBS news programs in breaking down the parochial perspective dominant at that time, and thereby facilitating the acceptance of multiculturalism in Australian media, cannot be underestimated. By foregrounding international news, SBS not only gave viewers access to international news that was not covered on other channels, thereby widening their world view, it also legitimised news from the home countries of many of Australia's migrants.

The success of SBS's international news paved the way for a transformation in the presentation of news in Australian television in general. Other broadcasters followed the lead of SBS and, while still maintaining the local, state and national news segments, increased their focus on international news items. In 2005, while 69.04 per cent of SBS news comprised international content, other major stations had reached a level of around 20–30 per cent international news coverage (Phillips & Tapsall 2007, p. 12), a very considerable increase from the situation of two decades previously.

Conclusion

Thus, it is evident that SBS has, through its active and sustained promotion of diversity in both policy interpretation and production practices, played an integral role in moving Australia from a largely white Anglo-Saxon public mindset, albeit with a history of accepting migrants into the country, to a populace that now has an enhanced awareness of its own cultural diversity and accepts this diversity as a normal part of life in Australia.

References

If no specific guidelines for your reference list are provided by your institution or lecturer, follow these rules:

- Begin the list of references on a new page immediately after the conclusion and before any appendices.
- Type 'References' in bold using the same font size as the text, and left-align it.
- List references in alphabetical order.
- Use single line spacing with a blank line between each reference.
- Ensure that the reference list includes all sources cited in-text and does not include any sources that are not cited in-text.

References

Brown, S 2008, 'Multicultural society, monocultural media: SBS—more special than ever', *The Sydney Papers*, vol. 20, no. 4, Summer, viewed 23 March 2010, <http://search .informit.com.au./documentSummary;dn=669290048617575;res=IELHSS>.

Cover, R 2013, 'Undoing attitudes: subjectivity and ethical change in the *Go back to where you come from* documentary', *Journal of Media & Cultural Studies,* vol. 27, no. 3, pp. 408–20.

Flew, T & Harrington, S 2010, 'Television', in S Cunningham & G Turner (eds), *The media and communications in Australia*, 3rd edn, Allen & Unwin, Crows Nest, NSW.

Hawkins, G & Ang, I 2007, 'Inventing SBS: televising the foreign', in L Jacka & T Dolin (eds), *Australian television history*, Network Books, Perth.

Meagher, B 2009, 'SBS: is there a role for a multicultural broadcaster in 2009 and beyond?' *Media International Australia, Incorporating Culture & Policy*, no. 133, November, pp. 19–23.

Phillips, G & Tapsall, SM 2007, *Australian television news trends: first results from a longitudinal study*, Centre for Public Culture and Ideas, Griffith University, Qld.

Roose, JM and Akbarzadeh, S 2013, 'The Special Broadcasting Service and the future of multiculturalism: an *Insight* into contemporary challenges and future direction, *Communication, Politics & Culture*, vol. 46, pp. 93–115.

'SBS reaps success with refugee reality show' 2011, *AdNews,* 24 June, viewed 30 October 2016 <http://www.adnews.com.au/adnews/sbs-reaps-success-with-refugee-reality-show>

Credits

Pages 91 and 93. Reproduced with kind permission of RMIT Publishing.
Page 96. Reproduced by permission of Transcript Verlag, Germany (2015).
Page 98. Reproduced with kind permission of Sydney University Press.
Page 100. Reproduced with permission from *The Conversation*.

15 APA Documentation

AT A *GLANCE*

- Use in-text citations (see 15a)
- Citations for print sources in APA style (see 15b to 15d)
- Citations for online sources in APA style (see 15e and 15f)

Social sciences disciplines—including government, linguistics, psychology, sociology and education—frequently use the American Psychological Association (APA) documentation style. The APA style is somewhat similar to the MLA: both styles use parenthetical citations in the body of the text, with complete bibliographical citations in the list of references at the end. If you have questions that the examples in this chapter do not address, consult the *Publication manual of the American Psychological Association*, 6th edition (2010).

APA Documentation Map

1 Collect the right information

For every source you need to have

- the name of the author or authors,
- the full title, and
- complete publication information.

For instructions go to the illustrated examples in Section 15b of the four major source types:

- **PERIODICAL SOURCES**
- **BOOKS AND NONPERIODICAL SOURCES**
- **ONLINE SOURCES**

For other kinds of sources such as visual and multimedia sources, see the Index of References on p. 135.

2 Cite sources in two places

Remember, this is a two-part process.

To create citations

(a) in **the body of your paper**, go to 15a.

(b) in a **list of References at the end of your paper**, go to 15b.

3 Find the right model citations

You'll find **illustrated examples of sources** in 15b.

Once you match your source to one of those examples, you can move on to more specific examples:

- **PERIODICAL SOURCES**, go to 15c.
- **BOOKS AND NONPERIODICAL SOURCES**, go to 15d.
- **ONLINE SOURCES**, go to 15e.

A complete list of examples is found in the Index of References on p. 135.

4 Format your paper

You will find pages from a **sample research paper in APA style** in 15g.

A note about footnotes:

APA style does not use footnotes for documentation. Use in-text citations instead (see 15a).

15a The Elements of APA Style

APA style emphasises the date of publication using author–date citations. When you cite an author's name in the body of your paper, always follow it with the date of publication. Notice too that APA style includes the abbreviation for page (p.) in front of the page number. A comma separates each element of the citation.

> Ambrosini (2016) found that about half of all Australian boys and girls eat at least two serves of fruit per day, which is the recommended amount. However, 'only 7% of girls and 23% of boys ate the recommended three serves of dairy' (p. 4).

If the author's name is not mentioned in the sentence, the reference looks like this:

> Researchers found that about half of all Australian boys and girls eat at least two serves of fruit per day, which is the recommended amount. However, 'only 7% of girls and 23% of boys ate the recommended three serves of dairy' (Ambrosini, 2016, p. 4).

The corresponding entry in the reference list would be

> Ambrosini, G. L. (2016). What do Australian teens really eat and is it important? *Nutridate, 27*(4), 3–9. Retrieved from http://search.informit.com.au/documentSummary;dn=312995095420840;res=IELHEA

Quotations forty words or longer

Orlean (2001) has attempted to explain the popularity of the painter Thomas Kinkade:

> People like to own things they think are valuable. . . . The high price of limited editions is part of their appeal; it implies that they are choice and exclusive, and that only a certain class of people will be able to afford them. (p. 128)

The sentence introducing the quotation names the author.

Note that the full stop appears before the parentheses in an indented 'block' quote.

The date appears in parentheses immediately following the author's name.

Index of in-text citations

1. **Author named in your text**

The influential political theorist Ulrich Beck (2012) defines *globality* as living in a world society where 'the notion of closed spaces has become illusory' (p. 35).

2. **Author not named in your text**

According to government figures, over 10 per cent of the population of the Philippines migrates overseas to work (Madinou & Miller, 2011, p. 459).

3. **Work by a single author**

(Bell, 1973, p. 3)

4. **Work by two authors**

List both authors' last names, joined with an ampersand.

(Wooley & Livingstone, 2010, p. 46)

5. **Work by three to five authors**

The authors' last names follow the order of the title page.

(Francisco, Vaughn, & Romano, 2012, p. 7)

Subsequent references can use the first name and *et al.*

(Francisco et al., 2012, p. 17)

6. **Work by six or more authors**

Use the first author's last name and *et al.* for all in-text references.

(Gainsbury et al., 2015, p. 13)

7. **Work by a group or organisation**

Identify the group in-text and place the page number in parentheses when it is referred to for the first time.

According to the Lowy Institute (2015), half of Australian adults believe that global warming is a 'serious and pressing problem' (p. 3).

Where the group is not identified in-text, it must be identified in parentheses and cited as follows when it is referred to for the first time.

50% of adults in Australia consider global warming to be a 'serious and pressing problem' (Lowy Institute [LI], 2015).

In both cases, subsequent references should be cited with the abbreviation of the group in brackets.

... (LI, 2015).

8. **Work by an unknown author**

Use a shortened version of the title (or the full title if it is short) in place of the author's name. Follow standard sentence capitalisation. If it is an article title, place it inside single quotation marks.

('Derailing the peace process', 2014, p. 44)

9. **Two works by one author published in the same year**

Assign the dates letters (*a*, *b*, etc.) according to their alphabetical arrangement in the reference list.

The majority of books written about co-authorship focus on partners of the same sex (Laird, 2007a, p. 351).

10. Parts of a digital source

If an online or other digital source does not provide page numbers, use the paragraph number preceded by the abbreviation *para.*

(Robinson, 2014, para. 7)

11. Two or more sources within the same sentence

Place each citation directly after the statement it supports.

Some researchers report that the incidence of gambling problems is high among the Australian younger population, including students (Cervini, 2013) and young adults prone to substance abuse issues (Hayatbakhsh et al., 2012).

If you need to cite two or more works within the same parentheses, list them in the order in which they appear in the reference list.

(Cervini, 2013; Hayatbakhsh et al., 2012)

12. Work quoted in another source

Castell's work on urban activism (as cited in Hutchins, 2016b)

Illustrated Examples and Index of References Entries in APA Style

Periodical sources

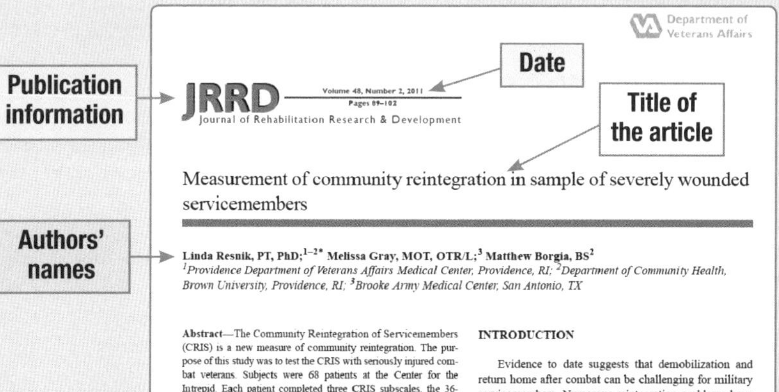

Department of Veterans Affairs

JRRD Volume 48, Number 2, 2011
Pages 89–102
Journal of Rehabilitation Research & Development

Measurement of community reintegration in sample of severely wounded servicemembers

Linda Resnik, PT, PhD;[1–2*] Melissa Gray, MOT, OTR/L;[3] Matthew Borgia, BS[2]
[1]Providence Department of Veterans Affairs Medical Center, Providence, RI; [2]Department of Community Health, Brown University, Providence, RI; [3]Brooke Army Medical Center, San Antonio, TX

Abstract—The Community Reintegration of Servicemembers (CRIS) is a new measure of community reintegration. The purpose of this study was to test the CRIS with seriously injured combat veterans. Subjects were 68 patients at the Center for the Intrepid. Each patient completed three CRIS subscales, the 36-Item Short Form Health Survey for Veterans (SF-36V), the Quality of Life Scale (QOLS), and two Craig Handicap Assessment and Reporting Technique subscales at visit 1 and the 3-month follow-up. Of the patients, 11 also completed the measures within 2 weeks of visit 1. We abstracted diagnoses and activities of daily living from the medical record. We evaluated test-retest reliability using intraclass correlation coefficients (ICCs). We evaluated concurrent validity with Pearson product moment correlations. We used multivariate analyses of variance to compare scores for subjects with and without posttraumatic stress disorder (PTSD), traumatic brain injury (TBI), and depression. Responsiveness analyses evaluated floor and ceiling effects, percent achieving minimal detectable change (MDC), effect size (ES), and the standardized response mean (SRM). CRIS subscale ICCs were 0.90 to 0.91. All subscales were moderately or strongly correlated with QOLS and SF-36V subscales. CRIS subscale scores were lower in PTSD and TBI groups ($p < 0.05$). CRIS Extent of Participation and Satisfaction with Participation subscales were lower for subjects with depression ($p < 0.05$). Of the sample, 17.4% to 23.2% had change greater than MDC. The ES ranged from 0.227 to 0.273 (SRM = 0.277–0.370), showing a small effect between visit 1 and the 3-month follow-up. Results suggest that the CRIS is a psychometrically sound choice for community reintegration measurement in severely wounded servicemembers.

Key words: community reintegration, disability, measurement, military healthcare, outcomes assessment, participation, psychometric testing, reliability, traumatic brain injury, veterans.

INTRODUCTION

Evidence to date suggests that demobilization and return home after combat can be challenging for military servicemembers. Numerous reintegration problems have been reported among veterans from the gulf war and more recent conflicts in Iraq and Afghanistan, including marital difficulties, financial difficulties, problems with alcohol or substance abuse, medical problems, behavioral problems such as depression or anxiety [1], homelessness [2], and motor vehicle accidents [3]. Readjustment to

Abbreviations: ADL = activity of daily living, ANOVA = analysis of variance, BAMC = Brooke Army Medical Center, CFI = Center for the Intrepid, CHART = Craig Handicap Assessment and Reporting Technique, CRIS = Community Reintegration of Servicemembers, ES = effect size, ICC = intraclass correlation coefficient, ICF = International Classification of Function, IED = improvised explosive device, MANOVA = multivariate analysis of variance, MDC = minimal detectable change, OEF = Operation Enduring Freedom, OIF = Operation Iraqi Freedom, PF-10 = 10-Item Physical Functioning Subscale, PTSD = posttraumatic stress disorder, QOLS = Quality of Life Scale, SD = standard deviation, SF-36V = 36-Item Short Form Health Survey for Veterans, SRM = standardized response mean, TBI = traumatic brain injury, VA = Department of Veterans Affairs.

***Address all correspondence to Linda Resnik, PT, PhD; Providence VA Medical Center, 830 Chalkstone Ave, Providence, RI 02908; 401-273-7100, ext 2368; fax: 401-863-3489. Email:** Linda_Resnik@brown.edu

DOI:10.1682/JRRD.2010.04.0070

Resnik, L., Gray, M., & Borgia, M. (2011). Measurement of community reintegration in sample of severely wounded servicemembers. *Journal of Rehabilitation Research and Development*, *48*, 89–102. doi:10.1682/JRRD.2010.04.0070

Elements of the citation

Author's name

The author's last name comes first, followed by the author's initials.

Join two authors' names with a comma and an ampersand.

Date of publication

Give the year the work was published in parentheses.

Newspapers and popular magazines are referenced by the year, month and day of publication.

Title of article

- Do not use quotation marks. If there is a book title in the article title, italicise it.
- Titles of articles in APA style follow standard sentence capitalisation.

Publication information

Name of journal

- Italicise the journal name.
- Put a comma after the journal name.

Volume, issue and page numbers

- Italicise the volume number.
- If each issue of the journal begins on page 1, give the issue number in parentheses, followed by a comma.
- If the article has been assigned a DOI (Digital Object Identifier), list it after the page numbers but without a full stop at the end.

Find the right example for your model (you may need to refer to more than one model)

What type of article do you have?

A scholarly journal article or abstract?

- For an article in a journal with continuous pagination, go to page 136, #17.
- For an article in a journal paginated by issue, go to page 136, #18.

A newspaper article?

- For a newspaper article, go to page 137, #20.

How many authors are listed?

- One, two or more authors: go to page 136, #13–15.
- Unknown author: go to page 136, #16.

Books and non-periodical sources

Author's name → Andrew T. Hickey

Title of the book → CITIES OF SIGNS

learning the logic of urban spaces

PETER LANG
New York • Washington, D.C./Baltimore • Bern
Frankfurt • Berlin • Brussels • Vienna • Oxford

Publisher and place of publication

Hickey, A. T. (2012). *Cities of signs: Learning the logic of urban spaces.* New York: Peter Lang Publishing.

Elements of the citation

Author's or editor's name

The author's last name comes first, followed by a comma and the author's initials.

If there is an editor, put the abbreviation *Ed.* in parentheses after the name, followed by a full stop. **Kavanagh, P. (Ed.).**

Year of publication

- Give the year the work was copyrighted in parentheses.
- If no year of publication is given, write n.d. ('no date') in parentheses.

Book title

- Italicise the title.
- Titles of books in APA style follow standard sentence capitalisation: capitalise only the first word, proper nouns and the first word after a colon.

Publication information

Place of publication

- For all books, list the city, state and country of the publisher. Locations within the US and Australia require only the city and the state.
- If more than one city is given on the title page, list only the first.
- Use a colon after the location.
- Insert a full stop after the publisher's name.

Publisher's name

Do not shorten or abbreviate words like *University* and *Press*. Omit words such as *Co.*, *Inc.* and *Publishers*.

Find the right example for your model (you may need to refer to more than one model)

How many authors are listed?
One, two or more authors: go to page 137, #21–24.

Do you have only a part of a book?

- For a chapter in an edited collection, go to page 138, #25.
- For an article in a reference work, go to page 138, #26.

Online sources

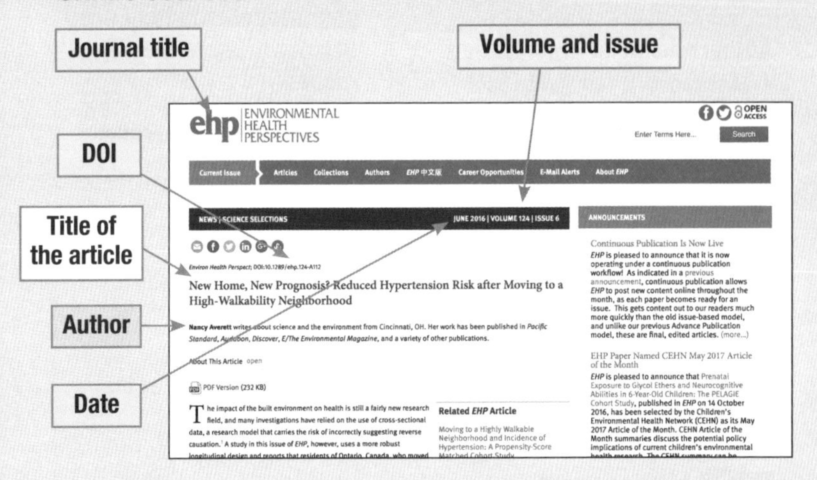

Averett, N. (2016). New home, new prognosis? Reduced hypertension risk after moving to a high-walkability neighborhood. *Environmental Health Perspectives, 124,* A112. doi:10.1289/ehp.124-A112

Elements of the citation

Author's name or organisation

- Authorship is sometimes hard to discern for online sources. If you have an author or a creator to cite, follow the rules for periodicals and books.
- If the only authority you find is a group or organisation, list its name as the author.

Dates

Give the date the site was produced or last revised (sometimes the copyright date) after the author.

Title of page or article

- Websites are often made up of many separate pages or articles. Each page or article on a website may or may not have a title.

URL

- Copy the address exactly as it appears in your browser window. You can even copy and paste the address into your text for greater accuracy.
- Break a URL at the end of a line *before* a mark of punctuation. Do not insert a hyphen.
- If the article has a DOI (Digital Object Identifier), give the DOI after the title. Do not list the URL.

Find the right example for your model (you may need to refer to more than one model)

What kind of publication do you have?

- For a publication in a database, go to pages 139–140, #29–#30.
- For an article with a DOI assigned, go to page 139, #34.
- For an article with no DOI assigned, go to page 140, #35.
- For an article in a newspaper or magazine, go to page 140, #36–#37.
- For a government publication, go to page 139, #33.

Do you have a source that is posted by an individual?

- For a blog, go to page 140, #38.
- For a post to a discussion list, go to page 140, #39.
- For email or text messaging, go to page 140, #40.

Index of References Entries

15c Periodical Sources 136

15d Book Sources 137

15e Online Sources 138

15f Visual and Multimedia Sources 141

15c Periodical Sources in the APA-Style Reference List

13. Article by one author

McCosker, A. (2014). Trolling as provocation: YouTube's agonistic publics. *Convergence: The International Journal of Research into New Media Technologies, 20*(2), 201–217.

14. Article by two authors

McClelland, D., & Eismann, K. (1998). [Follow with article title etc.]

15. Article by three or more authors

List last names and initials for up to seven authors, with an ampersand between the last two names. For works with eight or more authors, list the first six names, then an ellipsis, then the last author's name.

Andis, S., Franks, D., Gee, G., Ng, K., Orr, V., Ray, B., . . . Tate, L. [Follow with article title etc.]

16. Article by an unknown author

The green gene revolution. [Editorial]. (2004, February). *Scientific Australia, 291*, 8.

17. Article in a journal with continuous pagination

Include only the volume number and the year, not the issue number.

Croeser, S., & Highfield, T. (2015). Harbouring dissent: Greek independent and social media and the antifascist movement. *Fibreculture, 26*, 136–157.

18. Article in a journal paginated by issue

If each issue of the journal begins on page 1, give the issue number in parentheses (not italicised) after the volume number.

Bunyan, T. (2010). Just over the horizon—the surveillance society and the state in the EU. *Race and Class, 51*(3), 1–12.

19. Monthly publications

Barth, A. (2015, March). Brain science gets squishy. *Discover,* 11–12.

20. Newspaper article

Kaplan, S. (2016, September 12). Ocean and space scientists team up to look for alien life. *The Washington Post,* p. A16.

15d Books in the APA-Style Reference List

21. Book by one author

Fairfield, P. (2005). *Easy guide to Australian law*. Sydney, NSW: New Holland.

If an editor, put the abbreviation Ed. in parentheses after the name, followed by a full stop.

Marrapodi, M. (Ed.). (2016). *Shakespeare and Renaissance literary theories: Anglo-Italian transactions.* New York, NY: Routledge.

22. Two or more books by the same author

Arrange according to the date, with the earliest publication first.

DeLanda, M. (2006). *War in the age of intelligent machines*. New York, NY: Zone Books.

DeLanda, M. (2011). *Philosophy and simulation: The emergence of synthetic reason*. London, England: Continuum.

23. Book by two authors

Hardt, M., & Negri, A. (2000). *Empire.* Cambridge, MA: Harvard University Press.

24. Book by three or more authors

List last names and initials for up to seven authors, with an ampersand between the last two names. For works with eight or more authors, list the first six names, then an ellipsis, then the last author's name.

Anders, K., Child, H., David, K., Logan, O., Orr, J., Ray, B., ... Wood, G.

25. Chapter in an edited collection

Dehne, P. (2016). Profiting despite the Great War: Argentina's grain multinationals. In Smith, A., Tennent, K. D. & Mollan, S. (Eds.), *The impact of the First World War on international business* (pp. 67–86). New York, NY: Routledge.

26. Article in a reference work

Yothu Yindi. (1994). In D. Horton (General Ed.), *The encyclopaedia of Aboriginal Australia: Aboriginal and Torres Strait Islander history, society and culture*. Canberra, ACT: Aboriginal Studies Press for the Australian Institute of Aboriginal and Torres Strait Islander Studies.

27. Religious or classical texts

Reference entries are not required for major classical works or the Bible, but in the first in-text citation, identify the edition used.

John 3:16 (Modern Phrased Version)

28. E-books

Chaffe-Stengel, P., & Stengel, D. (2012). *Working with sample data: Exploration and inference*. http://dx.doi.org/10.4128/9781606492147

If the reference doesn't have a DOI assigned, include *Retrieved from* and the URL.

Burton, R. (1832). *The anatomy of melancholy*. Retrieved from http://etext.library.adelaide.edu.au/b/burton/robert/melancholy

15e Online Sources in the APA-Style Reference List

29. Document from a database

APA no longer requires listing the names of well-known databases. Include the name of the database only for hard-to-find books and other items.

Holloway, J. D. (2004). Protecting practitioners' autonomy. *Monitor on Psychology, 35*(1), 30.

If the source is not permanent, the removal date must be cited.

Australian Government Department of Foreign Affairs and Trade (2012, August 27). High Commissioner to Vanuatu. Retrieved from http://dfat.gov.au/releases/2012/ bc_mr_120824c.html

30. Abstract retrieved from a database

Putsis, W. P., & Bayus, B. L. (2001). An empirical analysis of firms' product line decisions. *Journal of Marketing Research*, *37*(8), 110–118. Abstract retrieved from PsycINFO database.

31. Online publication by a known author

Carr, A. (2003, May 22). *AAUW applauds Senate support of title IX resolution*. Retrieved from http://www.aauw.org/about/ newsroom/press_releases/030522.cfm

32. Online publication by a group or organisation

Girls Incorporated. (2003). *Girls' bill of rights*. Retrieved from http://www.girlsinc.org/ gc/ page.php?id=9

33. Online government publication

Australian Government. National Health and Medical Research Council Department of Age and Ageing. (2013, March 11). *Australian dietary guidelines: Providing the scientific evidence for healthier Australian diets*. Retrieved from https://www. nhmrc.gov.au/_files_nhmrc/publications/attachments/ n55_australian_dietary_guidelines_130530.pdf

34. Online article with DOI assigned

There is no need to list the database, the retrieval date or the URL if the DOI is listed.

Erdfelder, E. (2008). Experimental psychology: Good news. *Experimental Psychology, 55*(1), 1–2. doi:0.1027/1618-3169.55.1.1

35. Online article with no DOI assigned

Hudson, M. (2014). Music, knowledge and the sociology of sound. *Sociological Research Online, 19*(4). Retrieved from http://www.socresonline.org.uk

36. Article in an online newspaper

Mills, T. (2016, November 12). Super moon: Do the police believe lunar cycles are linked to violence?. *The Age*. Retrieved from http://www.theage.com.au

37. Article in an online magazine

Smith, B. (2015, June 1). A lifelong flu shot moves closer. *Cosmos.* Retrieved from http://www.cosmosmagazine.com

38. Blog entry

Soong, C. (2016, February 2). South Africa: Making memories at Gondwana Game Reserve [Web log post]. *The Hungry Australian*. Retrieved from https://hungryaustralian.com/2016/02/south-africa-gondwana-game-reserve/

39. Message posted to a newsgroup, online forum or discussion group

Tjelmeland, A. (2010, January 26). Zacate Creek [Electronic mailing list message]. Retrieved from http://server1.birdingonthe.net/mailinglists/TEXS.html#1264558433

40. Wiki

Mount Everest (n.d.). In *Wikipedia*. Retrieved November 12, 2013, from http://en.wikipedia.org/wiki/Mt._Everest

41. Email

Email sent from one individual to another should be cited as a personal communication. Personal communication is cited in-text but not included in the reference list.

(D. Jenkins, personal communication, July 12, 2014)

42. Twitter post, individual author

Duffy, A [astroduff]. (2016, November 10). Europe confirms space vision future w $2bn for new **#Ariane6** rocket, aiming to halve current launch costs [Tweet]. Retrieved from https://twitter.com/astroduff/status/796882524916092928

43. Social media (Facebook) page

The Daily Show. (2013, March 18). Political speeches contain much more than empty promises. [Facebook page]. Retrieved July 29, 2013, from https://www.facebook.com/thedailyshow

15f Visual and Multimedia Sources in the APA-Style Reference List

44. Lecture notes

Lecture notes are cited in-text and in the reference list. Include the following elements: name of author(s) or the institution, (year of publication). *Title and subtitle of document* [presentation media]. Unpublished manuscript, name of institution, location of institution (ensure you list the city, state and country—however, if the state is listed in the institution name, then do not repeat it in location).

Adams, C. (2012, July 26). Week five: Literary tools [Powerpoint slides]. Unpublished manuscript, SACW1001, Southern Cross University, Lismore, NSW.

If retrieved online, cite as follows.

Adams, C. (2012, July 26). Week five: Literary tools [Powerpoint slides]. Retrieved from SACW1001, MySCU: http://www.learn.scu.edu.au

45. Television program

Ball, A. (Writer), & Winant, S. (Director). (2008). The first taste [Television series episode]. In A. Ball (Producer), *True Blood*. New York, NY: HBO.

46. Film, video or DVD

Luhrmann, B. (Writer and Director). (2013). *The Great Gatsby* [Motion picture]. Sydney, Australia: Warner Bros.

47. Musical recording

Waits, T. (1980). Ruby's arms. On *Heart attack and vine* [CD]. New York, NY: Elektra Entertainment.

48. Graphic, audio or video file

Aretha Franklin: A life of soul. (2004, January 24). *NPR Online*. Retrieved from http://www.npr.org/features/feature.php?wfId=1472614

49. Photograph or work of art

American Heart Association. (2009). *Hands-only CPR graphic* [Photograph]. Retrieved from http://handsonlycpr.org/assets/files/Hands-only%20me.pdf

15g Sample Pages from a Research Paper with APA Documentation

Type the running head (the shortened title) in all caps, flush left at the top.

Running head: SURVEILLANOMICS 1

Surveillanomics: The Need for

Governmental Regulation of Video Surveillance

John M. Jones

The University of Melbourne

APA style uses a title page with a page number at the top right.

Centre the title, name of author(s) and name of university.

Continue to use the running head with the page number in the top right.

The abstract appears on a separate page with the title *Abstract*. An abstract may not exceed 150 words.

SURVEILLANOMICS 2

Abstract

Because recent technological advances have made it possible to use surveillance video to gather information about private citizens, and because unregulated data-mining has made this information economically valuable, the collection and use of video surveillance data should be regulated by the government. This regulation, based on the model introduced by Taylor (2002), should mandate that all video surveillance must be in accordance with the law, have a legitimate objective and be necessary for the maintenance of a free society. These guidelines would ensure that surveillance data could not be used for purposes other than those for which it was collected, and would make the primary concerns in debates over the use of surveillance democratic, not economic as they are now.

Do not indent the first line of the abstract.

Double-space the abstract.

The font should be Times Roman.

SURVEILLANOMICS 3

Surveillanomics: The Need for Governmental
Regulation of Video Surveillance

On 5 September 2005, the operators of the social networking site Facebook gave the service a facelift. One of the innovations they introduced was the 'news feed' feature, which 'automatically alerted users when their friends made changes to their online profiles', like changing personal details or adding new 'friends' (Meredith, 2006). This service, which was automatically installed for all accounts, outraged users, 700,000 of whom formed the group *Students Against Facebook News Feeds*. Before Facebook altered its implementation of this feature, the members of this group were preparing to protest the changes at the company's headquarters.

At first, this negative reaction by users took the company completely by surprise. As Schneier (2006) puts it, in their eyes, all they had done 'was take available data and aggregate it in a novel way for what [they] perceived was [their] customers' benefit'; however, users realised that this change 'made an enormous difference' to the way that their information could be aggregated, accessed and distributed. In other words, although Facebook news feeds did nothing more than take information that was already publicly available and repackage it in a new form, this new information source was seen by users as a massive invasion of their privacy.

In light of this reaction, it is interesting to note that right now companies referred to as 'data brokers' are creating …

Give the full title at the beginning of the body of the report.

Specify 2.5 cm margins.

Indent the first line of each paragraph 1.25 cm on the ruler in the word processing program.

Include the date in parentheses when you mention authors in the text.

Double-space the body of the report.

SURVEILLANOMICS 10

Centre *References* heading.

References

Alphabetise entries by last name of the author.

Double-space all entries.

Indent all but the first line of each entry five spaces.

Go through your text and make sure that everything you have cited, except for personal communications, is in the list of references.

Koskela, H. (2000). 'The gaze without eyes': Video-surveillance and the changing nature of urban space. *Progress in Human Geography*, *24*(2), 243–265.

Koskela, H. (2003). 'Cam era'—the contemporary urban panopticon. *Surveillance & Society*, 1(3), 292–313. Retrieved from http://www.surveillance-and-society.org

Lee, J. (2005, May 22). Caught on tape, then just caught: Private cameras transform police work. *The New York Times*. Retrieved from http://www.nytimes.com

Meredith, P. (2006, September 22). Facebook and the politics of privacy. *Mother Jones*. Retrieved from http://www.motherjones.com

Mieszkowski, K. (2003, September 25). We are all paparazzi now. *Salon*. Retrieved from http://archive.salon.com/tech/feature/2003/09/25/webcams/index.html

Nieto, M., Johnston-Dodds, K., & Simmons, C. W. (2002). *Public and private applications of video surveillance and biometric technologies*. Sacramento, CA: California Research Bureau, California State Library. Retrieved from http://www.library.ca.gov/CRB/02/06/02-006.pdf

O'Harrow, R. (2005). *No place to hide*. New York, NY: Free Press.

Schneier, B. (2006, September 21). Lessons from the Facebook riots. *Wired News*. Retrieved from http://www.wired.com/news/columns/0,71815-0.html

Credits

Page 129. Reproduced with permission from *Journal of Rehabilitation Research and Development*.
Page 131. Reproduced with kind permission of Peter Lang Publishing.
Page 133. Reproduced with permission from *Environmental Health Perspectives*.

16 MLA Documentation

AT A *GLANCE*

- Use in-text citation in MLA style (see 16a below)
- Use the new citation template (see 16b)
- Citations for print sources in MLA style (see 16c and 16d)
- Citations for online sources in MLA style (see 16e and 16f)
- Citations for multimedia sources in MLA style (see 16g)
- Main differences between the 7th and 8th editions (see p. 186)

The style developed by the Modern Language Association (MLA) follows an author–page method. It requires you to document each source in two places: an in-text citation in the body of your project, and a list of all works cited at the end.

16a The Elements of MLA Style

MLA style emphasises the author(s) and the page(s) of the source. When you quote, paraphrase or summarise a source, you can include the author's name either in the sentence through use of a signal phrase or in a parenthetical citation. The page number(s) should always be listed in an in-text citation. Note that in MLA style, no punctuation separates the author's surname and the page number(s) in an in-text citation.

For more information see the 8th edition of the *MLA Handbook* or visit the website www.mla.org.

Index of in-text citations

1. Author named in a signal phrase

Put the author's name in a signal phrase in your sentence.

Sociologist Gary Alan Fine argues that chess is a communal activity, not an individual one (16).

2. Author not named in your text

In 2014, 1.703 million viewers watched *Masterchef*'s finale. This was the biggest prime-time audience Channel Ten has had since July 2012 (Callaghan 13). This number reflects how pervasive cooking and food shows are in Australian television.

3. Work by one author

The author's last name comes first, followed by the page number. There is no comma.

(Fine 16)

4. Work by two or three authors

The authors' last names follow the order of the title page. If there are two authors, join the names with *and.* If there are three, use a comma between the first two names and a comma with *and* before the last name.

(Guzman, Vaughn, and Lynn 7)

5. Work by four or more authors

You may use the phrase *et al.* (meaning "and others" in Latin) for all names except the first, or you may write out all the names. Make sure you use the same method for both the in-text citations and the works-cited list.

(McGill et al.)

6. Author unknown

Use a shortened version of the title that includes at least the first important word. Your reader will use the shortened title to find the full title in the works-cited list.

A review in the *The Age* of Taika Waititi's new movie *Hunt for the Wilderpeople* praises 13-year-old Julian Dennison's performance. ("Hunt" 36).

Notice that "Hunt" is in quotation marks because it is the shortened title of an article. If it were a book, the short title would be in italics.

7. Quotations longer than four lines

Note: When using indented (block) quotations that are longer than four lines, the full stop appears *before* the parentheses enclosing the page number.

In her article "Art for Everybody," Susan Orlean attempts to explain the popularity of painter Thomas Kinkade:

> People like to own things they think are valuable. . . . The high price of limited editions is part of their appeal: it implies that they are choice and exclusive, and that only a certain class of people will be able to afford them. (128)

This same statement could also explain the popularity of phenomena like the BBC's *Antiques Road Show.*

8. Two or more works by the same author

Use the author's last name and then a shortened version of the title of each source.

> The majority of books written about co-authorship focus on partners of the same sex (Laird, *Women* 351).

Note that *Women* is italicised because it is the title of a book.

9. Different authors with the same last name

Include the initial of the first name in the parenthetical reference.

> Web surfing requires more mental involvement than channel surfing (S. Johnson 107).

10. Two or more sources within the same citation

If two sources support a single point, separate them with a semicolon.

> (McKibbin 39; Gore 92)

11. Work quoted in another source

When you do not have access to the original source of the material you wish to use and only an indirect source is available, put the abbreviation *qtd. in* (quoted in) before the information about the indirect source.

> National governments have become increasingly what Ulrich Beck, in a 1999 interview, calls "zombie institutions"—institutions which are "dead and still alive" (qtd. in Bauman 6).

12. One-page source

A page reference is unnecessary when you are citing a one-page work.

> Economists agree that automating routine work is the broad goal of globalization (Lohr).

13. Web sources including Web pages, blogs, podcasts, wikis, videos and other multimedia sources

MLA prefers that you mention the author in your text instead of putting the author's name in parentheses.

> Andrew Keen ironically used his own blog to claim that "blogs are boring to write (yawn), boring to read (yawn) and boring to discuss (yawn)."

14. Classic works

To supply a reference to classic works, you sometimes need more than a page number from a specific edition. Readers should be able to locate a quotation in any edition of the book. Give the page number from the edition that you are using, then a semicolon and other identifying information.

"Marriage is a house" is one of the most memorable lines in *Don Quixote* (546; pt. 2, bk. 3, ch. 19).

16b Illustrated Examples and Index of Works-Cited Entries in MLA Style

The latest edition of the MLA Handbook was updated to suit the era of digital publication. It proposes a template that is easily applied to any source. You don't have to fill in every field, but instead should aim to include as many fields as possible to make sure your readers can find all the sources you used in your paper. The key is to be consistent throughout your paper. This is the information you need to include in the works-cited list:

1. Author.
2. Title of source.
3. *Title of container,*
4. Other contributors,
5. Version,
6. Number,
7. Publisher,
8. Publication date,
9. Location.

When you cite a paper retrieved from a database, for example, you might need to include a bit more information in your citation to make sure your readers can easily find the material you've quoted. In these cases, list the title of the second container in italics and include, if available, the names of other contributors, the version, the publisher's name, the publication date and location.

Printed article

Scholarly journals usually list the publication information at the top or bottom of the first page. Popular magazines often do not list volume and issue numbers, but a few do. If that's the case, you can find the date of publication on the cover and the volume and issue on the spine or masthead's fine print.

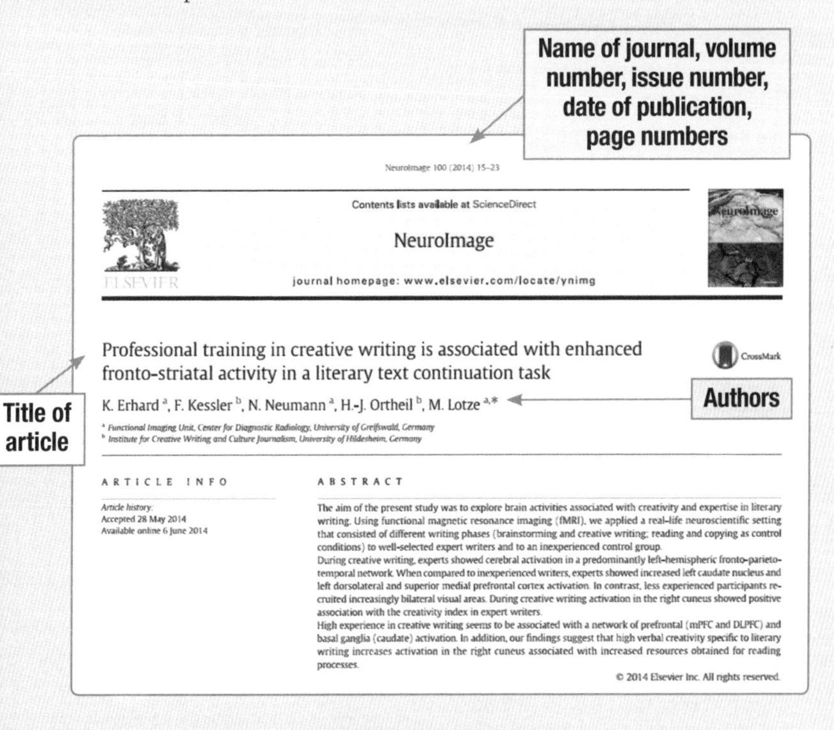

NeuroImage 100 (2014) 15–23

Contents lists available at ScienceDirect

NeuroImage

journal homepage: www.elsevier.com/locate/ynimg

ELSEVIER

Professional training in creative writing is associated with enhanced fronto-striatal activity in a literary text continuation task

K. Erhard [a], F. Kessler [b], N. Neumann [a], H.-J. Ortheil [b], M. Lotze [a,*]

[a] *Functional Imaging Unit, Center for Diagnostic Radiology, University of Greifswald, Germany*
[b] *Institute for Creative Writing and Culture Journalism, University of Hildesheim, Germany*

ARTICLE INFO

Article history:
Accepted 28 May 2014
Available online 6 June 2014

ABSTRACT

The aim of the present study was to explore brain activities associated with creativity and expertise in literary writing. Using functional magnetic resonance imaging (fMRI), we applied a real-life neuroscientific setting that consisted of different writing phases (brainstorming and creative writing; reading and copying as control conditions) to well-selected expert writers and to an inexperienced control group.
During creative writing, experts showed cerebral activation in a predominantly left-hemispheric fronto-parieto-temporal network. When compared to inexperienced writers, experts showed increased left caudate nucleus and left dorsolateral and superior medial prefrontal cortex activation. In contrast, less experienced participants recruited increasingly bilateral visual areas. During creative writing activation in the right cuneus showed positive association with the creativity index in expert writers.
High experience in creative writing seems to be associated with a network of prefrontal (mPFC and DLPFC) and basal ganglia (caudate) activation. In addition, our findings suggest that high verbal creativity specific to literary writing increases activation in the right cuneus associated with increased resources obtained for reading processes.

© 2014 Elsevier Inc. All rights reserved.

Citation in the List of Works Cited

Lotze, Martin et al. "Professional Training in Creative Writing is Associated with Enhanced Fronto-Striatal Activity in a Literary Text Continuation Task." *NeuroImage*, vol. 100, 2014, pp. 15–23.

Elements of the citation

Author's name

The author's last name comes first, followed by a comma and the first name.

For two or more works by the same author, see page 165.

Title of source

Use the exact title and put it inside double quotation marks. If a book title is part of the article's title, italicise the book title.

Publication information

Title of the container is, in this case, the name of the journal, newspaper or magazine in which the paper or article was published and it should be italicised. This is one of the new elements introduced in the 8th edition of MLA.

Number and location
For scholarly journals give the number (volume and number). Place a comma after the volume number.

Some scholarly journals use issue numbers only.

In this case, location refers to the page numbers for the entire article, not just the part you used.

Find the right example for your model (you may need to refer to more than one model)

What type of article do you have?

A scholarly journal article?
Go to page 162, #22–23.

A newspaper article, review, editorial or letter to the editor?

- For a newspaper article, go to pages 163–164, #27–31.
- For a review, go to page 164, #32.
- For an editorial, go to page 164, #34.
- For a letter to the editor, go to page 164, #33.

A government document?
Go to pages 164–165, #35–36.

How many authors are listed?

- One, two or more authors: go to page 161, #15–17.
- Unknown author: go to page 161, #18.

What kind of pagination is used?

- For a scholarly journal, go to page 162, #22.
- For a journal that starts every issue with page 1, go to page 162, #23.

Printed and digital books

Find the copyright date on the copyright page, which is on the back of the title page. Use the copyright date for the date of publication, not the date of printing.

MIT Press books may be purchased at special quantity discounts for business or sales promotional use. For information, please email special_sales@mitpress.mit.edu or write to Special Sales Department, The MIT Press, 55 Hayward Street, Cambridge, MA 02142.

This book was set in Stone Sans and Stone Serif by Toppan Best-set Premedia Limited, Hong Kong. Printed and bound in the United States of America.

Library of Congress Cataloging-in-Publication Data

Neuroscience of creativity / edited by Oshin Vartanian, Adam S. Bristol, and James C. Kaufman.
pages cm
Includes bibliographical references and index.
ISBN 978-0-262-01958-3 (hardcover : alk. paper)
1. Creative ability. 2. Cognitive neuroscience. I. Vartanian, Oshin, 1970–. II. Bristol, Adam S., 1975–.
BF408.N5196 2013
153.3'5—dc23
2013004389

10 9 8 7 6 5 4 3 2 1

Citation in the List of Works Cited

Printed edition:

Vartanian, Oshin, Adam S. Bristol, and James C. Kaufman, editors. *Neuroscience of Creativity*. MIT Press, 2013.

Digital edition:

Vartanian, Oshin, Adam S. Bristol, and James C. Kaufman, editors. *Neuroscience of Creativity*. Kindle Edition, MIT Press, 2013.

Elements of the citation

Author or editor's name

The author or editor's last name comes first, followed by a comma and the first name.

It's no longer necessary to abbreviate the word editor (or translator, when relevant).

Title of source

In the case of books, use the exact title as it appears on the title page (not the cover).

Italicise the title.

Publication information

Publisher
Publishers' names must be given in full.

In the case of university presses, the abbreviation *UP is still in use:* Melbourne UP.

If there are two or more publishers use a forward slash to separate their names.

When an organisation is the author and publisher, the organisation name is given just once as the publisher.

Publication date
Give the year as it appears on the copyright page.

If you find the date of publication in a reliable external source, you may include that information in square brackets.

Find the right example for your model (you may need to refer to more than one model)

How many authors are listed?

- One, two or more authors: go to pages 165–166, #38–41.
- Unknown author: go to page 166, #42.
- Group or organisation as the author: go to page 166, #43.

Do you have only a part of a book?

- For an introduction, foreword, preface or afterword, go to page 166, #44.
- For a chapter in an anthology or edited collection, go to page 166, #45.
- For more than one selection in an anthology or edited collection, go to page 166, #46.

Do you have two or more books by the same author?

- Go to page 165, #39.

E-books and other electronic editions

If you read this book on your Kindle, you need to acknowledge it. Electronic editions of printed books are considered versions. Name the e-reader device after the title of a book.

Note that according to the 8th edition of the MLA Handbook it's no longer necessary to include the city of publication, unless the book was printed before 1900 or is a rare book. Give the medium of publication.

Video

You may have found your topic or a quote in a TedTalk, online documentary or YouTube video. If that's the case you need to acknowledge it. Follow the same guidelines you use for citing print sources.

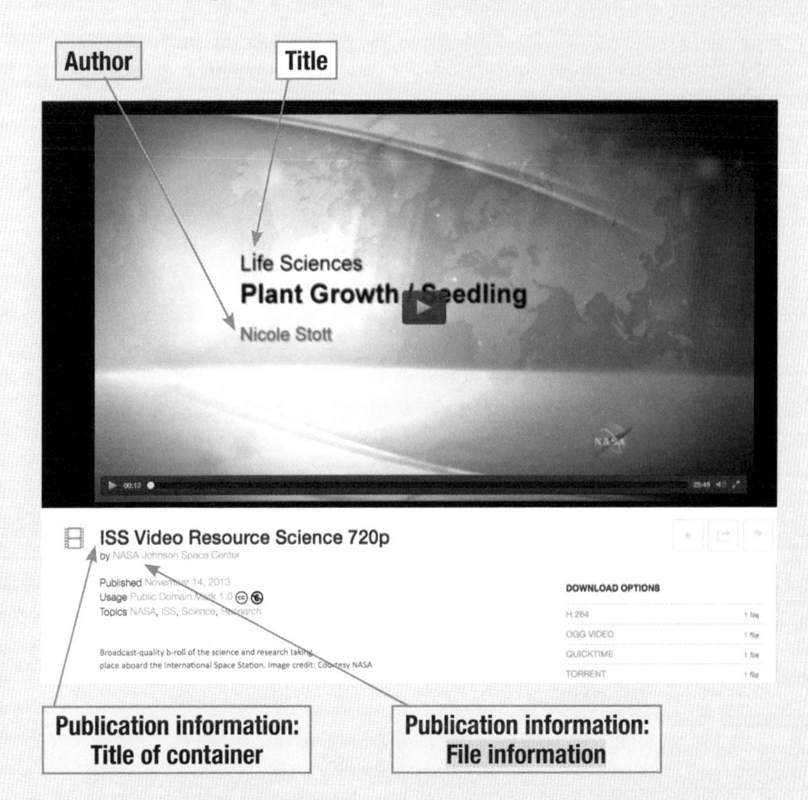

Citation in the List of Works Cited

Stott, Nicole. "Life Sciences: Plant Growth / Seedling." *ISS Video Resource,* uploaded Nov. 2013, https://archive.org/details/ISSVideoResourceScience720p

Elements of the citation

Start the citation with the name of the author followed by the title of the video. Include the title of the container in italics (that is YouTube, Vimeo or similar platforms) and include the URL without the http:// or https://.

Author's name

The author's last name comes first, followed by a comma and the first name.

Title of source

Use the exact title and put it inside double quotation marks.

Publication information for online video

Title of the container

Italicise the title of the site or platform the video was found on (YouTube, Vine, Facebook, Instagram, etc). Abbreviate the title if it commonly appears that way.

File information

If relevant, include the name of the host, director or performers after the title of the container. List the name of the publisher, publication date (or the day when it was uploaded), name of the database (if applicable) and the URL without the http:// or https://.

Find the right example for your model (you may need to refer to more than one model)

What kind of publication do you have?

- For an article in a scholarly journal, go to page 168, #55.
- For a magazine article, go to page 168, #56.
- For a newspaper article, go to page 169, #58.
- For a legal case, go to page 169, #59.

Do you have a publication with an unknown author?
Go to page 169, #57.

Web publication

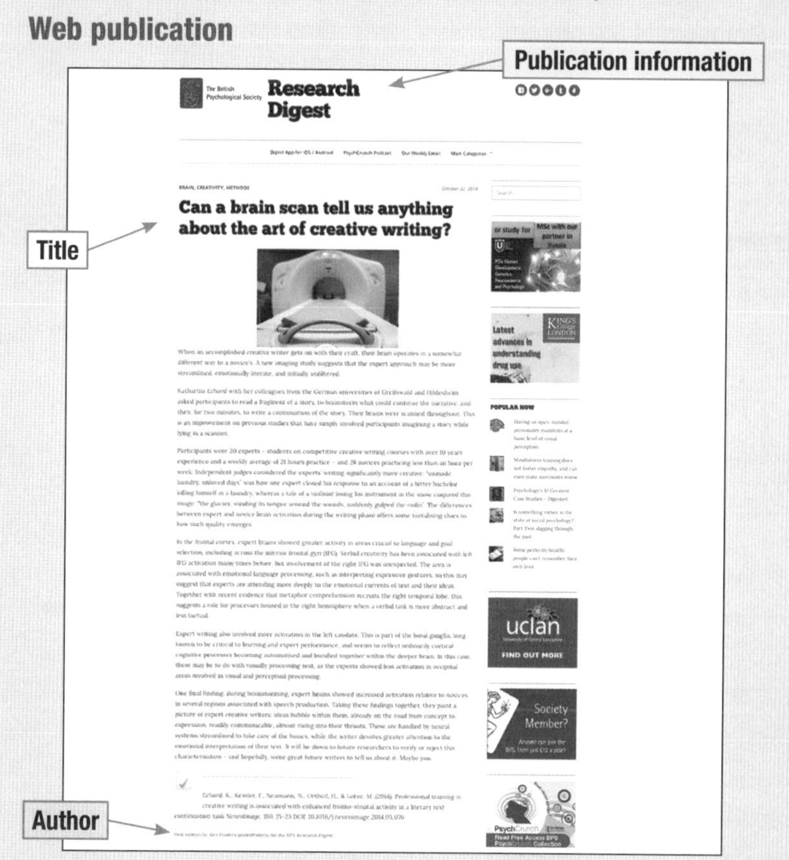

Citation in the List of Works Cited

Fradera, Alex. "Can a brain scan tell us anything about the art of creative writing?" *BPS Research Digest*, 22 Oct. 2014, digest.bps.org.uk/2014/10/22/can-a-brain-scan-tell-us-anything-about-the-art-of-creative-writing/.

When do you list a URL?

Always, unless a DOI or permalink is available, in that case include those. Make sure you include the complete web address for the site except for the *http://* or *https://*.

Elements of the citation

Author's name

Authorship is sometimes hard to discern for online sources. If you know the author or creator, follow the rules for books and journals.

If the only authority you find is a group or organisation, list its name before the date of publication.

Title of source

Place the title of the work inside quotation marks if it is part of a larger website.

Untitled works may be identified by a label (e.g. *Home page*, *Introduction*). List the label in the title slot without quotation marks or italics.

Italicise the name of the overall site if it is different from the work. The name of the overall website will usually be found on its index or home page.

Some websites are updated, so list the version if you find it (e.g. *Vers. 1.2*).

Publication information for Web sources

List the name of the publisher followed by a comma. If it isn't available, use *N.p.*

List the date of publication by day, month (abbreviate all months except May, June and July) and year.

Find the right example for your model

Do you have a Web page or an entire website?

- For an entire website, go to page 169, #61.
- For a page on a website, go to page 169, #60.

What kind of publication do you have, and who is the author?

- For a known author, go to page 170, #62.
- For a group or organisation as the author, go to page 170, #63.
- For a publication with print publication data, go to page 170, #64.
- For a PDF or digital file, go to page 170, #65.
- For an article in a scholarly journal, newspaper or magazine, go to pages 170–171, #66–68.

Do you have a source that is posted by an individual?

- For email or text messaging, go to page 172, #75.
- For a post to a discussion list, go to page 172, #76.
- For a personal home page, go to page 173, #78.
- For a blog, go to page 173, #79.
- For social media, go to page 172, #72.

Index of Works-Cited Entries

16c Journals, Magazines, Newspapers and Other Print Sources 161

16d Books 165

16e Library Database Sources 168

16f Online Sources 169

16h Visual and Multimedia Sources 173

16c Journals, Magazines, Newspapers and Other Print Sources in the MLA-Style Works-Cited List

JOURNAL AND MAGAZINE ARTICLES

15. Article by one author

Bhabha, Jacqueline. "The Child—What Sort of Human?" *PMLA,* vol. 121, no. 5, 2006, pp. 1526–35.

16. Article by two or three authors

The second and subsequent authors' names are printed first name first.

Kirsch, Gesa E., and Jacqueline J. Royster. "Feminist Rhetorical Practices: In Search of Excellence." *CCC,* vol. 61, no. 4, 2010, pp. 640–72.

Notice that a comma separates the authors' names.

17. Article by four or more authors

You may use the phrase *et al.* for all authors but the first, or you may write out all the names.

Breece, Katherine E., et al. "Patterns of mtDNA Diversity in Northwestern North America." *Human Biology,* vol. 76, no. 5, 2004, pp. 33–54.

18. Article by an unknown author

Begin the entry with the title.

"The Day the Great Barrier Reef Lost." *Australian Science and Environment,* 5 July 2014, pp. 20–9.

19. Article with a title within a title

If the title of the article contains the title of another short work, include it in single quotation marks. Italicise a title or a word that would normally be italicised.

Happel, Alison, and Jennifer Esposito. "Vampires, Vixens, and Feminists: An Analysis of *Twilight.*" *Educational Studies,* vol. 46, no. 5, 2010, pp. 524–31.

MONTHLY, WEEKLY AND BIWEEKLY MAGAZINES

20. Monthly or seasonal magazines or journals

Use the month (or season) and year in place of the volume. Abbreviate the names of all months except May, June and July.

Miklos, Anna. "Why We Still Need to Talk About Adoption." *Five Corners,* Spring, 2010, pp. 50–72.

21. Weekly or biweekly magazines

For weekly or biweekly magazines, give both the day and the month of publication, as listed on the issue.

Toobin, Jeffrey. "Crackdown." *The New Yorker,* 5 Nov. 2001, pp. 56–61.

DIFFERENT TYPES OF PAGINATION

22. Article in a scholarly journal

List the volume and issue numbers after the name of the journal.

Duncan, Mike. "Whatever Happened to the Paragraph?" *College English*, vol. 69, no. 5, 2007, pp. 470–95.

23. Article in a scholarly journal that uses only issue numbers

If a journal begins each issue on page 1, list the issue number after the name of the journal.

McCall, Sophie. "Double Vision Reading." *Canadian Literature,* issue 194, 2007, pp. 95–7.

REVIEWS, EDITORIALS, LETTERS TO THE EDITOR

24. Review

Provide the title and name the work reviewed. If there is no title, just name the work reviewed. Include the name of the author, director or artist if relevant to your paper. Italicise the titles of books, plays, television shows and films; use quotation marks for short stories or poems.

George, Jeff. "Saving the World One Word at a Time." Review of *Arrival*, director Denis Villeneuve, *Hawthorne Quarterly*, 1 Nov. 2016, pp. 27–30.

25. Letter to the editor

Add the word *Letter* after the name of the author.

Patai, Daphne. Letter. *Harper's Magazine,* Dec. 2011, p. 4.

26. Editorial

If the editorial is unsigned, put the title first. Add the word *Editorial* after the title. If the editorial is signed, add the word Editorial after the author's name.

"High Court Ruling Doesn't Mean Vouchers Will Work." Editorial. *Atlanta Journal and Constitution*, 28 June 2001, p. A19.

NEWSPAPER ARTICLES

27. Article by one author

Rojas, Rick. "For Young Sikhs, a Tie That Binds Them to Their Faith." *The Washington Post,* 20 June 2010, final ed., p. C03.

28. Article by two or three authors

The second and subsequent authors' names are printed in regular order, first name first.

Chazen, Guy, and Dana Cimilluca. "BP Amasses Cash for Oil-Spill Costs." *The Wall Street Journal,* 26 June 2010, p. A1.

29. Article by four or more authors

You may use the phrase *et al.* for all authors but the first, or you may write out all the names. Use the same method in the in-text citation as you do in the works-cited list.

Watson, Anne, et al. "Childhood Obesity on the Rise." *The Daily Missoulian,* 7 July 2003, p. B1.

30. Article by an unknown author

Begin the entry with the title.

"Democratic Candidates Debate Iraq War." *Austin American-Statesman,* 19 Jan. 2004, p. A6.

31. Article that continues to a non-consecutive page

Add a plus sign after the number of the first page.

> Kaplow, Larry, and Tasgola Karla Bruner. "U.S.: Don't Let Taliban Forces Flee." *Austin American-Statesman,* 20 Nov. 2001, final ed., p. A11+.

NEWSPAPER REVIEWS, EDITORIALS, LETTERS TO THE EDITOR

32. Review

List the reviewer's name and the title of the *review*. Then write review of followed by the title of the work, the word *by* and the author's name.

> Scott, A.O. "A Midlife Crisis for a Harried Former Assassin," review of *Jason Bourne*, directed by Paul Greengrass. *The New York Times,* 29 July 2016, p. C13.

If your paper is about the performance of Matt Damon in the Jason Bourne series, you could alter the citation to suit your topic:

> Scott, A.O. "A Midlife Crisis for a Harried Former Assassin," review of *Jason Bourne*, performance by Matt Damon. *The New York Times,* 29 July 2016, p. C13.

33. Letter to the editor

> Leach, Richard E. Letter. *Boston Globe,* 2 Apr. 2007, first ed., p. A10.

34. Editorial

If the editorial is unsigned, put the title first.

> "High Court Ruling Doesn't Mean Vouchers Will Work." Editorial. *Atlanta Journal and Constitution,* 28 June 2002, home ed., p. A19.

GOVERNMENT DOCUMENTS

35. Government document

> Australian Bureau of Statistics. *Characteristics of People Using Mental Health Services and Prescription Medication, 2011*. ABS, 2014.

36. *Hansard*

Hansard is the official report of parliamentary debates in Australia.

Australia, Senate 2000, *Debates*, vol. S25, p. 65.

DISSERTATIONS

37. **Published dissertation or thesis**

Ball, Benjamin. *Hearing with Light, Seeing with Sound: Aesthetic Journalism as a Place for Depth and Difficulty in a Media Life.* Dissertation, University of Technology Sydney, 2014.

16d Books in the MLA-Style Works-Cited List

ONE AUTHOR

38. **Book by one author**

Mayer-Schönberger, Viktor. *Delete: The Virtue of Forgetting in the Digital Age*. Princeton UP, 2009.

39. **Two or more books by the same author**

In the entry for the first book, include the author's name. In the second entry, substitute three hyphens and a full stop for the author's name. List the titles of books by the same author in alphabetical order.

Krakauer, Jon. *Into the Wild*. Villard, 1996.

—. *Where Men Win Glory: The Odyssey of Pat Tillman*. Doubleday, 2009.

MULTIPLE AUTHORS

40. **Book by two or three authors**

The second and subsequent authors' names appear first name first.

Burger, Edward B., and Michael Starbird. *Coincidences, Chaos, and All That Math Jazz*. Norton, 2006.

41. Book by four or more authors

You may use the phrase *et al.* (meaning 'and others') for all authors except the first, or you may write out all the names. Use the same method in the in-text citation as you do in the works-cited list.

North, Stephen M., et al. *Refiguring the Ph.D. in English Studies.* NCTE, 2000.

ANONYMOUS AND GROUP AUTHORS

42. Book by an unknown author

Begin the entry with the title.

Encyclopedia of Australia. Oxford UP, 2001.

43. Book by a group or organisation

Treat the group as the author of the work.

Australian Human Rights Commission. *What Does the Children's Rights Report 2015 Say?/National Children's Commissioner.* Sydney Australian Human Rights Commission, 2015.

PARTS OF BOOKS

44. Introduction, foreword, preface or afterword

Benstock, Sheri. Introduction. *The House of Mirth*, by Edith Wharton. Bedford-St. Martin's, 2002, pp. 3–24.

45. Chapter in an anthology or edited collection

Garner, Helen. "This Old Self." *The Best Australian Essays 2016*, edited by Geordie Williamson, Black Inc, 2016, pp. 54–68.

46. More than one selection from an anthology or edited collection

Multiple selections from a single anthology can be handled by creating a complete entry for the anthology and shortened cross-references for individual works in that anthology.

Hay, Ashley, editor. *The Best Australian Science Writing 2014*. University of New South Wales Press, 2014.

Phillips, Nicky. "Survival in the City." Hay, pp. 20–5.

Suddendorf, Thomas. "Uniquely Human." Hay, pp. 180–7.

47. Article in a reference work

"Utilitarianism." *The Columbia Encyclopedia*. 6th ed., 2001.

THE BIBLE AND OTHER SACRED TEXTS

48. Sacred texts

The New Oxford Annotated Bible. Edited by Bruce M. Metzger and Roland E. Murphy. Oxford UP, 1991.

Use a full stop to separate the chapter and verse in the in-text note: (John 3.16)

EDITIONS, TRANSLATIONS AND ILLUSTRATED BOOKS

49. Book with an editor—focus on the editor

Lewis, Gifford, editor. *The Big House of Inver*, by Edith Somerville and Martin Ross. Farmar, 2000.

50. Book with an editor—focus on the author

Somerville, Edith, and Martin Ross. *The Big House of Inver*, edited by Gifford Lewis. Farmar, 2000.

51. Book with a translator

Mallarmé, Stéphane. *Divagations*, translated by Barbara Johnson. Harvard UP, 2007.

52. Second or subsequent edition of a book

Hawthorn, Jeremy, editor. *A Concise Glossary of Contemporary Literary Theory*. 3rd ed., Arnold, 2001.

53. Illustrated book or graphic narrative

After the title of the book, give the illustrator's name. If the emphasis is on the illustrator's work, place the illustrator's name first, and list the author after the title, preceded by the word *By*.

Strunk, William, Jr., and E. B. White. *The Elements of Style Illustrated*, illustrated by Maira Kalman. Penguin, 2005.

MULTIVOLUME WORKS

54. One volume of a multivolume work

Samuel, Raphael. *Theatres of Memory*. Vol. 1. Verso, 1999.

16e Library Database Sources in the MLA-Style Works-Cited List

All articles retrieved from databases have two containers (the periodical itself and the database or Google Books), so make sure you follow the new template and include all relevant information for the second container. Remember that you don't have to fill in all the fields, just those relevant to the source. Be consistent and if you have questions, ask your lecturer.

55. Scholarly journal article from a library database

Strangio, Paun. "The Ancestry of the Australian Prime Ministership: 'The Blue Ribbon of the Highest Possible Ambition'." *Australian Journal of Politics & History*, vol. 61, no. 1, pp. 19–36. *Academic Search Complete*, doi: 10.1111/ajph.12084.

56. Magazine article from a library database

You can add the access date at the end of the citation or you can omit it. If you decide to include the access date, you have to be consistent throughout your list of works cited. Remember that the 8th edition encourages its users to include the URL. Consult your lecturer if you have questions.

Chacos, Brad. "Facebook is Finally Building a Dislike Button." *PC World*, Nov. 2015, pp. 65–6. *Academic Search Complete*, search.ebscohost.com/login.aspx?direct=true&db=a9h&AN=110843240&site=ehost-live&scope=site.

57. Article with unknown author from a library database

"The Real Cost of That 'Free App' Just Might Be Your Privacy." *St. Joseph News – Pres,* 12 Oct. 2012, *ProQuest,* search.proquest.com.ezproxy/usnews/docview/1104985762/13429F3377C4469EPQ/7?accountid=14205.

58. Newspaper article from a library database

Lo Dico, Joy. "Between a Nice Rock and a Legal Place." *Evening Standard*, 24 Mar. 2016, p. 16. *EBSCOhost*, search.ebscohost.com/login.aspx?direct=true&db=nfh&AN=113947709&site=ehost-live&scope=site

59. Legal case from a library database

"People v. Aaron". *NW 2d*. Supreme Court of Michigan, vol. 299, 1980, *Google Scholar*, scholar.google.com/scholar_case?case=5726386068390560061&q=murder&hl=en&as_sdt=4,115,199

16f Online Sources in the MLA-Style Works-Cited List

WEBSITES

60. Page on a website

Follow the new template and include the author or editor, the title of the page, the title of the site in italics, the publisher of the site, publishing date, the URL (without http://), and any other information that may be useful to your readers.

Ossola, Alexandra. "Recycled Packing Peanuts Could Make Batteries Better." *Australian Popular Science*, 24 Mar. 2015, www.popsci.com.au/science/energy/page9.

61. Entire website

Research. RMIT University, 20 July 2016, www.rmit.edu.au/research.

PUBLICATIONS ON THE WEB

62. Publication by a known author

Low, Nic. "New Writing for the Real Australia." *Southerly*, 21 Nov. 2016, southerlyjournal.com.au/2016/11/21/new-writing-for-the-real-australia.

63. Publication by a group or organisation

If a work has no author's or editor's name listed, begin the entry with the title.

"Adopt a Wild Koala." *Koala Hospital*. Koala Preservation Society Australia Incorporated, 2013, www.koalahospital.org.au/adopt-a-koala.

64. Publication on the Web with print publication data

Include the print publication information, give the name of the website or database in italics and list the URL.

Kirsch, Irwin S., et al. *Adult Literacy in Australia*. Diane, 1993. *Google Scholar*, rer.sagepub.com/content/82/1/276.short.

65. PDFs and digital files

Glaser, Edward L., and Albert Saiz. "The Rise of the Skilled City." Discussion Paper No. 2025. Harvard Institute of Economic Research. Harvard U, 2003, papers.ssrn.com/sol3/papers.cfm?abstract_id=569867.

PERIODICALS ON THE WEB

66. Article in a scholarly journal on the Web

Some scholarly journals are published on the Web only. List articles by author, title, name of journal in italics, volume and issue number, year of publication and DOI or URL.

Fleckenstein, Kristie. "Who's Writing? Aristotelian Ethos and the Author Position in Digital Poetics." *Kairos*, vol. 11, no. 3, 2007, kairos.technorhetoric.net/11.3/topoi/fleckenstein/index.html.

67. Article in a newspaper on the Web

Brown, Patricia Leigh. "Australia in Sonoma." *The New York Times*, 5 July 2008, www.nytimes.com/2008/07/03/garden/03australia.html3.

68. Article in a popular magazine on the Web

DePalma, Anthony. "How Fake News Created the Myth of Fidel Castro as Latin Robin Hood." *Newsweek*, 26 Nov. 2016, europe.newsweek.com/fake-news-myth-fidel-castro-robin-hood-525527

BOOKS, ARCHIVES AND GOVERNMENT PUBLICATIONS ON THE WEB

69. Book on a database

Sumner, David E., and Holly G. Miller. *Feature and Magazine Writing: Action, Angle, and Anecdotes*. 3rd ed. Wiley-Blackwell, 2013. *Google Books*, books.google.com.au/books?id=806mWThQHkwC&lpg=PT80&ots=29F16D4zLw&dq=masthead's%20fineprint&pg=PT10#v=onepage&q=masthead's%20fineprint&f=false.

70. Document within an archive on the Web

Give the print information, then the title of the scholarly project or archive in italics.

"New York Quiet." *Franklin Repository,* 5 Aug. 1863, 1. *Valley of the Shadow*, www2.vcdh.virginia.edu/saxon/servlet/SaxonServlet?source=/xml_docs/valley_news/newspaper_catalog.xml&style=/xml_docs/valley_news/news_cat.xsl&level=edition&paper=fr&year=1863&month=08&day=05&edition=fr1863/pa.fr.fr.1863.08.05.xml.

71. Government publication

If you cannot locate the author of the document, give the name of the government and the agency that published it.

Australian Government. Dept. of Social Services. *Beginning a Life in Australia*. Dept. of Immigration and Citizenship, Sept. 2016, www.dss.gov.au/our-responsibilities/settlement-services/beginning-a-life-in-australia.

UNEDITED ONLINE SOURCES

72. Posting on social media

Many organisations now use Facebook and other social media. Give the author, title, name of the organisation, name of the container (Facebook in this case, but it could be other platform) and date of publication.

> Eklund, Dung. "Dedicated to Myself." Metropolitan Museum of Art. Facebook, 14 Mar. 2013, www.facebook.com/metmuseum/posts/149503738548617?pnref=story.

73. Posting on Twitter

Use the Twitter handle instead of the author's name, include the tweet verbatim in quotations and register the time of posting.

> @Dr.Olaf. "Super Trawler gone. It is worth fighting for change. Now it is time to ban super trawlers in Australian waters..." *Twitter.* 1 Dec. 2016, 10:11 a.m., twitter.com/DrOlaf_/status/804100585989533696.

74. Wiki entry

Wiki content is written collaboratively, hence no author is listed. Because the content on a wiki changes frequently, wikis are not considered reliable scholarly sources.

> "Sandboarding." *Wikipedia*. Wikimedia Foundation, 2016, en.wikipedia.org/wiki/Sandboarding.

75. Email and text messaging

Give the name of the writer, the subject line in quotation marks, include the phrase *received by* before the name of the recipient and write the date the message was sent.

> Grant, Holly. "Re: Final Assignment Comparative Literature." Received by Bronwyn Winter. 25 Oct. 2014.

76. Posting to a discussion list

Give the name of the writer and his/her screen name in square brackets if available, the subject line in quotation marks, the name of the site in italics, the publisher, the date of the posting and the URL. Treat screen names as author names if the latter are not known.

Janinew [Janine Wright]. "Life Skills Students in 2-Unit Mathematics Class." *AAMT Mathematics Education Discussion List*, 21 Jan. 2016, groups.google.com/a/aamt.edu.au/forum/?fromgroups#!topic/discuss/B5cJIjmggoI. Accessed 3 Mar. 2017.

77. Course home page

"Bachelor of Advanced Science." Course home page. University of Technology Sydney, 18 Jan. 2016, www.uts.edu.au/future-students/find-a-course/courses/c10347.

78. Personal home page

Graff, Harvey J. Home page. Dept. of Comparative Studies, Ohio State University, comparativestudies.osu.edu/people/graff.40.

79. Blog entry

The Flying PhD. "Looking for Death in Little Cells." *The Flying PhD*. 29 Jan. 2016, theflyingphd.wordpress.com/2016/01/29/looking-for-death-in-little-cells/.

16g Visual and Multimedia Sources in the MLA-Style Works-Cited List

80. Cartoon or comic strip

Trudeau, G. B. "Doonesbury." Comic strip. *The Washington Post,* 21 Apr. 2008, p. C15.

81. Advertisement

Begin with the name of the advertiser or product, then the word *Advertisement.*

Toyota. Advertisement. Channel 9. 3 Oct. 2010. Television.

82. **Map, graph or chart**

Specify *Map*, *Graph*, or *Chart* after the title.

Brisbane Sunshine Coast. Map. RACQ, 2004.

83. **Painting, sculpture or photograph**

Give the artist's name if available, the title of the work in italics, its date of creation, the medium of composition, the name of the institution that houses the work and the city, or the name of the collection.

Manet, Edouard. *Olympia*. 1863. Oil on canvas. Musée d'Orsay, Paris.

VISUAL SOURCES ON THE WEB

84. **Photograph on the Web**

Give the photographer's name, the title of the image in italics, the date, the name of the website in italics, the URL, and the date of access.

Stones, Darren. *Split Point Lighthouse, Aireys Inlet, Victoria, Australia*. 2009. *Flickr.com*, www.flickr.com/photos/photojour/3759949355/. 24 Feb. 2017.

85. **Photograph from an archive**

Give the photographer's name, the title of the image in italics, the date, the name of the archive, the URL, and the date of access.

Murray, Neil. *Memorials - The Eureka Stockade Obelisk, Ballarat*. 1956. National Archives of Australia, recordsearch.naa.gov.au/SearchNRetrieve/Interface/Viewimage.aspx?B=11145731. 24 Feb. 2017.

86. **Video on the Web**

Begin the entry with a title if you cannot find a creator, include the name of the person or organisation who uploaded the video if this is different from the name of the creator.

"MLA Citations (8th Edition)." *YouTube*, uploaded by McMaster Libraries, 28 Sep. 2016, www.youtube.com/watch?v=ZDGDUOi_92A.

87. Work of art on the Web

Include the artist, the title of the work in italics and the year it was created. If you know which technique was used, state it after the year of creation.

Nolan, Sidney. *Ned Kelly.* 1946, enamel paint on composition board, National Gallery of Victoria, Melbourne, artsearch.nga.gov.au/Detail.cfm?IRN=28926.

88. Map on the Web

"An Elusive Enemy" Map. *National Geographic,* 2015, ngm.nationalgeographic.com/2015/07/ebola/outbreak-map.

89. Cartoon or comic strip on the Web

First Dog on the Moon. "A Piece of String, a Banana, and a Cassowary walk into Scott Morrison's Bar." *The Guardian*, 26 Aug. 2016, www.theguardian.com/commentisfree/2016/aug/26/a-piece-of-string-a-banana-and-a-cassowary-walk-into-scott-morrisons-bar.

MULTIMEDIA SOURCES ON THE WEB

90. Sound recording (Spotify and CD)

Britton, Connie. "Buried Under." *The Music of Nashville Original Soundtrack*, track 1, Lions Gate Television, 2012, *Spotify,* play.spotify.com/album/2GHpt591m6b9jcsvl8Hfop.

Cohen, Leonard. "Leaving the Table." *You Want It Darker,* Columbia, 2016.

91. Podcast

O'Neal, Jeff. "Who Moved My Cheese That I Learned About In Kindergarten While I Was Eating Soup for My Soul?" *The Book Riot Podcast*, 29 July 2013, bookriot.com/2013/07/29/the-book-riot-podcast-episode-12-who-moved-my-cheese-that-i-learned-about-in-kindergarten-while-i-was-eating-soup-for-my-soul/.

92. Film

Begin with the title in italics. List the director, the distributor, and the date. Other data, such as the names of the screenwriters and performers, is optional if you want to highlight a specific aspect of the film. To emphasise the director, start with his/her name.

Two Days, One Night. Performance by Marion Cotillard. Les Films du Fleuve, 2014.

Dardenne, Jean-Pierre and Luc Dardenne. *Two Days, One Night*, Les Films du Fleuve, 2014.

93. DVD

No Country for Old Men. Directed by Joel and Ethan Coen. Paramount, 2007.

94. Television, Netflix (or other streaming service) or radio program

"Kaisha." *The Sopranos*. HBO, 4 June 2006.

"Scientia Potentia Est." *The Crown*, directed by Benjamin Caron, season 1, episode 7, Netflix, 4 Nov. 2016.

95. Telephone interview

Minogue, Kylie. Telephone interview. 5 Mar. 2008.

96. Speech, debate, mediated discussion or public talk

Gillard, Julia. "Misogyny Speech." Canberra, 9 Oct. 2012. Parliamentary speech.

97. Lecture notes

Lecture notes are cited in-text and in the works-cited list. Include the following elements in the list of works cited: last name, first name. "title of presentation." lecture, institution, city. date.

Adams, Charles. "Week 5: Literary Tools." SACW1001 Lecture. Southern Cross University, Lismore. 22 Apr. 2012.

If retrieved online, add the URL.

Adams, Charles. "Week 5: Literary Tools." SACW1001 Lecture. Southern Cross University, Lismore. 22 Apr. 2012

16h Sample Pages from a Research Paper with MLA Documentation

FORMATTING A RESEARCH PAPER IN MLA STYLE

MLA offers these general guidelines for formatting a research paper.

- **Use white A4 paper**. Don't use coloured or lined paper.
- **Double-space everything—the title, headings, body of the paper, quotations and works-cited list**. Set the line spacing on your word processor for double spacing and leave it there.
- **Put your last name and the page number at the top of every page, aligned with the right margin, 1.25 cm from the top of the page**. Your word processor has a header command that will automatically put a header with the page number on every page.
- **Specify 2.5 cm margins**. 2.5 cm margins are the default setting for most word processors.
- **Do not justify (make even) the right margin**. Justifying the right margin throws off the spacing between words and makes your paper harder to read. Use the left-align setting instead.
- **Indent the first line of each paragraph 1.25 cm (5 spaces)**. Set the paragraph indent command or the tab on the ruler of your word processor at 1.25 cm.
- **Use the same readable typeface throughout your paper**. Use a standard typeface such as Times New Roman, 12 point.
- **Use block format for quotations longer than four lines**. See p. 148.
- **MLA does not require a title page**. Unless your lecturer asks for a separate title page, put, at 2.5 cm from the top of the page: your name, your lecturer's name, the course and the date on separate lines. Centre your title on the next line. Do not underline your title or put it inside quotation marks.

2.5 cm

1.25 cm

Harvey 1

MLA style does not require a title page. Check with your lecturer whether you need one.

Louise Harvey

Professor Christie

Creativity Studies

6 May 2016

Scientists Must Continue to Study Creativity

Centre the title. Do not underline it, put in quotation marks or type it in capital letters.

1.25 cm

2.5 cm

Curie. Mozart. Van Gogh. Beethoven. Chaplin. Einstein. Lovelace. Each of them achieved genius in their own right. Each left a legacy that to this day continues to awe those who watch, explore, study or listen to their life's work. Their personalities and quirks have inspired conversations, studies and even films. But their lives are shrouded in fundamental mysteries: What happened in their brains when they were being creative? Where does creativity come from? Scientists have been working hard to find an answer, but they still need more information.

Do not include page numbers for items without pagination, such as websites.

Specify 2.5 cm margins all around. Double-space everything.

For centuries, the creative spark (the famous *Eureka* moment that is so well depicted by the anecdote of Sir Isaac Newtown and the falling apple that gave birth to his Law of Universal Gravitation) was something attributed to the muses or chance. Today, however, science reveals that creativity is a much deeper mystery.

In the 1960s, Robert Sperry (1913–1994) and his colleagues conducted a series of experiments known as the Split-Brain Experiments. In these, the researchers cut off the corpus callosum of patients with severe epilepsy ("Split Brain"). Their experiments demonstrated that the left and right hemispheres of the brain specialise in different tasks. For this discovery, the first to point out the differences between the hemispheres of the brain, Sperry went on to win the Nobel Prize in Physiology in 1981. His study gave birth to the popular notion that the left side of the brain performs more

Sources not identified with an author are referenced by a shorter title.

2.5 cm

2.5 cm

Give page numbers for paraphrases as well as direct quotations.

Use a signal phrase to include the author's name before a quotation from a source

Indent each paragraph five spaces.

Harvey 2

logical tasks while the right hemisphere is more creative and thus more artistic (Diedrich 35).

The inaccurate notion of a brain split between a creative and a logical hemisphere gained a life of its own and was quickly disseminated through popular media. Magazines, public lectures and even Internet memes have told people how to tap on their "creative potential" (Dietrich 23). As Novotney explains, this misinterpretation of scientific facts was taken at face value because of well-intentioned psychology enthusiast who misread Sperry's studies and pegged personality types to brain hemispheres. "There's something seductively simple about labelling yourself and others as either a logical left-brainer or a free-spirited right brainer."

More studies have followed Sperry's pioneering efforts. After analysing 1,011 scans from individuals between the ages of 7 and 29, researchers found that although the left hemisphere has a dominance for language and the right hemisphere for visuospatial tasks (the processing of the visual perception of the spatial relationships of objects), there is no evidence to suggest that the left side of brain is more logical and the right one more creative (Nielsen et al.). "The neuroscience community has never accepted the idea of the 'left-dominant' or 'right-dominant' personality types. Lesion studies don't support it, and the truth is that it would be highly inefficient for one half of the brain to consistently be more active than the other." (Anderson in Novotney).

"It takes two hemispheres to be logical—or be creative" (Federmerier in Lombrozo), and this is exactly what creativity researchers are currently exploring.

Harvey 3

However, to fully understand how the creative process works, we first need to define what creativity is. For the purposes of this essay, we will define a creative act as "the production of something both novel and useful" (Jung et al.; Vartanian, Bristol, and Kaufman xii). This definition is often referenced and applies not only to the creative arts, but to other areas such as engineering, technology and even sports. After all, the study of creativity is not exclusive to artistic endeavours.

Over the past 20 years, neuroscientists worldwide have made use of new technologies such as functional MRIs (fMRI) to try to understand how creativity takes place in the brain (Abraham, 3). In 2003, Charles Limb used an fMRI scanner to study the brains of jazz musicians. The musicians had to play either a written melody or improvise a tune while lying inside an fMRI scanner. Limb modified a keyboard and arranged a set of mirrors that allowed the musicians to see the instrument when inside the machine. Limb and his colleagues measured the blood flow to different areas of the brain and were able to identify the areas that light up when musicians are working.

Harvey mentions a TedTalk video and the signal phrase leads to the entry in Works Cited.

In a TedTalk recorded in Atlanta in 2010, Limb explained that he used improvisation as a means to measure creativity because when musicians think on their feet, they have to come up with a completely new melody each time (00:07:32–00:08:16). The researcher found that different areas of the brain turn on and off during the creative process and when the musicians are just interpreting a given tune. Limb calls this phenomenon dissociated frontal activity state because of the dissociation generated in the frontal lobe. It is this state which decreases inhibition to generate novelty (Stamberg).

Harvey includes the range of minutes she referenced in her paper.

Harvey 4

Limb's results are consistent with those found by Martin Lotze in a 2014 study conducted with writers. Neuroscientists used fMRI scanners to track the brain activity of writers, both professional and amateur. Their results also suggest that there is activity in both hemispheres of the brain when someone is writing, which suggests the brain works more like a network in which different areas are activated according to the task at hand (Lotze et al.).

Surprisingly, the activated areas also differ between non-professional and experienced writers. Even though all of the volunteers' brains showed activity in language areas, amateurs showed activity in visual areas when they were brainstorming, while professionals showed more activity in verbal areas (Lotze et al.). The researcher explained that both groups seem to be using different strategies to come up with the stories. The experienced writers' scans showed more activation of brain areas associated with speech whereas the novices showed activation in areas that have to do with images—it almost seemed as if the second group was watching a movie (Zimmer).

Studies such as Lotze and Limb's have given us a glimpse of how the creative brain works, but their field is still in its infancy. When Limb conducted the jazz experiment almost 20 years ago, there wasn't enough scientific literature he could compare his discoveries with (McManus).

The last two decades have seen a boom in this type of studies and their results not only try to depict an accurate image of what happens in the brain when someone is creating, they are also showing a way of helping people to be better at problem solving, which is a creative endeavour in itself. Others have pointed out that creativity is matter of hard work and training (Onarheim and Friis-Olivarius), which has real-life implications for how people can approach creative tasks.

But as Dietrich suggests, to fully understand creativity, researchers have first to put an end to outdated ideas, such the left- and right-hemisphere personalities, divergent thinking or altered states of consciousness that facilitate creativity (Dietrich 27).

Although the field is new and promising, researching creativity faces many obstacles. The first issue is funding. These scientists are not trying to find a cure, they are analysing the brain and sometimes finding resources for such efforts is challenging (Limb in McManus). Second, the way in which the experiments are conducted has to be improved and new sets of guidelines and protocols need to be established. How can a musician or a writer get 'in the zone' if they are uncomfortably lying on their backs inside a machine? New methods have to be put in place. But, perhaps, the most important challenge for neuroscientists studying creativity today is making sure that everyone understands that the brain and its cognitive and neural processes aren't cookie cut.

Harvey 6

Works Cited

Centre "Works Cited" on a new page.

Abraham, A. "The Promises and Perils of the Neuroscience of Creativity." *Frontiers in Human Neuroscience*, vol. 7, no. 247, 2013, pp. 1–9.

Diedrich, Jennifer, et al. "Are Creative Ideas Novel And Useful?" *Psychology of Aesthetics, Creativity and the Arts*, vol. 9, no. 1, Feb 2015, pp. 35–40.

Dietrich, Arne. "Who's Afraid of a Cognitive Neuroscience of Creativity?" *Methods*, vol. 42, 2007, pp. 22–27.

Jung, Rex et al. "The Structure of Creative Cognition in the Human Brain." *Frontiers*, 2013, dx.doi.org/10.3389/fnhum.2013.00330.

Limb, Charles. "Your Brain on Improv." *TedTalk,* Nov. 2010, www.ted.com/talks/charles_limb_your_brain_on_improv.

Lombrozo, Tania. "The Truth About the Left Brain/Right Brain Relationship." NPR. 2 Dec. 2013. www.npr.org/sections/13.7/2013/12/02/248089436/the-truth-about-the-left-brain-right-brain-relationship.

Lotze, Martin, et al. "Neural correlates of verbal creativity: differences in resting-state functional connectivity associated with expertise in creative writing." *Frontiers in Human Neuroscience*, vol. 8, 2014, doi.org/10.3389/fnhum.2014.00516.

McManus, Emily. "Hip-hop, Creativity and the Brain: Q&A with Dr. Charles Limb." *TedBlog*, 18 Jan. 2011, blog.ted.com/hip-hop-creativity-and-the-brain-qa-with-dr-charles-limb.

Nielsen, J.A., et al. "An Evaluation of the Left-Brain vs. Right-Brain Hypothesis with Resting State Functional Connectivity

Go through your text and make sure that all the sources you have used are in the list of works cited.

Double-space all entries. Indent all but the first line in each entry 1.25 cm.

Blog entry

Harvey 7

Magnetic Resonance Imaging." *PloS One*, vol. 8, no. 8, 2013, 10.1371/journal.pone.0071275.

Novotney, Amy. "Despite What You've Been Told, You Aren't 'Left-Brained' Or 'Right-Brained'." *The Guardian*, 16 Nov. 2013, www.theguardian.com/commentisfree/2013/nov/16/left-right-brain-distinction-myth.

Onarheim, Balder, and Morten Friis-Olivarius. "Applying the Neuroscience of Creativity to Creativity Training." *Frontiers in Human Neuroscience*, vol. 7, 2013, dx.doi.org/10.3389/fnhum.2013.00656.

"The Split Brain Experiments." *NobelPrize.org*. Nobel Media AB 2014, nobelprize.org/educational/medicine/split-brain/background.html.

Stamberg, Susan. "Study Jazz Improv Cranks Up Brain's Creativity." *NPR*, 22 Mar. 2008, www.npr.org/templates/story/story.php?storyId=88827029.

Vartanian, Oshin, Adam S. Bristol, and James C. Kaufman, editors. *Neuroscience of Creativity*. MIT Press, 2013.

Zimmer, Carl. "This Is Your Brain on Writing." *The New York Times*, 20 June 2014, p. D3.

FORMATTING THE WORKS CITED IN MLA STYLE

- **Begin the works-cited list on a new page.** Insert a page break with your word processor before you start the works-cited page.
- **Centre 'Works Cited' on the first line at the top of the page.**
- **Double-space all entries.**
- **Alphabetise each entry by the last name of the author or, if no author is listed, by the first content word in the title (ignore *A*, *An*, *The*).**
- **Indent all but the first line in each entry 1.25 cm (five spaces)**
- **Italicise the titles of books and periodicals.**
- **If an author has more than one entry, list the entries in alphabetical order by title. Use three hyphens in place of the author's name for the second and subsequent entries.**

  Murphy, Dervla. *Cameroon with Egbert*. Woodstock: Overlook, 1990. Print.

  —. *Full Tilt: Ireland to India with a Bicycle*. London: Murray, 1965. Print.

- **Go through your paper to check that each source you have used is in the works-cited list.**

SMARTER WRITING

The 8th edition of the MLA Handbook was develop to adapt to the digital age and to offer researchers and students a logical and easy-to-use method of citing print and digital sources, with a clear emphasis on the latter. Whereas there is almost no change in the in-text citations, the elements of the list of works cited changed a lot. If you are familiar with the 7th edition and need to update your research papers, here are some of the things that you should take into consideration when proofing your work:

- Eliminate the city of publication.
- When a publication has more than three authors, list the name of the first author and then use *et al.*
- Spell out editor and translator instead of using abbreviations.
- Don't include the medium of publication unless needed for clarity.
- Always include the URL (without http:// or https://) or DOI.
- Include the abbreviation p. or pp. before the page numbers in the works-cited list but not in the body of the text.
- It's optional to include the date on which you accessed an online paper. If you choose to include it, remember that you'll have to be consistent throughout your paper.
- When a printed source begins with the articles A, An or The, include the article as part of the title in text citations and in the works-cited list (i.e. *The Sydney Morning Herald, The Age, The New York Times* in all contexts).
- It's not necessary to include n.d. (no date) when the publication date is not available.
- Use this model to identify a journal's volume, issue and pages "vol. 75, no. 1, pp. 56–79" instead of "75.1 (56–79)".

Credits

Page 151. Reprinted with permission from Elsevier.
Page 153. Screenshots of cover image and copyright page, © 2013, by permission of The MIT Press
Page 155. Screenshot © NASA. Reproduced with kind permission of NASA.
Page 157. Reproduced with permission of the British Psychological Society.

17 CMS Documentation

AT A *GLANCE*

- Use footnotes or endnotes for print sources in CMS style (see 17a to 17c)
- Use footnotes or endnotes for online sources in CMS style (see 17d)

Writers who publish in business, social sciences, fine arts and humanities outside the discipline of English often use *The Chicago Manual of Style* (CMS) method of documentation. CMS guidelines offer a clear way of using notes (rather than in-text citations as used in the MLA and APA methods) for citing the sources of quotations, summaries and paraphrases. If you have questions after consulting this chapter, you can consult *The Chicago Manual of Style*, 16th edition (Chicago: University of Chicago Press, 2010), or visit the website (www.chicagomanualofstyle.org).

17a The Elements of CMS Documentation

CMS describes two systems of documentation, one similar to APA and the other a style that uses notes, which is the focus of this chapter. In the note style, CMS uses a superscript number directly after any quotation, paraphrase or summary. Notes are numbered consecutively throughout the essay, article or chapter.

In *Australian Television Culture*, O'Regan points out that in late 1986 the impending introduction of the domestic satellite resulted in the television industry undertaking "fundamental rethinking of existing policy settings including ownership and control, audience boundaries, program deliveries, connections between places and the number of stations sustainable in broadcast markets".[1]

Note

1. Tom O'Regan, *Australian Television Culture* (St Leonards, NSW: Allen & Unwin, 1993), 26.

Bibliography

O'Regan, Tom. *Australian Television Culture*. St Leonards, NSW: Allen & Unwin, 1993.

Footnote and endnote placement

Notes appear at the bottom of the page on which each citation appears. Begin your note four lines from the last line of text on the page and double-space.

CMS bibliography

Because notes in CMS format contain complete citation information, a separate list of references is often optional. This list of references can be called the *Bibliography*, or if it has only works referenced in your text, *Works Cited, Literature Cited or References.* For academic writing, it is likely that you will be required to include a bibliography.

Index of CMS documentation

17b Periodical Sources

17c Books and Non-Periodical Sources

17d Online Sources

17b Periodical Sources in CMS Style

Note

1. Michael Hutt, "A Nepalese Triangle: Monarchists, Maoists, and Political Parties," *Asian Affairs* 38 (2007): 16.

Bibliography

Hutt, Michael. "A Nepalese Triangle: Monarchists, Maoists, and Political Parties." *Asian Affairs* 38 (2007): 11–22.

Author's or editor's name

In a note, the author's name is listed in normal order.

In a bibliography, list the author's surname first.

Title of article

- Put the article title in double quotation marks. If there is a title of a book within the article title, italicise the book title.
- Capitalise nouns, verbs, adjectives, adverbs and pronouns, and the first word of the title and subtitle.

Publication information

Name of journal

- Italicise the name of the journal.
- Journal titles are normally not abbreviated in the arts and humanities unless the title of the journal is an abbreviation (*PMLA*, *ELH*).

Volume, issue and page numbers

- Place the volume number after the journal title without intervening punctuation.
- For journals that are paginated from issue to issue within a volume, do not list the issue number.

Date

- The date or year of publication is given in parentheses after the volume number, or issue number, if provided.

Sample citations for periodical sources

1. Article by one author

Note

1. Catherine R. Cooper, "Cultural Brokers: How Immigrant Youth in Multicultural Societies Navigate and Negotiate their Pathways to College Identities," *Learning, Culture and Social Interaction* 3 (2014): 170–176.

Bibliography

Cooper, Catherine R. "Cultural Brokers: How Immigrant Youth in Multicultural Societies Navigate and Negotiate their Pathways to College Identities." *Learning, Culture and Social Interaction* 3 (2014): 170–176.

2. Article by two or three authors

Note

1. Hyena Kim and Daehyun Kim, "A Critical Reflection on Topology of Interdisciplinarity in University Focusing on Cultural Studies," *Procedia - Social and Behavioral Sciences* 174 (2015): 1991–1993.

Bibliography

Kim, Hyena and Daehyun Kim. "A Critical Reflection on Topology of Interdisciplinarity in University Focusing on Cultural Studies." *Procedia - Social and Behavioral Science* 174 (2015): 1991–1993.

3. Article by more than three authors

Note

Include the name of the first listed author, followed by *et al.*

5. Samantha Simpson et al., "Validation of a Culturally Adapted Developmental Screening Tool for Australian Aboriginal Children: Early Findings and Next Steps," *Early Human Development* 103 (2016): 91–95.

Bibliography

Include all authors' names. Use reverse order for the first author only.

Simpson, Samantha, Anita D'Aprano, Collette Tayler, Siek Toon Khoo, Roxanne Highfold. "Validation of a Culturally Adapted Developmental Screening Tool for Australian Aboriginal Children: Early Findings and Next Steps." *Early Human Development* 103 (2016): 91–95.

4. **Journals paginated by volume**

Note

In a note, list the specific page number(s) for the quote, paraphrase or summary.

4. Francisco Vaz da Silva, "The Invention of Fairy Tales," *Journal of American Folklore* 123 (2010): 420.

Bibliography

In a bibliography, list the entire page range for the journal article.

Vaz da Silva, Francisco. "Invention of Fairy Tales." *Journal of American Folklore* 123 (2010): 398–425.

5. **Journals paginated by issue**

Note

In a note, list the specific page number(s) for the quote, paraphrase or summary.

5. Tzvetan Todorov, "The New World Disorder," *South Central Review* 19, no. 2 (2002): 28–32.

Bibliography

In a bibliography, list the entire page range for the journal article.

Todorov, Tzvetan. "The New World Disorder." *South Central Review* 19, no. 2 (2002): 28–32.

6. **Weekly and biweekly magazines**

Note

5. Malcolm Gladwell, "Pandora's Briefcase," *New Yorker*, 10 May 2010, 72–78.

Bibliography

Magazine articles are commonly omitted from the bibliography. Use the following style if you choose to cite it in your bibliography.

Gladwell, Malcolm. "Pandora's Briefcase." *New Yorker*, 10 May 2010.

7. **Newspaper article**

If the name of the newspaper begins with 'The', you should omit it in your citation.

Note

1. Melena Ryzik, "Off the Beaten Beat," *New York Times*, 11 May 2007, late edition, sec. E.

Bibliography

Like magazine articles, newspaper articles are often omitted from the bibliography. If you choose to include it, use the following style.

Farrelly, Elizabeth. "Australia's Fall from Lucky Country to Cruel Country." *Age*, 4 November 2016.

Books and Non-Periodical Sources in CMS Style

Note

1. Bruce Moore, *Speaking Our Language: The Story of Australian English* (South Melbourne: Oxford University Press, 2010), 5.

Bibliography

Moore, Bruce. *Speaking Our Language: The Story of Australian English.* South Melbourne: Oxford University Press, 2010.

Author's or editor's name

In a note, the author's name is listed in normal order.

In the bibliography, give the author's surname first. If you are referring to an editor, put *ed*. after the name.

Bahn, Paul ed. *The History of Archaeology: An Introduction.* Abingdon-New York: Routledge, 2014.

Book title

Use the exact title as it appears on the title page (not the cover).

Italicise the title.

Capitalise all nouns, verbs, adjectives, adverbs and pronouns, and the first word of the title and subtitle.

Anderson, Elijah. *The Cosmopolitan Canopy: Race and Civility in Everyday Life.* New York: W.W Norton & Co. 2011

Publication information

In a note, the place of publication, publisher and year of publication are in parentheses.

Place of Publication

- Add the state's postal abbreviation or the country when the city is not well-known or ambiguous (Melbourne, US, or Melbourne, AU).
- If more than one city is given on the title page, use the first one listed.

Publisher's name

- You may use acceptable abbreviations (e.g. Co. for Company).
- Elijah Anderson. The Cosmopolitan Canopy: Race and Civility in Everyday Life (New York: WW Norton & Co. 2011)

Year of publication

- If no year of publication is given, write n.d. ('no date') in place of the date.

Sample citations for books and non-periodical sources

8. Book by one author

In a note, the author's name is listed in normal order.

1. Robin Hamley, *A Field Guide for Immersion Writing: Memoir, Journalism and Travel* (Athens, Georgia: University of Georgia Press, 2012), 120.

In subsequent references, cite the author's surname only.

2. Hamley, 10.

If the reference is to the same work as the preceding note, you can use the abbreviation *Ibid.*

3. Ibid., 10.

In the bibliography, list the author's name in reverse order.

Hamley, Robin. *A Field Guide for Immersion Writing: Memoir, Journalism and Travel.* Athens Georgia: University of Georgia Press, 2012.

For edited books, put *ed.* after the name.

Chen, Kuan-Hsing, ed. *Trajectories: Inter-Asia Cultural Studies.* London: Routledge, 1998.

9. Book by multiple authors

In a note for books with two or three authors, cite the names in the order listed on the title page. Include all authors' names in normal order. For subsequent references, use only the authors' surnames.

4. Mark L. Knapp, Judith A. Hall and Terrence G. Horgan, *Nonverbal Communication in Human Interaction* (Boston: Wadsworth Cengage Learning, 2014), 67.

In the bibliography, use reverse order for the first author and normal order for subsequent authors.

Knapp, Mark L, Judith A. Hall and Terrence G. Horgan. *Nonverbal Communication in Human Interaction*. Boston: Wadsworth Cengage Learning, 2014.

In a note for more than three authors, include the name of the first author listed, followed by *et al.*. List all authors in the bibliography.

10. Book by a group or organisation

Note

7. World Health Organization, *Advancing Safe Motherhood through Human Rights* (Geneva, Switzerland: World Health Organization, 2001), 18.

Bibliography

World Health Organization. *Advancing Safe Motherhood through Human Rights*. Geneva, Switzerland: World Health Organization, 2001.

11. A selection in an anthology or a chapter in an edited collection

Note

2. Hanna Wirman, "Princess Peach Loves Your Enemies, Too," in *Game Love Essays on Play and Affection,* ed. Jessica Enevold and Esther MacCallum-Stewart (Jefferson, North Carolina: McFarland & Company, Inc., 2015), 131–148.

Bibliography

Wirman, Hanna. "Princess Peach Loves Your Enemies, Too." In *Game Love Essays on Play and Affection,* edited by Jessica Enevold and Esther MacCallum, 131–148. Jefferson, North Carolina: McFarland & Company, Inc., 2015.

12. Book with an editor

Note

1. Thomas Hardy, *Jude the Obscure,* ed. Norman Page (New York: Norton, 1999), 35.

Bibliography

Hardy, Thomas. *Jude the Obscure.* Edited by Norman Page. New York: Norton, 1999.

13. Government document

Note

5. Australian Bureau of Statistics, *Youth, Australia: A Social Report* (Canberra: ABS, 1997), 11.

Bibliography

Australian Bureau of Statistics. *Migration Australia 2009–2010: Age Structure of Interstate Migrants.* Canberra: Australian Government, 2011.

14. Religious texts

Citations from religious texts appear in the notes but not in the bibliography. Give the version in parentheses in the first citation only.

Note

4. John 3:16 (King James Version).

17d Online Sources in CMS Style

15. Document or page from a website

To cite original content from within a website, include as many descriptive elements as you can: author of the page, title of the page, title and owner of the website, and the URL. Include the date accessed only if the site is time-sensitive or is frequently updated. If you cannot locate an individual author, the owner of the site can stand in for the author.

Note

11. National Organization for Women, "NOW History," accessed 8 October 2010, http://www.now.org/history/history.html.

Bibliography

National Organization for Women. "NOW History." Accessed 8 October 2010. http://www.now.org.history/history.html.

16. Online book

Note

12. Angelina Grimké, *Appeal to the Christian Women of the South* (New York: New York Anti-Slavery Society, 1836), accessed 2 November 2015, http://history.furman.edu/~benson/docs/grimke2.htm.

Bibliography

Grimké, Angelina. *Appeal to the Christian Women of the South*. New York: New York Anti-Slavery Society, 1836. Accessed 2 November 2015. http://history.furman.edu/~benson/docs/grimke2.htm.

17. Online article

Note

13. Theodore A. Alston and Daniel B. Carr, "George Bernard Shaw on Anesthesia," *Journal of Anesthesia History* 2, no. 2 (2016): 37–41, doi: http://dx.doi.org/10.1016/j.janh.2016.01.005.

Bibliography

Alston, Theodore A and Daniel B. Carr. "George Bernard Shaw on Anesthesia." *Journal of Anesthesia History* 2, no. 2 (2016): 37–41. doi:10.1632/pmla.2010.125.3.657.

18. Posting to a discussion list or group

Note

16. Ken Silburn, post to Open Forum in Innovation, 10 January 2016, http://openforum.com.au/innovation-featured-forum#comment-5308.

19. Email

Because personal emails are not available to the public, they are not usually listed in the bibliography. Instead, list the email in the text or in a note.

Note

19. Erin P. Riley, "US Politics and Australia," email to author, 16 October 2013.

20. Twitter feed

Although not a common source in academic writing, Twitter handles of universities, goverments, esteemed organisations and public figures may provide useful information for your paper. You can incorporate the information in the text.

The United Nations posted on Twitter on November 20, 2016 that "2.4 billion people lack access to basic sanitation services"

Note

17. United Nations, Twitter post, November 20, 2016, 4:03 a.m., https://twitter.com/UN/status/800021649886248961

21. Online video

Note

Derek Muller, *World's Roundest Object!*, YouTube video, 11:40, March 25, 2013, https://www.youtube.com/watch?v=ZMByI4s-D-Y

Bibliography

15. Muller, Derek. *World's Roundest Object!*. YouTube video, 11:40. March 25, 2013. https://www.youtube.com/watch?v=ZMByI4s-D-Y

Sample Pages from a Research Paper with CMS Documentation

Laker 1

Jason Laker

Politics and Culture

1 June 2014

Biometrics in Australia: Does It Really Make Us Safer?

Biometrics are 'automated methods for identifying and/or verifying an individual on the basis of some biological or behavioural unique characteristic of the individual'.[1] This means that data can be used to verify identity through both physical attributes and behaviour.[2] Fingerprints, facial recognition, walking gait, voice and DNA are all examples of ways in which biometric technologies can authenticate one's identity. One argument for the use of biometric technologies is to increase safety and security for citizens, as governments can use the information that is gathered and stored to secure borders. There are many benefits of biometrics, such as an increased sense of confidence that the individual nature of the technologies provides an error-proof system of identification and thus protection of one's identity.[3] This is a benefit often given by governments for justifying the use of these technologies, along with biometric collection methods that are non-invasive and low-risk.[4] But what if instead of safety, these technologies are used to control citizens? Despite the benefits, the growing use of biometrics in Australia also presents many risks to privacy and security.

The use of biometrics for authentication and identification presents a great many technological risks, from false positives and false negatives to identity theft and fraud. There have been cases of misidentification because facial recognition systems often inaccurately identify ethnicity and age.[5] Once data is in the biometric system, it is difficult to correct any errors. This is one reason that moving from a single biometric system to multiple systems is troubling. Biometric technologies are not 100 per cent accurate, and there are unclear rules in Australia about when data is collected and how long the data is kept.

Laker 6

NOTES

1. Yue Liu, "Privacy Regulations on Biometrics in Australia," *Computer Law & Security Review,* 26.4 (2010): 355–367, http://www.sciencedirect.com/science/article/pii/ S0267364910000798.

2. Electronic Frontier Foundation, "Biometrics", accessed 22 May 2012, https://www.eff.org/issues/biometrics.

3. Lawrence Lessig, *Code: Version 2.0* (New York: BasicBooks, 2006), 42.

4. David Lyon, "Biometrics, Identification and Surveillance," *Bioethics* 22.9 (2009): 499–508, doi:10.1111/j.1467-8519.2008.00697.x.

5. Jennifer Lynch, "From Fingerprints to DNA: Biometric Data Collection in US Immigrant Communities and Beyond," *Immigration Policy Center Special Report,* accessed 18 May 2012, http://www.immigrationpolicy.org/special-reports/fingerprints-dna-biometric-data-collection-us-immigrant-communities-and-beyond.

Laker 7

BIBLIOGRAPHY

Electronic Frontier Foundation. "Biometrics". Accessed 22 May 2012. https://www.eff. org/issues/biometrics.

Lessig, Lawrence. *Code: Version 2.0.* New York: BasicBooks, 2006.

Liu, Yue. "Privacy Regulations on Biometrics in Australia," *Computer Law & Security Review,* 26.4 (2010): 355–367, http://www.sciencedirect.com/ science/article/pii/ S0267364910000798.

Lynch, Jennifer. "From Fingerprints to DNA: Biometric Data Collection in US Immigrant Communities and Beyond". *Immigration Policy Center Special Report.* Accessed 18 May 2012. http://www.immigrationpolicy.org/special-reports/fingerprints-dna-biometric-data-collection-us-immigrant-communities-and-beyond.

Lyon, David. "Biometrics, Identification and Surveillance," *Bioethics* 22.9 (2009): 499–508, doi:10.1111/j.1467-8519.2008.00697.x.

PART 4 Effective Style and Language

18 Write with Power 202

19 Write Concisely 207

20 Write with Emphasis 212

21 Find the Right Words 217

18 Write with Power

AT A *GLANCE*

- Make your writing active (see below)
- Use agents in your writing (see 18d)
- Vary your sentences (see 18e)

In photographs

You imagine actions when subjects are captured in motion.

In writing

Your readers expect actions to be expressed in verbs:
gallop, canter, trot, run, sprint, dash, bound, thunder, tear away.

In photographs

Viewers interpret the most prominent person or thing as the subject—what the photograph is about.

In writing

Readers interpret the first person or thing they meet in a sentence as what the sentence is about (the jockey, the horse). They expect that person or thing to perform the action expressed in the verb.

Recognise Active and Passive Voice

In the **active voice** the subject of the sentence is the actor. In the **passive voice** the subject is being acted upon.

The best way to distinguish the active from the passive in your writing is to notice the different forms of verbs used. The passive form uses the verb(s) 'to be' (is/are, was/were, or am), plus a past form of the main action verb (the past participle). The active form only uses an action verb.

Active ***Leonardo da Vinci*** painted *Mona Lisa* between 1503 and 1506.

Passive ***Mona Lisa*** was painted by Leonardo da Vinci between 1503 and 1506.

To write with power, use the active voice. Observe the difference:

Passive The pear tree in the front yard was **demolished** by the unexpected storm.

Active The unexpected storm demolished the pear tree in the front yard.

18b When to use the passive?

Passive The study was analysed.

Reasons to use it:

- In some formal written genres such as scientific report writing, using the passive might be required stylistically to avoid using the personal pronoun: 'Two case studies were selected . . .' *rather than*:

  'I selected two case studies . . .'

- Foregrounding the important topic in a sentence (e.g. we want to foreground 'sampling bias') : '**Sampling bias** was controlled by . . .' *rather than:*

  'The controls for **sampling bias** consisted of . . .'.

Use Action Verbs

Where are the action words in the following sentences?

> Dr Karl Kruszelnicki, a medical doctor, science communicator and media celebrity with a penchant for colourful shirts, holds a number of awards for the promotion of science. In the 2001 Australian honours list, he was the winner of the Centenary Medal 'for major service in raising public awareness of the importance of science and technology' and in the 2006 honours list, he became a Member of the Order of Australia. One of Kruszelnicki's more notable undertakings was his part in a research project on belly-button fluff, for which he was a recipient of the tongue-in-cheek Ig Nobel Prize in 2002. He was the Australian Father of the Year in 2003. In 2007, he was the Australian Skeptic Of The Year and in 2012, in a ceremony held by the National Trust of Australia, he became a National Living Treasure. In 2014, he became the ninth-most trusted person in Australia according to a poll of *Reader's Digest* readers. In 2016, he officially became 'Dr Karl' after receiving an honorary Doctorate from the University of the Sunshine Coast.

No action words here! The passage describes a series of actions, yet most of the verbs are *is*, *was* and *became*. Think about what the actions are and choose powerful verbs that express those actions.

> Dr Karl Kruszelnicki, a medical doctor, science communicator and media celebrity with a penchant for colourful shirts, **holds** a number of awards for his promotion of science. In the 2001 Australian honours list, he was **awarded** the Centenary Medal 'for major service in raising public awareness of the importance of science and technology' and in the 2006 honours list, he was **inducted** as a Member of the Order of Australia. One of Kruszelnicki's more notable undertakings was his part in a research project on belly-button fluff, for which he **received** the tongue-in-cheek Ig Nobel Prize in 2002. He **won** the Australian Father of the Year award in 2003. In 2007, the Australian Skeptics **recognised** him as the Australian Skeptic Of The Year and in 2012, Kruszelnicki was **named** a National Living Treasure by the National Trust of Australia. In 2014, *Reader's Digest* readers **voted** Kruszelnicki the ninth-most trusted person in Australia. In 2016, he was **awarded** an honorary Doctorate by the University of the Sunshine Coast and is now officially called 'Dr Karl'.

Many sentences contain words that express action, but those words are nouns rather than verbs. Often the nouns can be changed into verbs. For example:

> The arson unit ~~conducted an investigation of~~ investigated the mysterious fire.

> The committee ~~had a debate over~~ debated how best to spend the surplus funds.

Notice that changing nouns into verbs also eliminates unnecessary words.

18d Find Agents

The **agent** is the person or thing that does the action. Powerful writing puts the agents in sentences.

Focus on people

Read the following sentence aloud:

> The use of a MIDI keyboard for playing the song will facilitate capturing it in digital form on a laptop for the subsequent purpose of uploading it to a website.

It sounds dead, doesn't it? Putting people into the sentence makes it come alive:

> By playing the song on a MIDI keyboard, we can record the digitised sound on our laptop and then upload it to our website.

Including people makes your writing more emphatic. Most readers relate better to people than to abstractions. Putting people in your sentences also introduces active verbs because people do things.

Identify characters

If people are not your subject, then keep the focus on other types of characters.

Without characters	The celebration of Australia Day had to be cancelled because of inclement weather.
With characters	A severe cyclone forced the city to cancel the Australia Day celebration.

18e Vary Your Sentences

Read the following passage.

> On the first day Garth, Jim and I paddled fourteen kilometres down Johnstone Strait. We headed down the strait about five more kilometres to Robson Bight. It is a well-known place for seeing dolphins. The bight is a small bay. We paddled out into the strait so we could see the entire bight. There were no dolphins to be seen. By this time we were getting tired. We were hungry. The clouds assumed a wintry dark thickness. The wind was kicking up against us. Our heads were down going into the cold spray.

The subject matter is interesting, but the writing isn't. The passage is a series of short sentences, one after the other. When you have too many short sentences one after the other, try combining a few of them.

The result of combining some (but not all) short sentences is a paragraph with sentences that match the interest of the subject.

> On the first day Garth, Jim and I paddled 14 kilometres down Johnstone Strait. We headed down the strait about five more kilometres to Robson Bight, a small bay well known for seeing dolphins. We paddled out into the strait so we could see the entire bight, but there were no dolphins to be seen. By this time we were tired and hungry, the clouds had assumed a wintry dark thickness and the wind was kicking up against us—our heads dropped going into the cold spray.

19 Write Concisely

AT A *GLANCE*

- Eliminate unnecessary words (see 19a below)
- Reduce wordy phrases (see 19b)
- Simplify tangled sentences (see 19c)

19a Eliminate Unnecessary Words

Clutter creeps into our lives every day. Clutter also creeps into writing through unnecessary words, inflated constructions and excessive jargon.

> **In regards to** the website, the content is **pretty** successful in **consideration of** the topic. The site is **fairly** good **writing-wise** and is **very** unique in telling you how to adjust the rear derailleur one step at a time.

The words in **red** are clutter. Get rid of the clutter. You can say the same thing with half the words and have a greater effect as a result.

> The well-written website on bicycle repair provides step-by-step instructions on adjusting your rear derailleur.

Redundancy

Some words act as modifiers, but when you look closely at them they repeat the meaning of the word they pretend to modify. Have you heard someone refer to a *personal friend?* Aren't all friends personal? Likewise, you may have heard such as *red in colour, small in size, round in shape* or *honest truth*. Imagine red not referring to colour or round not referring to shape.

19b Reduce Wordy Phrases

Many inexperienced writers use phrases like 'It is my opinion that' or 'I think that' to begin sentences. These phrases are deadly to read. If you find them in your prose, cut them. Unless a writer is citing a source, we can assume that the ideas are the writer's.

Coaches are among the worst at using many words for what could be said in a few:

> After much deliberation about Brown's future in rugby with regard to possible permanent injuries, I came to the conclusion that it would be in his best interest not to continue his pursuit of playing rugby again.

The coach might have said simply:

> Brown risks permanent injury if he plays rugby again, so I decided to release him from the team.

Perhaps the coach wanted to sound impressive, authoritative or thoughtful. But the result is the opposite. Speakers and writers who impress us are those who use words efficiently.

COMMON ERRORS

Empty intensifiers

Intensifiers modify verbs, adjectives and other adverbs, and they are often overused. One of the most overused intensifiers is *very*. Take the following sentence as an example:

> Her clothing style was **very unique**.

If something is unique, it is one of a kind. The word *very* doesn't make something more than unique.

> Her clothing style was **unique**.

or

> Her clothing style was **strange**.

COMMON ERRORS

Very and *totally* are but two of a list of empty intensifiers that can usually be eliminated with no loss of meaning. Other empty intensifiers include *absolutely, awfully, definitely, incredibly, particularly* and *really*.

Remember: When you use *very, totally* or another intensifier before an adjective or adverb, always ask yourself whether there is a more accurate adjective or adverb you could use instead to express the same thought.

WORDY PHRASES

Certain stock phrases plague writing in the workplace, in the media and in academia. Many can be replaced by one or two words with no loss in meaning.

Wordy	**Concise**
at this point in time	now
due to the fact that	because
for the purpose of	for
have the ability to	can
in order to	to
in spite of the fact that	although
in the event that	if

19c Simplify Tangled Sentences

Long sentences can be graceful and forceful. Such sentences, however, often require several revisions before they achieve elegance. Too often, long sentences reflect wandering thoughts that the writer didn't bother to go back and sort out. Two of the most important strategies for untangling long sentences are described in Chapter 18: Use action verbs (Section 18c) and Find agents (Section 18d). Here are some other strategies.

Revise 'dummy subjects'

Dummy subjects are empty words that can occupy the subject position in a sentence. The most frequently used dummy subjects are *there is*, *there are* and *it is*.

Wordy **There were** several important differences between the positions raised by the candidates in the debate.

To simplify the sentence, find the agent and make it the subject.

Revised The two candidates raised several important differences between their positions in the debate.

A few kinds of sentences—for example, *It is raining*—do require you to use a dummy subject. In most cases, however, dummy subjects add unnecessary words, and sentences will read better without them.

Use positive constructions

Sentences become wordy and hard to read when they include two or more negatives such as the words *no, not* and *nor*, and the prefixes *un-* and *mis-*. For example:

Difficult A **not un**common complaint among employers of new university graduates is that they cannot communicate effectively in writing.

Revised Employers frequently complain that new university graduates cannot write effectively.

Even simpler Employers value the rare university graduate who can write well.

Phrasing sentences positively usually makes them more economical. Moreover, it makes your style more forceful and direct.

Simplify sentence structure

Long sentences can be hard to read, not because they are long but because they are convoluted and hide the relationships between ideas. Take the following sentence as an example.

When the cessation of eight years of hostility in the Iran–Iraq war occurred in 1988, it was not the result of one side's defeating the other but the exhaustion of both after losing thousands of people and much of their military capability.

This sentence is hard to read. To rewrite sentences like this one, find the main ideas, then determine the relationships between them.

After examining the sentence, you decide there are two key ideas:

1 Iran and Iraq stopped fighting in 1988 after eight years.

2 Both sides were exhausted from losing people and equipment.

Next ask what the relationship is between the two ideas. When you identify the key ideas, the relationship is often obvious. In this case, (2) is the cause of (1), thus the word you want to connect the two ideas is *because*.

> Iran and Iraq stopped fighting after eight years of an indecisive war because both sides had lost thousands of people and most of their equipment.

The revised sentence is both clearer and more concise, reducing the number of words from 43 to 25.

Start sentences with the agent, not the main verb posing as a noun

Be careful not to bury the agent within the sentence. It is clearer if the agent is stated at the beginning. Two types of sentence beginnings that can lead to awkward constructions of this type are the following:

1. Gerunds (*-ing* verbs) posing as noun subjects

   Example:

   Difficult Emerging from the participant's comments was the developing relationship between the different stakeholders.

   Revised The developing relationship between the different stakeholders **emerged** from the participant's comments.

2. **Main verbs** posing as noun subjects

   Example:

   Difficult The implementation of the strategy is the role of the participants.

   Revised The participants' role is to **implement** the strategy.

20 Write with Emphasis

AT A *GLANCE*

- Manage emphasis (see 20a)
- Forge links across sentences (see 20b)
- Balance sentences using parallel structure (see 20c)

Photographs and writing gain energy when key ideas are emphasised.

In visuals

Photographers create emphasis by composing the image to direct the attention of the viewer. Putting people and objects in the foreground and making them stand out against the background give them emphasis.

In writing

Writers have many tools for creating emphasis. Writers can design a page to gain emphasis by using headings, white space, type size, colour and boldfacing. Just as important, learning the craft of structuring sentences will empower you to give your writing emphasis.

Manage Emphasis within Sentences

Put your main ideas in main clauses

Placing more important information in **main clauses** and less important information in subordinate clauses emphasises what is important.

In the following paragraph, all the sentences are main clauses:

> Lotteries have been used to raise money for hundreds of years. Some lotteries ran into trouble. They were run by private companies. Sometimes the companies took off with the money. They didn't pay the winners.

This paragraph is grammatically correct, but it doesn't help the reader understand which pieces of information the author wants to emphasise. Combining the simple sentences into main and subordinate clauses and phrases can significantly improve the paragraph.

First, identify the main ideas:

> Lotteries have been used to raise money for hundreds of years. Some lotteries ran into trouble.

These ideas can be combined into one sentence:

> Lotteries have been used to raise money for hundreds of years, but some ran into trouble.

Now think about the relationship of the three remaining sentences to the main ideas. These sentences explain why lotteries ran into trouble, thus the relationship is *because.*

> Lotteries have been used to raise money for hundreds of years, but some ran into trouble because they were run by private companies that sometimes took off with the money instead of paying the winners.

Put key ideas at the beginning and end of sentences

Read these sentences aloud:

1. The Cottingley Fairies, a series of five photographs taken in 1917 by Elsie Wright and Frances Griffiths, depicts the girls interacting with what seem to be fairies.

2 A series of photographs showing two girls interacting with what seem to be fairies, known as the Cottingley Fairies, was taken by Elsie Wright and Frances Griffiths in 1917.

3 The series of photos Elsie Wright and Frances Griffiths took in 1917 showing them interacting with what seem to be fairies is called the Cottingley Fairies.

Most readers put the primary emphasis on words at the beginning and end of a sentence. The front of a sentence usually gives what is known: the topic. At the back is the new information about the topic. Subordinate information is in the middle. If a paragraph is about the Cottingley Fairies, we would not expect the writer to choose sentence 2 over sentence 1 or 3. In sentence 2, the reference to the Cottingley Fairies is buried in the middle.

20b Forge Links across Sentences

When your writing maintains a focus of attention across sentences, the reader can distinguish the important ideas and how they relate to each other. To achieve this coherence, you need to control which ideas occupy the positions of greatest emphasis. The words you repeat from sentence to sentence act as links.

Link sentences from front to front

In front-to-front linkage, the subject of the sentence remains the focus from one sentence to the next. In the following sequence, sentences 1 to 5 are all about Arthur Wright. The subject of each sentence refers to the first sentence with the pronouns *he* and *his*.

1 Arthur Wright was one of the first electrical engineers in England.

2 He loaned his camera to his daughter Elsie, who took the fairy pictures in the garden behind their house.

3 His opinion was that the pictures were fake.

4 However, his wife, Polly, was convinced that they were real.

5 Nevertheless, he banned Elsie from ever using his camera again.

Each sentence adds more information about the repeated topic, Arthur Wright.

Link sentences from back to front

In back-to-front linkage, the new information at the end of the sentence is used as the topic of the next sentence. Back-to-front linkage allows new material to be introduced and commented on.

1. By the summer of 1919, the girls and their photographs had become so well known that author Sir Arthur Conan Doyle even wrote an article for a leading magazine claiming that the photos and the fairies were real.
2. Not everyone believed that the Cottingley Fairies were authentic, however, and other public figures wrote to the papers calling the photographs a hoax.
3. The hoax continued until the 1980s, when both Elsie and Frances finally admitted that all but one of the pictures were fake.

Back-to-front linkage is useful when ideas need to be advanced quickly, as when you are telling stories. Rarely, however, will you use either front-to-front linkage or back-to-front linkage continuously throughout a piece of writing. Use front-to-front linkage to add more information and back-to-front linkage to move the topic along.

Check the links between your sentences to find any gaps that will cause your readers to stumble.

20c Use Parallel Structure with Parallel Ideas

What if Genesis 31 from the Bible were written 'He who lives by the sword will be killed by a sword'? Would we remember those words today? We remember the words 'he who lives by the sword dies by the sword' because the same verb forms (lives and dies) are used to make the structure parallel. Writers who use parallel structure often create memorable sentences.

Use parallelism with *and*, or, *nor*, *but*

When you join elements at the same level with coordinating conjunctions, including *for, and, nor, but, or, yet* and *so*, normally you should use parallel grammatical structure for these elements.

Awkward

In today's global economy, the method of production and where factories are located has become relatively unimportant in comparison with the creation of new concepts and marketing those concepts.

Parallel

In today's global economy, how goods are made and where they are produced has become relatively unimportant in comparison with creating new concepts and marketing those concepts.

Use parallelism with *either/or*, not *only/but*

Make identical in structure the parts of sentences linked by correlative conjunctions: *either ... or, neither ... nor, not only ... but also, whether ... or.*

Awkward

Purchasing the undeveloped land not only **gives us a new park** but also it **is something that our children will benefit from in the future.**

Parallel

Purchasing the undeveloped land will not only give our city a new park but will also leave our children a lasting inheritance.

The more structural elements you match, the stronger the effect of parallelism.

COMMON ERRORS

Faulty parallel structure

When writers neglect to use parallel structure, the result can be jarring. Reading your writing aloud will help you catch problems in parallelism. Read this sentence aloud:

At our club meeting we identified problems in finding new members, publicising our activities and **maintenance** of our website.

The end of the sentence doesn't sound right because the parallel structure is broken. We expect to find another verb + *ing* following *finding* and *publicising*. Instead, we run into *maintenance*, a noun. The problem is easy to fix: change the noun to the *-ing* verb form.

At our club meeting we identified problems in finding new members, publicising our activities and maintaining our website.

Remember: Use parallel structure for parallel ideas.

21 Find the Right Words

AT A *GLANCE*

- Choose the right level of formality (see 21a below)
- Write to be inclusive (see 21d)

Be Aware of Levels of Formality

While you may get plenty of practice in informal writing—emails and notes to friends and family members—mastering formal writing is essential in academic and professional settings. How formal or informal should your writing be? That depends on your audience and the writing task at hand.

DECIDE HOW FORMAL YOUR WRITING SHOULD BE

- Who is your audience?
- What is the occasion?
- What level of formality is your audience accustomed to in similar situations?
- What impression of yourself do you want to give?

Colloquialisms

Colloquialisms are words or expressions that are used informally, often in conversation but less often in writing.

I'm not happy with my essay mark, but that's life.

Liz is always running off at the mouth about something.

I enjoyed the restaurant, but it was nothing to write home about.

In academic and professional writing, colloquialisms often suggest a flippant attitude, carelessness or even thoughtlessness. Sometimes colloquialisms can be used for ironic or humorous effect, but as a general rule, avoid using them if you want to be taken seriously.

Avoiding colloquialisms doesn't mean, however, that you should use big words when small ones will do as well, or that you should use ten words instead of two. Formality doesn't mean being pretentious or wordy.

Wordy

One could argue that the beaches on Australia's west coast are far superior in every particular to their counterparts on the east coast.

Better

Australia's west coast beaches are better in every way than those on the east coast.

Slang

The most conspicuous kind of language that is usually avoided in formal writing is slang. The next time a friend talks to you, listen closely to the words he or she uses. Chances are you will notice several words that you probably wouldn't use in a university writing assignment. Slang words are created by and for a particular group—even if that group is just you and your friend.

The movie was ace, except for all the ankle biters.

Shannon's new ride is totally pimped out.

Slang is used to indicate membership in a particular group. But because slang excludes readers who are not members of the group, it is best to avoid using any in academic writing.

21b Be Aware of Denotation and Connotation

Words have both literal meanings, called **denotations**, and associated meanings, called **connotations**. The contrast is evident in words that mean roughly the same thing but have different connotations. For example, some people are set in their opinions, a quality that can be described positively as *persistent, firm* and *steadfast* or negatively as *stubborn, bull-headed* and *intransigent.*

In academic and professional writing, writers are expected to not rely on the connotations of words to make important points. For example, the statement *It's only common sense to have good schools* carries high positive connotations. Most people believe in common sense, and most people want good schools. What is common sense for one person, however, isn't common sense for another; how a good school is defined varies greatly. You have an obligation in academic writing to support any judgment with evidence.

Use Specific Language

Be precise

Effective writing conveys information clearly and precisely. Words such as *situation*, *sort*, *thing*, *aspect* and *kind* often signal undeveloped or even lazy thinking.

Vague The violence aspect determines how computer games are rated.

Better The level of violence determines how computer games are rated.

When citing numbers or quantities, be as exact as possible. A precise number, if known, is always better than slippery words such as *several* or *many*, which some writers use to cloak the fact that they don't know the quantity in question.

Use a dictionary

There is no greater tool for writers than the dictionary. Always have a dictionary handy when you write—either a book or an online version—and get into the habit of using it. In addition to checking spelling, you can find additional meanings of a word that perhaps you hadn't considered, and you can find the etymology—the origins of a word. In many cases, knowing the etymology of a word can help you use it to better effect. For example, if you want to argue that universities as institutions have succeeded because they bring people together in contexts that prepare them for their professional lives, you might point out the etymology of *university*. *University* can be traced back to the late Latin word *universitas*, which means 'society or guild', thus emphasising the idea of a community of learning.

21d Write to Be Inclusive

While the conventions of inclusiveness change continually, three guidelines for inclusive language towards all groups remain constant:

- Don't point out people's differences unless those differences are relevant to your argument.
- Call people whatever they prefer to be called.
- When given a choice of terms, choose the more accurate one. (*Vietnamese*, for example, is preferable to *Asian*.)

Be inclusive about gender

Don't use masculine nouns and pronouns to refer to both men and women. *He, his, him, man* and *mankind* are outmoded and inaccurate terms for both genders. Eliminate gender bias by using the following tips:

- Don't say *boy* when you can say *child*.
- Use *men and women* or *people* instead of *man*.
- Use *humanity* or *humankind* in place of *mankind*.

Eliminating *he, his* and *him* when referring to both men and women is more complicated. Many readers consider *he/she* to be an awkward alternative. Try one of the following instead:

- Make the noun and its corresponding pronoun plural. The pronoun will change from *he, him* or *his* to *they, them* or *theirs*.

Biased masculine pronouns

An undercover police officer won't reveal **his** identity, even to other officers, if **he** thinks it will jeopardise the case.

Better

Undercover police officers won't reveal their identities, even to other officers, if they think it will jeopardise the case.

- Replace the pronoun with an article (*the, a* or *an*)

Biased masculine pronoun

Each prospective driving instructor must pass a test before receiving **his** licence.

Better

Each prospective driving instructor must pass a test before receiving a licence.

Professional titles that indicate gender—*chairman*, *waitress*—falsely imply that the gender of the person doing the job changes the essence of the job being done. Terms such as *woman doctor* and *male nurse* imply that a woman working as a doctor and a man working as a nurse are out of the ordinary. Instead, simply write *doctor* and *nurse*.

Be inclusive about race and ethnicity

'*Australian*' is a generic and inclusive term used to refer to all people who were born in Australia or who have Australian citizenship, regardless of their cultural background. If it is necessary to indicate the ethnic identity of a particular group—for example, those of Vietnamese heritage—use *Vietnamese Australians, Vietnamese-speaking Australians* or *Australians of Vietnamese descent.* If making comparisons between ethnic groups, use parallel terms—*Chinese Australians* and *Anglo Australians.*

Take care not to inaccurately generalise religion with ethnicity, as not everyone from a particular ethnic group will have the same religion. While most Thais are Buddhists, not all Thais are Buddhists and not all Buddhists are Thai.

'*Indigenous*' is a generic and inclusive word used to refer to all Aboriginal and Torres Strait Islander peoples. *Indigenous* is capitalised when it refers to the first peoples of Australia but not when used as an adjective to generally describe the original inhabitants of other countries.

Australia's First Peoples is an alternative term for Australia's **Indigenous** community of Aboriginals and Torres Strait Islanders.

If referring collectively to Aboriginal and Torres Strait Islander peoples, the full term must be used. An abbreviation is not acceptable. Other acceptable general terms are *Indigenous Australians, Aboriginal people(s), Torres Strait Islanders, the first Australians* and *the first people of Australia.*

Ideally, however, Indigenous peoples should be referred to using the terms they use to describe themselves, which may relate to their family structure and the area from which they originate.

There are several such regional terms, and some of the more widely used include:

Koori	New South Wales
Koorie	Victoria
Murri	Queensland
Anangu	northern South Australia and bordering parts of the Northern Territory and Western Australia

Within these larger groups, Indigenous people may identify with particular land areas and language groups. For example, an Anangu person may be Pitjantjatjara or Yankunytjatjara.

Note that these terms apply to particular groups and are not synonyms for each other or for the more general terms Aboriginal or Indigenous.

Be inclusive about people with disabilities

Refer to people as having a disability, not as being disabled. Write *people who are deaf* instead of *the deaf* and *a student who is quadriplegic* instead of *a quadriplegic student.*

Be inclusive about people of different ages

Avoid bias by choosing accurate terms to describe age. If possible, use the person's age. *Eighty-year-old Margaret Brown* is better than *elderly Margaret Brown.*

21e Recognise International Varieties of English

English comes in various forms. Many applied linguists now speak of 'World Englishes' in the plural, to highlight the diversity of the English language as it is used worldwide today.

English has long been established as the dominant language in Australia, Canada, New Zealand, the United Kingdom and the United States, although many people in those countries also use other languages at home and in their communities. Englishes used in these countries share many characteristics, but there also are some differences in sentence structure, vocabulary, spelling and punctuation. For example:

Australian English	I stepped off the footpath.
US English	I stepped off of the pavement.
Australian English	What's the price of petrol (petroleum) these days?
US English	What's the price of gas (gasoline) these days?

Newer varieties of English have emerged outside traditionally English-speaking countries. Many former British and US colonies—Hong Kong, India, Malaysia, Nigeria, Papua New Guinea, the Philippines, Singapore and others—continue to use a local variety of English for both public and private communication. Englishes used in many of these countries are based primarily on the British variety, but they also include many features that reflect the local context.

Australian English	Turn on the air conditioner.
Indian English	Open the air conditioner.
Australian English	I was selected to lead the discussion.
Singaporean English	I was arrowed to lead the discussion.

Remember that perceptions of correctness differ from one variety of English to another. For example, each of the expressions above is correctly used within its own cultural and linguistic context.

PART 5 Understanding Grammar

22 Fragments, Run-ons and Comma Splices

AT A *GLANCE*

- Identify and correct fragments (see 22b)
- Identify and correct run-on sentences (see 22c)
- Identify and correct comma splices (see 22d)

22a Common Sentence Construction Errors

This section presents some of the most common errors in formal writing and how to fix them when they occur in your writing. The glossary at the end of this book provides definitions for all of the highlighted grammar terms for your easy reference, so look at these as you come across terms you are not familiar with in this section. Before reading, you might like to check your understanding of the following grammar terms in the glossary: 'subject', 'object', 'complete verb', 'participle', 'auxiliary verb', 'phrase', 'clause', 'subordinate clause', 'main clause'.

22b Fragments

Fragments are incomplete sentences. They are punctuated to look like sentences, but they lack a key element—often a subject or a verb—or else they are subordinate clauses or phrases. Consider this example of a full sentence followed by a fragment:

> The university's enrolment rose unexpectedly during the second semester. Because the percentage of students who accepted offers of admission was much higher than in previous years and fewer students than usual dropped out or transferred.

When a sentence starts with *because*, we expect to find a main clause later. Instead, the *because* clause in this example refers back to the previous sentence. The writer no doubt knew that the fragment gave the reasons why enrolment rose, but a reader must stop to determine the connection.

You should avoid fragments in formal writing. Readers expect words punctuated as a sentence to be a complete sentence. They expect writers to complete their thoughts rather than force readers to guess the missing element.

Basic strategies for turning fragments into sentences

Incorporate the fragment into an adjoining sentence

In many cases you can incorporate the fragment into an adjoining sentence.

game, playing

I was hooked on the ~~game. Playing~~ day and night.

Add the missing element

If you cannot incorporate a fragment into another sentence, add the missing element.

investors should think

When aiming for the highest returns, ~~and~~ also ~~thinking~~ about the possible losses.

COMMON ERRORS

e Edit Help

If you are not certain of the meaning of the grammar terms, look them up in the glossary (where they are given in blue).

Recognising fragments

If you can spot fragments, you can fix them. Grammar checkers can find some of them, but they miss many fragments and may incorrectly identify other sentences as fragments. Ask these questions when you are checking for sentence fragments.

- **Does the sentence have a subject?** Except for commands, sentences need subjects:

    Jane spent every cent of credit she had available. **And then applied for more cards.**

- **Does the sentence have a complete verb?** Sentences require complete verbs. Verbs that end in *-ing* must have an auxiliary verb to be complete.

    Robert keeps changing courses. **He trying to figure out what he really wants to do after university.**

- **If the sentence begins with a subordinate clause, is there a main clause in the same sentence?**

    Even though it is cheaper to watch a DVD than visit a movie theatre, it is the total experience that moviegoers enjoy. **Which is one reason people continue to go to the movies.**

(continued on next page)

COMMON ERRORS *(continued)*

Remember:

1. A sentence must have a subject and a complete verb.

2. A subordinate clause cannot stand alone as a sentence.

Run-on Sentences

While fragments are incomplete sentences, run-ons fuse together two or more sentences, failing to separate them with appropriate punctuation. Run-ons are also known as 'fused sentences'.

Fixing run-on sentences

Take three steps to fix run-on sentences: (1) identify the problem, (2) determine where the run-on sentence needs to be divided, and (3) choose the punctuation that best indicates the relationship between the main clauses.

COMMON ERRORS

Recognising run-on sentences

When you read this sentence, you realise something is wrong.

> **I don't recall what kind of printer it was all I remember is that it could sort, staple and print a packet at the same time.**

The problem is that two main clauses aren't separated by punctuation. The reader must look carefully to determine where one main clause stops and the next one begins.

> I don't recall what kind of printer it was | all I remember is that it could sort, staple and print a packet at the same time.

The most common way to correct this run-on is to place a full stop after *was*, and then begin the next sentence with a capital letter:

> I don't recall what kind of printer it was. All I remember is that it could sort, staple and print a packet at the same time.

COMMON ERRORS

Run-on sentences are major errors because they force the reader to re-read the sentence in order to understand it.

Remember: Two main clauses must be separated by correct punctuation.

1. Identify the problem

When you read your writing aloud, run-on sentences will often trip you up, just as they confuse readers. If you find two main clauses with no punctuation separating them, you have a run-on sentence. You can also search for subject and verb pairs to check for run-ons.

> [SUBJ: Internet businesses] [VERB: are] not [bound] to specific locations or old ways of running a business [S: they] [V: are] more flexible in allowing employees to telecommute and to determine the hours they work.

2. Determine where the run-on sentence needs to be divided

> Internet businesses are not bound to specific locations or old ways of running a business | they are more flexible in allowing employees to telecommute and to determine the hours they work.

3. Determine the relationship between the main clauses

You will be able to revise a run-on more effectively if you first determine the relationship between the main clauses and understand the effect or point you are trying to make. There are several punctuation strategies for fixing run-ons.

- **Insert a full stop**. This is the simplest way to fix a run-on sentence.

  Internet businesses are not bound to specific locations or old ways of running a business. They are more flexible in allowing employees to telecommute and to determine the hours they work.

  However, if you want to indicate more clearly a closer relationship between the two main clauses, you may want to choose one of the following strategies.

- **Insert a semicolon.** A less common option is to use a semicolon, but this is done rarely, when you want to link the two sentences because the second sentence continues the same idea, as in the following example:

  It is not correct to use a comma in this example; commas cannot be used to connect two sentences.

- **Insert a semicolon and a transitional word specifying the relationship between the two main clauses.**

  Internet businesses are not bound to specific locations or old ways of running a business; therefore, they are more flexible in allowing employees to telecommute and to determine the hours they work.

- **Insert a comma and a coordinating conjunction (*for, and, nor, but, or, yet, so*—the acronym to remember these is F.A.N.B.O.Y.S.).**

  Internet businesses are not bound to specific locations or old ways of running a business, so they are more flexible in allowing employees to telecommute and to determine the hours they work.

- **Make one of the clauses subordinate.**

  Because Internet businesses are not bound to specific locations or old ways of running a business, they are more flexible in allowing employees to telecommute and to determine the hours they work.

22d Comma Splices

Comma splices occur when two or more sentences that could stand on their own are incorrectly joined by a comma. In this example, the comma following 'classes' should be a full stop.

> **Most of us were taking the same classes, if someone had a question, we would all help out.**

Such sentences include a punctuation mark—a comma—separating two main clauses. However, a comma isn't a strong enough punctuation mark to separate two main clauses.

Fixing comma splices

You have several options for fixing comma splices. Select the one that best fits where the sentence is located and the effect you are trying to achieve.

1. Change the comma to a full stop

Most comma splices can be fixed by changing the comma to a full stop.

> It didn't matter that I worked in a windowless room for 40 hours a ~~week, on~~ *week; on* the Web I was exploring and learning more about distant people and places than I ever had before.

COMMON ERROR

Recognising comma splices

When you edit your writing, look carefully at sentences that contain commas. Does the sentence contain two main clauses? If so, are the main clauses joined by a comma and coordinating conjunction (*for, and, nor, but, or, yet, so*)?

Incorrect The **concept** [SUBJ] of 'nature' **depends** [VERB] on the concept of human 'culture', the **problem** [SUBJ] **is** [V] that 'culture' is itself shaped by 'nature'. [Two main clauses joined by only a comma]

Correct **Even** though the concept of 'nature' depends on the concept of human 'culture', 'culture' is itself shaped by 'nature'. [Subordinate clause plus a main clause]

Correct The concept of 'nature' depends on the concept of human 'culture', **but** 'culture' is itself shaped by 'nature'. [Two main clauses joined by a comma and coordinating conjunction]

The word *however* produces some of the most common comma splice errors. *However* usually functions to begin a main clause, and when it does it should be preceded by a semicolon rather than a comma. However, when 'however' appears at the beginning of a sentence, it is incorrect to precede it with a semicolon. Some students, however, like to use 'however' as an interrupter. In this case, it is bracketed by commas.

Incorrect The foreign affairs minister repeatedly vowed that the government wasn't choosing a side between the two

(continued on next page)

COMMON ERRORS *(continued)*

countries embroiled in conflict, **however** the developing foreign policy suggested otherwise.

Correct The foreign affairs minister repeatedly vowed that the government wasn't choosing a side between the two countries embroiled in conflict; **however,** the developing foreign policy suggested otherwise. [Two main clauses joined by a semicolon]

Remember: Don't use a comma as a full stop.

2. Change the comma to a semicolon

A semicolon indicates a close connection between two main clauses.

> It didn't matter that I worked in a windowless room for 40 hours a ~~week,~~ *week;* on the Web I was exploring and learning more about distant people and places than I ever had before.

3. Insert a coordinating conjunction

Other comma splices can be repaired by inserting a coordinating conjunction (for, and, nor, *but, or, yet, so*) to indicate the relationship between the two main clauses. The coordinating conjunction must be preceded by a comma.

> Digital technologies have intensified a global culture that affects us daily in large and small ways, **yet** their impact remains poorly understood.

4. Make one of the main clauses a subordinate clause

If a comma splice includes one main clause that is subordinate to the other, rewrite the sentence using a subordinating conjunction.

> *Because community* ~~Community~~ is the vision of a great society trimmed down to the size of a small town, it is a powerful metaphor for real estate developers who sell a mini-utopia along with a house or an apartment.

5. Make one of the main clauses a phrase

You can also rewrite one of the main clauses as a phrase.

> Community—**the vision of a great society trimmed down to the size of a small town**—is a powerful metaphor for real estate developers who sell a mini-utopia along with a house or an apartment.

23 Subject–Verb Agreement

AT A *GLANCE*

- Decide whether a subject is singular or plural (see 23c)
- Choose the right verb for indefinite pronouns (see 23d)

23a Agreement of Subjects and Verbs

In English a **verb** and its **subject** need to match, or 'agree' in terms of **singular** and **plural**, e.g., The stud***y*** involve***s***…, *but* the stud**ies** involve…, and also in terms of **person** (first, second or third person), e.g., I stud***y***, you stud***y***, *but* he, she, *or* it stud***ies***. Depending on the tense and construction of the sentence, there are added complications which arise in determining correct agreement. Note: You might like to check your understanding of some of the bolded terms in the Glossary.

23b Agreement in the Present Tense

When your verb is in the present tense, agreement in number is straightforward: the subject takes the base form of the verb in all but the third person singular. For example, the verb *walk*, in the present tense, agrees in number with most subjects in its base form.

First person singular	I walk
Second person singular	You walk
First person plural	We walk
Second person plural	You walk
Third person plural	They walk

Third person singular subjects are the exception to this rule. When your subject is in the third person singular (*he, it, Lucky, Lucy, Mr Jones*) you need to add *-s* or *-es* to the base form of the verb.

Third person singular (add *-s*)	He walks. It walks. Lucky walks.
Third person singular (add *-es*)	Lucy goes. Mr Jones goes.

23c Singular and Plural Subjects

Follow these rules when you have trouble determining whether to use a singular or a plural verb form.

Subjects joined by *and*

When two subjects are joined by *and*, treat them as a compound (plural) subject.

The teacher and the solicitor are headed west to start a commune.

Some compound subjects work together as a single noun and are treated as singular. Although they appear to be compound and therefore plural, these subjects take the singular form of the verb.

Rock and roll remains the devil's music, even in the twenty-first century.

When two nouns linked by *and* are modified by *every* or *each*, these two nouns are likewise treated as one singular subject.

Each night and day brings no new news of you.

An exception to this rule arises when the word *each* follows a compound subject. In these cases, usage varies depending on the number of the direct object.

The army and the navy each have their own planes.

The owl and the pussycat each has a personal claim to fame.

Subjects joined by *or*, *either . . . or*, or *neither . . . nor*

When a subject is joined by *or*, *either . . . or*, or *neither . . . nor*, make sure the verb agrees with the subject closest to the verb.

SING PLURAL PL
Is it **the sky or the mountains** that are blue?

PLURAL SING SING
Is it **the mountains or the sky** that surrounds us?

PLURAL SING SING
Neither the animals nor the zookeeper knows how to relock the gate.

SING PLURAL PL
Either a dingo or several dogs were howling last night.

Subjects along with another noun

Verbs agree with the subject of a sentence, even when a subject is linked to another noun with a phrase like *as well as, along with* or *alongside*. These modifying phrases are usually set off from the main subject with commas.

IGNORE THIS PHRASE

Chicken, alongside various steamed vegetables, is my favourite meal.

IGNORE THIS PHRASE

Besides B.B. King, **John Lee Hooker and Muddy Waters** are my favourite blues artists of all time.

COMMON ERRORS

Subjects separated from verbs

The most common agreement errors occur when words come between the subject and the verb. These intervening words don't affect subject–verb agreement. To ensure that you use the correct verb form, identify the subject and the verb. Ignore any phrases that come between them.

IGNORE THIS PHRASE

Incorrect **Students** at inner-city Sydney High **reads** more than suburban students.

Correct **Students** at inner-city Sydney High read more than suburban students.

Students is plural and *read* is plural; subject and verb agree.

Incorrect **The whale shark**, the largest of all sharks, **feed** on plankton.

Correct **The whale shark**, the largest of all sharks, feeds on plankton.

The plural noun *sharks* that appears between the subject *the whale shark* and the verb *feeds* doesn't change the number of the subject. The subject is singular and the verb is singular. Subject and verb agree.

Remember: When you check for subject–verb agreement, identify the subject and the verb. Ignore any words that come between them.

23d Indefinite Pronouns as Subjects

The choice of a singular or plural pronoun is determined by the **antecedent**—the noun that pronoun refers to. Indefinite pronouns, such as *some, few, all, someone, everyone* and *each*, often don't refer to identifiable subjects;

hence they have no antecedents. Most indefinite pronouns are singular and agree with the singular forms of verbs. Some, like *both* and *many*, are always plural and agree with the plural forms of verbs. Other indefinite pronouns are variable and can agree with either singular or plural verb forms, depending on the context of the sentence.

COMMON ERRORS

Agreement errors using *each*

When a pronoun is singular, its verb must be singular. A common stumbling block to this rule is the pronoun *each*. *Each* is always treated as a singular pronoun in academic writing. When *each* stands alone, the choice is easy to make:

Incorrect	**Each** **are** an outstanding student.
Correct	**Each** is an outstanding student.

But when *each* is modified by a phrase that includes a plural noun, the choice of a singular verb form becomes less obvious:

Incorrect	**Each** of the girls **are** fit.
Correct	**Each** of the girls is fit.
Incorrect	**Each** of our dogs **get** a present.
Correct	**Each** of our dogs gets a present.

Remember: *Each* is always singular.

23e Collective Nouns as Subjects

Collective nouns refer to groups (*audience, class, committee, crowd, family, government, group, jury, public, team*). When members of a group are considered as a unit, use singular verbs and singular pronouns.

The **crowd** is unusually quiet at the moment, but it will get noisy soon.

When members of a group are considered as individuals, use plural verbs and plural pronouns.

The **staff** have **their** differing opinions on how to address the problems caused by reduced government support.

Sometimes collective nouns can be singular in one context and plural in another. Writers must decide which verb form to use based on sentence context.

The **number** of people who live in the inner city is increasing.

A **number** of people are moving into the inner city from the suburbs.

23f Inverted Word Order

In English a sentence's subject usually comes before the verb: *The nights are tender.* Sometimes, however, you will come across a sentence with inverted word order: *Tender are the nights.* Here the subject of the sentence, *nights*, comes after the verb, *are*. Writers use inverted word order most often in forming questions. The statement *Cats are friendly* becomes a question when you invert the subject and the verb: *Are cats friendly?* Writers also use inverted word order for added emphasis or for style considerations.

Don't be confused by inverted word order. Locate the subject of your sentence, then make sure your verb agrees with that subject.

23g Amounts, Numbers and Pairs

Subjects that describe amounts of money, time, distance or measurement are singular and require singular verbs.

Three days is never long enough to unwind.

Some subjects, such as courses of study, academic specialisations, illnesses and even some nations, are treated as singular subjects even though their names end in *-s* or *-es*. For *example, economics, news, ethics, measles* and *the Philippines* all end in *-s* but are all singular subjects.

Economics is a rich field of study.

Other subjects require a plural verb form even though they refer to single items, such as *jeans, slacks, glasses, scissors* and *tweezers*. These items are all pairs.

My **glasses** are scratched.

24 Verbs

AT A *GLANCE*

- Understand basic verb forms (see 24a below)
- Distinguish forms of transitive and intransitive verbs (see 24c)

24a Basic Verb Forms

Almost all verbs in English have five possible forms. The exception is the verb *be* (which consists of a group of verbs that vary in form depending on the corresponding subject noun: *be, am, is, are, was, were, been*). For example, I am/I was/I have been..., She is..., They are..., etc.

Regular verbs follow this basic pattern:

Base form	Third person singular	Past tense	Past participle*	Present participle*
jump	jumps	jumped	jumped	jumping
like	likes	liked	liked	liking
talk	talks	talked	talked	talking
wish	wishes	wished	wished	wishing

*Note: participle means 'part of a verb'. To complete the verb form, an **auxiliary** verb needs to be added to it; e.g., It *had* jumped. I *was* jumping.

Base form

The base form of the verb is the one you find listed in the dictionary. This form indicates an action or condition in the present.

I like Darwin in June.

Third person singular

Third person singular subjects include *he*, *she*, *it*, and the nouns they replace, as well as other pronouns, including *someone, anybody* and *everything*. Present tense verbs in the third person singular end with *s* or *es*.

Ms Nessan speaks in riddles.

Past tense

The past tense describes an action or condition that occurred in the past. For most verbs, the past tense is formed by adding *-d* or *-ed* to the base form of the verb.

> She inhaled the night air.

Many verbs, however, have irregular past tense forms. (See Section 24b.)

Past participle

The past participle is used with *have* or *had* to form verbs in the present perfect and past perfect tenses, with *be* to form verbs in the passive voice (see Section 18a), and to form adjectives derived from verbs.

Present	I have seen it recently.
Past perfect	They had gone to the supermarket the previous day.
Passive	The book was written 30 years before it was published.
Adjective	In the 1980s, teased hair was fashionable.

COMMON ERRORS

Missing verb endings

Verb endings are not always pronounced in speech, especially in some dialects of English. It is also easy to omit these endings when you are writing quickly. Spelling checkers won't mark these errors, so you have to find them while proofreading.

Incorrect	Jeremy feel as if he's catching a cold.
Correct	Jeremy feels as if he's catching a cold.
Incorrect	Sarah hope she would get the day off.
Correct	Sarah hoped she would get the day off.

Remember: Check verbs carefully for missing *-s* or *-es* endings in the present tense and missing *-d* or *-ed* endings in the past tense.

Present participle

The present participle functions in one of three ways. Used with an auxiliary verb, it can describe a continuing action. The present participle can also function as a noun, known as a **gerund**, or as an adjective. The present participle is formed by adding *ing* to the base form of a verb.

Present participle	Wild camels **are** competing for limited food resources.
Gerund	Sailing around the Cape of Good Hope is rumoured to bring good luck.
Adjective	We looked for shells in the ebbing tide.

24b Irregular Verbs

A verb is **regular** when its past and past participle forms are created by adding *-ed* or *-d* to the base form. If this rule doesn't apply, the verb is considered an **irregular** verb. Here are selected common irregular verbs and their basic conjugations.

Base form	Past tense	Past participle
be (is, am, are)	was, were	been
become	became	become
bring	brought	brought
come	came	come
do	did	done
get	got	got or gotten
have	had	had
go	went	gone
know	knew	known
see	saw	seen

COMMON ERRORS

Past tense forms of irregular verbs

The past tense and past participle forms of irregular verbs are often confused. The most frequent error is using a past tense form instead of the past participle with *has/have* or *had*.

PAST TENSE
Incorrect She has never **rode** a horse before.

PAST PARTICIPLE
Correct She has never **ridden** a horse before.

PAST TENSE
Incorrect He had **saw** many crocodiles in Kakadu.

PAST PARTICIPLE
Correct He had **seen** many crocodiles in Kakadu.

Remember: Change any past tense verbs preceded by *has/have* or *had* to past participles.

24c Transitive and Intransitive Verbs

Lay/lie, set/sit and *raise/rise*

Do your house keys lay or lie on the kitchen table? Does a book set or sit on the shelf? *Raise/rise, lay/lie and set/sit* are transitive/intransitive verb pairs that writers frequently confuse. **Transitive verbs** take direct objects—nouns that receive the action of the verb. **Intransitive verbs** act in sentences that lack direct objects.

Transitive Henry **sets** the book [direct object, the book being set] on the shelf.

Intransitive Henry **sits** down to read the book.

The following charts list the trickiest pairs of transitive and intransitive verbs and the correct forms for each verb tense. Pay special attention to *lay* and *lie*, which are irregular.

	lay (put something down)	lie (recline)
Present	lay, lays	lie, lies
Present participle	laying	lying
Past	laid	lay
Past participle	laid	lain

Transitive When you complete your test, please lay your pencil [direct object, the thing being laid down] on the desk.

Intransitive The *Titanic* lies upright in two pieces at a depth of 4000 metres.

	raise (elevate something)	rise (get up)
Present	raise, raises	rise, rises
Present participle	raising	rising
Past	raised	rose
Past participle	raised	risen

Transitive We raise our glasses [direct object, the things being raised] to toast Uncle Han.

Intransitive The sun rises over the bay.

	set (place something)	sit (take a seat)
Present	set, sets	sit, sits
Present participle	setting	sitting
Past	set	sat
Past participle	set	sat

Transitive Every morning Stanley sets two dollars [direct object, the things being set] on the table for his daughter's bus fare.

Intransitive I sit in the front seat if it's available.

25 Pronouns

AT A *GLANCE*

- Chose the correct pronoun case (see 25a below)
- Identify and correct errors in pronoun agreement (see 25b)

25a Pronoun Case

Subjective pronouns function as the subjects of sentences. **Objective pronouns** function as direct or indirect objects. **Possessive pronouns** indicate ownership.

Subjective pronouns	Objective pronouns	Possessive pronouns
I	me	my, mine
we	us	our, ours
you	you	your, yours
he	him	his
she	her	her, hers
it	it	its
they	them	their, theirs
who	whom	whose

Pronouns in compound phrases

Picking the right pronoun can sometimes be confusing when the pronoun appears in a compound phrase.

> If we work together, you and **me** can get the job done quickly.

> If we work together, you and **I** can get the job done quickly.

Which is correct—*me* or *I*? Removing the other pronoun usually makes the choice clear.

Incorrect	**Me** can get the job done quickly.
Correct	I can get the job done quickly.

We and *us* before nouns

Another pair of pronouns that can cause difficulty is *we* and *us* before nouns.

Us friends must stick together.

We friends must stick together.

Which is correct—*us* or *we?* Removing the noun indicates the correct choice.

Incorrect	**Us** must stick together.
Correct	We must stick together.

Who versus *whom*

Choosing between *who* and *whom* is often difficult, even for experienced writers. The distinction between *who* and *whom* is disappearing from spoken language. *Who* is more often used in spoken language, even when *whom* is correct. However, *who* is increasingly used instead of *whom* in written as well as spoken English. In any case, you are unlikely to use this type of personal pronoun construction in academic writing.

Possessive pronouns

Possessive pronouns are confusing at times because possessive nouns are formed with apostrophes, but possessive pronouns don't require apostrophes. Pronouns that use apostrophes are always **contractions**.

It's	=	It is
Who's	=	Who is
They're	=	They are

The test for whether to use an apostrophe is to determine whether the pronoun is possessive or a contraction. The most confusing pair is *its* and *it's*.

Incorrect	**Its** a sure thing she will be elected. [Contraction needed]
Correct	It's a sure thing she will be elected. [It is a sure thing.]
Incorrect	The dog lost **it's** collar. [Possessive needed]
Correct	The dog lost its collar.

25b Pronoun Agreement

Because pronouns usually replace or refer to other nouns, they must match those nouns in number and gender. The noun that the pronoun replaces is called its **antecedent**. If pronoun and antecedent match, they are in **agreement**. When a pronoun is close to the antecedent, usually there is no problem.

Maria forgot her coat.

The band **members** collected their uniforms.

Pronoun agreement errors often happen when pronouns and the nouns they replace are separated by several words.

Incorrect

The **players**, exhausted from the double-overtime game, picked up **his** tracksuit and walked towards the club rooms.

Correct

The **players**, exhausted from the double-overtime game, picked up their tracksuits and walked towards the club rooms.

Careful writers make sure that pronouns match their antecedents.

COMMON ERRORS

Indefinite pronouns

Indefinite pronouns (such as *anybody, anything, each, either, everybody, everything, neither, none, somebody, something*) refer to unspecified people or things. Most take singular pronouns.

Incorrect	Everybody can choose **their** flatmates.
Correct	Everybody can choose **his or her** flatmate.
Correct alternative	All students can choose **their** flatmates.

A few indefinite pronouns (*all, any, either, more, most, neither, none, some*) can take either singular or plural pronouns.

Correct	**Some** of the shipment was damaged when it became overheated.
Correct	**All** thought they should have a good seat at the concert.

A few pronouns are always plural (*few, many, several*).

Correct	**Several** want refunds.

Remember: Words that begin with *any, some* and *every* are usually singular

Collective nouns

Collective nouns (such as *audience, class, committee, crowd, family, herd, jury, team*) can be singular or plural depending on whether the emphasis is on the group or on its individual members.

Correct	The **committee** was unanimous in its decision.
Correct	The **committee** put their opinions ahead of the goals of the unit.

COMMON ERRORS

Pronoun agreement with compound antecedents

Antecedents joined by *and* take plural pronouns.

Correct *Moncef and Driss* practised their music.

Exception: When compound antecedents are preceded by *each* or *every*, use a singular pronoun.

Correct **Every male cardinal and warbler** arrives before the female to define its territory.

When compound antecedents are connected by *or* or *nor*, the pronoun agrees with the antecedent closer to it.

Incorrect **Either the Ross twins or Angela** should bring their CDs.

Correct **Either the Ross twins or Angela** should bring her CDs.

Better **Either Angela or the Ross twins** should bring their CDs.

When you put the plural *twins* last, the correct choice becomes the plural pronoun *their*.

Remember:

1. Use plural pronouns for antecedents joined by *and*.
2. Use singular pronouns for antecedents preceded by *each* or *every*.
3. Use a pronoun that agrees with the nearest antecedent when compound antecedents are joined by *or* or *nor*.

25c Avoid Sexist Pronouns

English doesn't have a neutral singular pronoun for a group of mixed genders or a person of unknown gender. Referring to a group of mixed genders using male pronouns is unacceptable to many people. Unless the school in the following example is all male, many readers would object to the use of *his*.

Sexist **Each student** must select his courses using the online registration system.

One strategy is to use *her or his* or *his or her* instead of *his.*

Correct **Each student** must select his or her courses using the online registration system.

Often you can avoid using *his or her* by changing the noun to the plural form.

Better **All students** must select their courses using the online registration system.

In some cases, however, using *his or her* is necessary.

25d Vague Reference

Pronouns can sometimes refer to more than one noun, thus confusing readers.

The **coach** rushed past the injured **player** to yell at the **referee.** She was hit in the face by a stray elbow.

You have to guess which person *she* refers to—the coach, the player or the referee. Sometimes you cannot even guess the antecedent of a pronoun.

The new subdivision destroyed the last remaining habitat for wildlife within the city limits. They have ruined our city with their unchecked greed.

To whom does *they* refer? The mayor and city council? The developers? The people who live in the subdivision? Or all of the above?

Pronouns should never leave the reader guessing about antecedents. If different nouns can be confused as the antecedent, then the ambiguity should be clarified.

Vague Siham's pet python crawled across Tonya's foot. She was mortified.

Better When Siham's pet python crawled across Tonya's foot, Siham was mortified.

COMMON ERRORS

Vague use of *this*

Always use a noun immediately after *this, that, these, those* and *some.*

Vague Enrique asked Meg to remove the viruses on his computer. **This** was a bad idea.

Was it a bad idea for Enrique to ask Meg because she was insulted? Because she didn't know how? Because removing viruses would destroy some of Enrique's files?

Better Enrique asked Meg to remove the viruses on his computer. **This imposition** on Meg's time was a bad idea.

Remember: Ask yourself 'this *what*?' and add the noun that *this* refers to.

26 Shifts

AT A *GLANCE*

- Identify and correct verb tense shifts (see 26a below)
- Identify and correct shifts in mood (26b), voice (26c), and person and number (see 26d)

Shifts in Tense

Appropriate shifts in verb tense

Changes in verb tense are sometimes necessary to indicate a shift in time.

Past to future Because Kimiko won (PAST TENSE) the lottery, she will quit (FUTURE TENSE) her job at the hospital as soon as her supervisor finds (PRESENT TENSE) a qualified replacement

Inappropriate shifts in verb tense

Be careful to avoid confusing your reader with shifts in verb tense.

Incorrect While Brazil looks (PRESENT TENSE) to ecotourism to fund rainforest preservation, other South American nations relied (PAST TENSE) on foreign aid and conservation efforts.

The shift from present tense (*looks*) to past tense (*relied*) is confusing. Correct the mistake by putting both verbs in the present tense.

Correct While Brazil looks (PRESENT TENSE) to ecotourism to fund rainforest preservation, other South American nations rely (PRESENT TENSE) on foreign aid and conservation efforts.

COMMON ERRORS

Unnecessary tense shift

Notice the tense shift in the following example.

Incorrect

PAST TENSE
On census night 2016, a cyber attack crippled the
PAST TENSE
Australian Bureau of Statistics web server and irritated
PRESENT TENSE
millions of Australians. As the attack threatens security
PRESENT TENSE PRESENT TENSE
and inconveniences millions of people, the Bureau is
forced to shut down its web site.

The second sentence shifts unnecessarily to the present tense, confusing the reader. Did the Australian Bureau of Statistics shut down the server in the past, or is it doing this now? Changing the verbs in the second sentence to the past tense eliminates the confusion.

Correct

PAST TENSE
On census night 2016 a cyber attack crippled the
PAST TENSE
Australian Bureau of Statistics web server and irritated
PAST TENSE
millions of Australians. As the attack threatened security
PAST TENSE PAST TENSE
and inconvenienced millions of people, the Bureau was
forced to shut down its web site.

Remember: Shift verb tense only when you are referring to different time periods.

 Shifts in Mood

Verbs can be categorised into three moods—indicative, imperative and subjunctive—defined by the functions they serve.

Indicative verbs state facts, opinions and questions.

Fact Qantas plans to boost its domestic seat capacity to make up for losses incurred during the global financial crisis.

Imperative verbs make commands, give advice and make requests.

Command	Make up for losses incurred during the global financial crisis by boosting domestic seat capacity.

Subjunctive verbs express wishes, unlikely or untrue situations, hypothetical situations, requests with *that* clauses, and suggestions.

Unlikely or untrue situation	If improving profitability were as simple as merely increasing seat capacity, Qantas would be assured of making up for losses incurred during the global financial crisis.

Be careful not to shift from one mood to another in mid-sentence.

Incorrect	If Qantas **were** to boost its domestic seat capacity, it **is** difficult for other airlines to maintain market share.

The sudden shift from subjunctive to indicative mood in this sentence is confusing. Is it difficult for the other airlines to maintain market share now, or is difficulty in maintaining market share a likely result of Qantas boosting its seat capacity? Revise the sentence to keep both verbs in the subjunctive.

Correct	If Qantas **were** to boost its domestic seat capacity, it would be difficult for other airlines to maintain market share.

26c Shifts in Voice

Watch for unintended shifts from active voice (*I ate the biscuits*) to passive voice (*the biscuits were eaten*).

Incorrect	The sudden storm toppled several trees and numerous windows **were shattered.**

The unexpected shift from active voice (*toppled*) to passive voice (*were shattered*) forces readers to wonder whether it was the sudden storm, or something else, that broke the windows.

Correct	The sudden storm toppled several trees and shattered numerous windows.

Revising the sentence to eliminate the shift to passive voice (see Section 18a) also improves its parallel structure (see Section 20c).

 Shifts in Person and Number

Sudden shifts from third person (*he, she, it, one*) to first (*I, we*) or second (*you*) are confusing to readers and often indicate a writer's uncertainty about how to address a reader. We often make such shifts in spoken English, but in formal writing shifts in person need to be recognised and corrected.

Incorrect When **one** is reading a magazine, **you** often see several different fonts used on a single page.

The shift from third person to second person in this sentence is confusing.

Correct When reading a magazine, you often see several different fonts used on a single page.

Shifts from singular to plural subjects (see Section 23a) within a single sentence also confuse readers.

Incorrect Administrators often make more money than lecturers, but only **a lecturer** has frequent contact with students.

Correct Administrators often make more money than lecturers, but only lecturers have frequent contact with students.

The revised sentence eliminates a distracting and unnecessary shift from plural to singular.

27 Modifiers

AT A *GLANCE*

- Choose the correct modifier (see 27a below)
- Place adjectives (see 27b)
- Revise dangling modifiers (see 27c)
- Place adverbs carefully (see 27d)
- Use hyphens correctly (see 27e)

 Choose the Correct Modifier

Modifiers come in two varieties: adjectives and adverbs. The same words can function as adjectives or adverbs, depending on what they modify.

Adjectives modify:

nouns—*iced* tea, *fast* runner
pronouns—He is *brash*.

Adverbs modify:

verbs—*barely* reach, drive *carefully*
adjectives—*truly* brave activist, *shockingly* red lipstick
other adverbs—*not* soon, *more* rapidly
clauses—*Honestly*, I find ballet boring.

Adjectives answer the questions *Which one? How many?* and *What kind?* Adverbs answer the questions *How often? To what extent? When? Where? How?* and *Why?*

Handy tip: A way to check whether a word is an adjective (not an adverb) is to see if it can be followed by the verb 'to be' and make a complete meaningful clause:

Correct He is brash. It is fast.

Incorrect *But not:* It is barely. It is truly.

Use the correct forms of comparatives and superlatives

Comparative modifiers weigh one thing against another. They either end in *-er* or are preceded by *more.*

Road bikes are faster on bitumen than mountain bikes.

The more courageous juggler tossed flaming torches.

Superlative modifiers compare three or more items. They either end in *-est* or are preceded by *most.*

May and June are the hottest months in New Delhi.

Wounded animals are the most ferocious.

Some frequently used comparatives and superlatives are irregular. The following list can help you become familiar with them.

Adjective	**Comparative**	**Superlative**
good	better	best
bad	worse	worst
little (amount)	less	least
many, much	more	most
Adverb	**Comparative**	**Superlative**
well	better	best
badly	worse	worst

Don't use both a suffix (*-er* or *-est*) and *more* or *most.*

Incorrect The service at Jane's Restaurant is more slower than the service at Alphonso's.

Correct The service at Jane's Restaurant is slower than the service at Alphonso's.

Absolute modifiers are words that represent an unvarying condition and thus aren't subject to the degrees that comparative and superlative constructions convey. Common absolute modifiers include *complete, ultimate* and *unique. Unique*, for example, means 'one of a kind'. There is nothing else like it. Thus something cannot be *very unique* or *totally unique*. It is either unique or it isn't. Absolute modifiers shouldn't be modified by comparatives (*more* + modifier or modifier + *-er*) or superlatives (*most* + modifier or modifier + *-est*).

Double negatives

Avoid using the following negative words together in a sentence or you will create ambiguous meanings:

barely	nobody	nothing
hardly	none	scarcely
neither	no one	

Incorrect, double negative	**Barely no one** noticed that the pop star lip-synched during the whole performance.
Correct, single negative	Barely anyone noticed that the pop star lip-synched during the whole performance.
Incorrect, double negative	When the minister asked if anyone had objections to the marriage, **nobody** said **nothing**.
Correct, single negative	When the minister asked if anyone had objections to the marriage, nobody said anything.

27b Place Adjectives Carefully

As a general rule, the closer you place a modifier to the word it modifies, the less likely it is that you will confuse your reader. The following is called a 'dangling modifier'.

Confusing	**Watching from the ground below**, the eagles circled high above the observers.

Are the eagles watching from the ground below? You can fix the problem by putting the modified subject immediately after the modifier or placing the modifier next to the modified subject.

Better	The eagles circled high above the **observers** who were watching from the ground below.
Better	Watching from the ground below, the **observers** saw eagles circling high above them.

27c Revise Dangling Modifiers

Some modifiers are ambiguous because they could apply to more than one word or clause. Dangling modifiers are ambiguous for the opposite reason: they don't have a word to modify. In such cases, the modifier is usually an introductory clause or phrase. What is being modified should immediately follow the phrase, but in the following sentence it is absent.

> **After bowling a perfect game**, Surfside Bowling Alley hung Marco's photo on the wall.

You can eliminate a dangling modifier in two ways:

1. Insert the noun or pronoun being modified immediately after the introductory modifying phrase.

   After bowling a perfect game, Marco was honoured by having his photo hung on the wall at Surfside Bowling Alley.

2. Rewrite the introductory phrase as an introductory clause to include the noun or pronoun.

   After Marco bowled a perfect game, Surfside Bowling Alley hung his photo on the wall.

COMMON ERRORS

Dangling modifiers

A dangling modifier doesn't seem to modify anything in a sentence; it dangles, unconnected to the word or words it presumably is intended to modify. Frequently, it produces funny results:

> I saw four kangaroos **driving down the road**.

It sounds as if *the kangaroos* were driving. The problem is that the subject, *I*, is missing:

> I saw four Kangaroos while I was driving down the road.

Remember: Modifiers should be clearly connected to the words they modify, especially at the beginning of sentences.

27d Place Adverbs Carefully

Single-word adverbs and adverbial clauses and phrases can usually sit comfortably either before or after the words they modify.

Dimitri quietly **walked** down the hall.

Dimitri **walked** quietly down the hall.

Conjunctive adverbs—*also, however, instead, likewise, then, therefore, thus* and others—are adverbs that show how ideas relate to one another. They prepare a reader for contrasts, exceptions, additions, conclusions and other shifts in an argument. Conjunctive adverbs can usually fit well into more than one place in the sentence. In the following example, *however* could fit in three different places.

Between two main clauses

Professional football players earn very high salaries; however, they pay for their wealth with lifetimes of chronic pain and debilitating injuries.

Within second main clause

Professional football players earn very high salaries; they pay for their wealth, however, with lifetimes of chronic pain and debilitating injuries.

At end of second main clause

Professional football players earn very high salaries; they pay for their wealth with lifetimes of chronic pain and debilitating injuries, however.

Subordinating conjunctions—words such as *after, although, because, if, since, than, that, though, when and where*—often begin **adverb clauses**. Notice that we can place adverb clauses with subordinating conjunctions either before or after the word(s) being modified:

After someone in the audience yelled, he **forgot** the lyrics.

He **forgot** the lyrics after someone in the audience yelled.

Note: In the first example above a comma is required because a subordinate clause begins the sentence. The comma signals to the reader that the main clause 'he forgot the lyrics' is yet to come.

COMMON ERRORS

Placement of limiting modifiers

Words such as *almost, even, hardly, just, merely, nearly, not, only* and *simply* are called limiting modifiers. Although people often speak ungrammatically in everyday speech, limiting modifiers should always go immediately before the word or words they modify in your writing. Like other limiting modifiers, *only* should be placed immediately before the word it modifies.

Incorrect The Gross Domestic Product **only** gives one indicator of economic growth.

Correct The Gross Domestic Product gives **only** one indicator of economic growth.

The word *only* modifies *one* in this sentence, not *Gross Domestic Product.*

Remember: Place limiting modifiers immediately before the word(s) they modify.

Hyphens with Compound Modifiers

When to hyphenate

Hyphenate a compound modifier that precedes a noun

When a compound modifier precedes a noun, you should usually hyphenate the modifier. A **compound modifier** consists of words that join together as a unit to modify a noun.

middle-class values   self-fulfilling prophecy

Hyphenate a phrase when it is used as a modifier that precedes a noun

all-you-can-eat buffet step-by-step instructions

Hyphenate the prefixes *pro-*, *anti-*, *post-*, *pre-*, *neo-* and *mid-* before proper nouns and some common nouns

neo-Nazi racism mid-Pacific storms

Hyphenate a compound modifier with a number when it precedes a noun

eighteenth-century drama one-way street

When not to hyphenate

Don't hyphenate a compound modifier that follows a noun

The tutor's approach is student centred.

Don't hyphenate compound modifiers when the first word is *very* or ends in *-ly*

newly recorded data very cold day

28 Grammar for Multilingual Writers

AT A *GLANCE*

- Learn more about nouns (see 28a below)
- Using articles correctly (see 28b)
- Using verbs correctly (see 28c)

28a Nouns

Handy tip to recognise nouns*: A way to check whether a word is a noun when you are a native English speaker, or a highly proficient in English, is to put **'the', 'an'** or **'a'** in front of the singular form (not plural form); e.g. **a boy, the institution, an ideal**.

If it 'sounds right', then it is a noun.

However, it is often not so simple for speakers for whom English is not a first language because they may not have had as much exposure to the language to internalise these patterns.

Perhaps the most troublesome conventions are those that guide usage of the common articles *the*, *a* and *an*. To understand how articles work in English, you must first understand how the language uses nouns.

Kinds of nouns

There are two basic kinds of nouns. A **proper noun** begins with a capital letter and names a unique person, place or thing: *Ian Thorpe, Indonesia, Melbourne Cricket Ground.*

The other basic kind of noun is called a **common noun**. Common nouns don't name a unique person, place or thing: *man, country, sportsground.*

Countable and uncountable nouns

Common nouns can be classified as either *countable* or *uncountable*. **Countable nouns** can be made plural, usually by adding *-s* (*finger, fingers*) or by using

*Note this tip does not apply to most proper nouns, e.g. people's names, the names of cities etc. (they are readily recognisable anyway).

their plural forms (*person, people; datum, data*). **Uncountable nouns** cannot be counted directly and cannot take the plural form (*information*, but not *informations*; *garbage*, but not *garbages*). Some nouns can be either countable or uncountable, depending on how they are used. *Hair* can refer to either a strand of hair, where it serves as a countable noun, or a mass of hair, where it becomes an uncountable noun. This variable category of noun is sometimes called a 'variable noun'.

COMMON ERRORS

Singular and plural forms of countable nouns

Countable nouns are simpler to quantify than uncountable nouns, but remember that English requires you to state both singular and plural forms of nouns explicitly. Look at the following sentences.

Incorrect The three **cyclist** shaved their **leg** before the big race.

Correct The three cyclists shaved their legs before the big race.

Remember: English requires you to use plural forms of countable nouns even if a plural number is otherwise indicated.

28b Articles

Articles indicate that a noun is about to appear, and they clarify what the noun refers to. There are only two kinds of articles in English: definite and indefinite.

1. **the:** *The* is a **definite article**, meaning that it refers to (1) a specific object already known to the reader, (2) one about to be made known to the reader, or (3) a unique object.
2. **a, an:** The **indefinite articles** *a* and *an* refer to an object whose specific identity isn't known to the reader. The only difference between *a* and *an* is that a is used before a consonant **sound** (a ***m**an,* a ***f**riend*). Note that a consonant sound may also be spelled with a vowel **'letter'** (*a **e**uro,* a ***u**niversity*). The indefinite article *an* is used before a vowel **sound** (an ***a**nimal,* an ***e**nemy,* an ***o**range*).

COMMON ERRORS

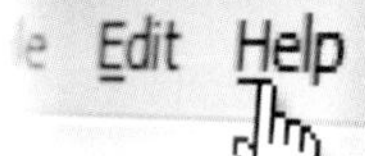

Articles with countable and uncountable nouns

Knowing how to distinguish between countable and uncountable nouns can help you decide which article to use. Uncountable nouns are never used with the indefinite articles *a* or *an*.

Incorrect	Maria jumped into a water.
Correct	Maria jumped into the water.

However, variable nouns—which are sometimes uncountable in some contexts, but have a countable meaning in other contexts—can be used with the indefinite articles *a* or *an*.

Correct	**Maria drank a beer**
Correct	**Maria drank the beer**
Correct	**Maria drank three beers**

No articles are used with uncountable and plural countable nouns when you wish to state something that has a general application.

Incorrect	The water is a precious natural resource.
Correct	Water is a precious natural resource.

Remember:

1. **Uncountable nouns are never used with *a* and *an*.**
2. **Uncountable and plural nouns used to make general statements don't use articles.**

28c Verbs

Handy tip to recognise verbs*: A word is a **verb** if you can put **'to'** in front of the present form of it; **e.g. to play, to love, to have, to fluctuate**—*and it 'sounds right'*.

*Note: Some words in English can be categorised as more than one part of speech; e.g., ship (verb or noun). For these words, check the position of the word in **context**. For example, *The cargo was shipped by ship*. The first 'shipped' is in the position of a verb. The second 'ship' is in the position of a noun.

The only exception is the verb forms of **'to be'** (*am, are, is, was, were*).

'To am' doesn't sound right.

The verb system in English can be divided between simple verbs such as *run, speak* and *look*, and verb phrases such as *may have run, have spoken* and *will be looking*. In these examples, the words that appear before the main verbs—*may, have, will* and *be*—are called **auxiliary verbs** (or **helping verbs**).

Indicating tense and voice with be verbs

Like the other auxiliary verbs *have* and *do*, *be* changes form to signal tense. In addition to *be* itself, the **be verbs** are *is, am, are, was, were* and *been*. To show ongoing action, be verbs are followed by the present participle, which is a verb with an *-ing* ending.

Incorrect I **am think** of all the things I'd rather **be do**.

Correct I am thinking of all the things I'd rather be doing.

To show that an action is being done to, rather than by, the subject, follow *be* verbs with the past participle (a verb usually ending in *-ed*, *-en* or *-t*). See Section 18a on the passive form.

Incorrect The movie **was direct** by Baz Luhrmann.

Correct The movie was directed by Baz Luhrmann.

Modal auxiliary verbs

Modal auxiliary verbs *will, would, can, could, may, might, shall, must* and *should* express conditions such as possibility, permission, speculation, expectation, obligation and necessity. Unlike the auxiliary verbs *be, have* and *do*, modal verbs don't change form based on the grammatical subject of the sentence (*I, you, she, he, it, we, they*).

Two basic rules apply to all uses of modal verbs. First, modal verbs are always followed by the simple form of the verb. The simple form is the verb by itself, in the present tense, such as *have*, but not *had, having* or *to have*.

Incorrect She should **studies** harder to pass the exam.

Correct She should study harder to pass the exam.

The second rule is that you should not use modals consecutively.

Incorrect	If you work harder at writing, you **might could** improve.
Correct	If you work harder at writing, you might improve.

Phrasal (multi-word) verbs

Verbs do not need to be single words. There are a number of **word groups** that can be treated as single verbs, such as the following:

To *turn up*. To *put up with*. To *get by*. . . and so on.

Phrasal verbs are formed by combining a verb with one or more prepositions such as *by, on, in, up, out, through*, etc. (These words are called 'prepositions' because they are often used in the 'pre-position' of a noun.)

Phrasal verbs are seldom used in the **academic writing genre** as they are more a spoken form and their meaning often depends on shared context between speakers that may not exist in the case of a reader and writer. For this reason, the meaning of phrasal verbs can sometimes be ambiguous in written texts.

So, in academic writing we select an action verb instead. Replacements for the above phrasal verbs could be:

To *turn up*	to arrive/increase.
To *put up with*	to tolerate.
To *get by*	to survive.

PART 6

Understanding Punctuation and Mechanics

29 Commas

AT A *GLANCE*

- Using commas in introductory elements (see 29a below)
- Using commas in compound clauses (see 29b)
- Using commas with non-restrictive modifiers (see 29c)
- Using commas in a series (see 29d), with adjectives (see 29e), with with quotations (see 29f), with dates, numbers, titles and addresses (see 29g)

29a Commas with Introductory Elements

Introductory words or phrases signal a shift in ideas or a particular arrangement of ideas; they help direct the reader's attention to the writer's most important points. Introductory elements usually need to be set off by commas.

When a conjunctive adverb (see Section 27d) or an introductory phrase begins a sentence, the comma follows.

> **Therefore**, the suspect could not have been at the scene of the crime.

> **Above all**, remember to let water drip from the taps if the temperature drops below freezing.

When a conjunctive adverb comes in the middle of a sentence, set it off with commas preceding and following.

> If you really want to prevent your pipes from freezing, **however**, you should insulate them before the start of winter.

Occasionally the conjunctive adverb or phrase blends into a sentence so smoothly that a pause would sound awkward.

Awkward	Even if you take every precaution, the pipes in your home may freeze, **nevertheless**.
Better	Even if you take every precaution, the pipes in your home may freeze **nevertheless**.

COMMON ERRORS

e Edit Help

Commas with long introductory modifiers

Long subordinate clauses or phrases that begin sentences should be followed by a comma. The following sentence lacks the needed comma.

Incorrect Because teens and younger adults are so comfortable with and reliant on mobile phone devices texting while driving does not immediately seem like an irresponsible and possibly deadly act.

When you read this sentence, you probably had to go back to sort it out. The words *mobile phone devices* and *texting* tend to run together. When the comma is added, the sentence is easier to understand because the reader knows where the subordinate clause ends and where the main clause begins:

Correct Because teens and younger adults are so comfortable with, and reliant on mobile phone devices, texting while driving does not immediately seem like an irresponsible and possibly deadly act.

How long is a long introductory modifier? Short introductory adverbial phrases and clauses of five words or fewer can get by without the comma if the omission doesn't mislead the reader. Using the comma is still correct after short introductory adverbial phrases and clauses:

Correct In the long run shares have always done better than bonds.

Correct In the long run, shares have always done better than bonds.

Remember: Put commas after long introductory modifiers.

29b Commas with Compound Clauses

Two main clauses joined by a coordinating conjunction (*for, and, nor, but, or, yet, so*) form a compound sentence. Writers sometimes get confused about when to insert a comma before a coordinating conjunction.

Use a comma and a coordinating conjunction to separate main clauses

Main clauses carry enough grammatical weight to be punctuated as sentences. When two main clauses are joined by a coordinating conjunction, place a comma before the coordinating conjunction in order to distinguish them.

> Sandy borrowed two boxes full of DVDs on Tuesday, and she returned them on Friday.

Very short main clauses joined by a coordinating conjunction don't need commas.

> She called and she called, but no one answered.

Don't use a comma to separate two verbs with the same subject

Incorrect Sandy borrowed two boxes full of DVDs on Tuesday, and returned them on Friday.

Sandy is the subject of both *borrowed* and *returned*. This sentence has only one main clause; it should not be punctuated as a compound sentence.

Correct Sandy borrowed two boxes full of DVDs on Tuesday and returned them on Friday.

Don't use a comma to separate a main clause from a restrictive clause or phrase

When clauses and phrases that follow the main clause are essential to the meaning of a sentence, they should not be set off with a comma.

Incorrect Sandy plans to borrow Amanda's DVD collection, while Felicia is on holiday.

Correct Sandy plans to borrow Amanda's DVD collection while Felicia is on holiday.

COMMON ERRORS

Commas in compound sentences

The easiest way to distinguish between compound sentences and sentences with phrases that follow the main clause is to isolate the part that comes after the conjunction. If the part that follows the conjunction can stand on its own as a complete sentence, insert a comma. If it cannot, omit the comma.

Main clause plus phrases

Marcus thinks he lost his passport on the bus **or** by absentmindedly leaving it on the counter when he checked into the hostel.

Look at what comes after the coordinating conjunction *or*:

by absentmindedly leaving it on the counter when he checked into the hostel

This group of words isn't a main clause and cannot stand on its own as a complete sentence. Don't set it off with a comma.

Main clauses joined with a conjunction

On Saturday Marcus went to the Australian embassy to get a new passport, but the officer told him that replacement passports couldn't be issued on weekends.

Read the clause after the coordinating conjunction *but*:

the officer told him that replacement passports couldn't be issued on weekends

This group of words can stand on its own as a complete sentence. Thus, it is a main clause. Place a comma before *but*.

Remember:

1. **Place a comma before the coordinating conjunction (*for, and, nor, but, or, yet, so*) when there are two main clauses.**
2. **Don't use a comma before the coordinating conjunction when there is only one main clause.**

COMMON ERRORS

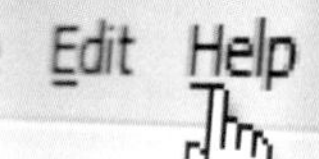

Don't use a comma to set off a *because* clause that follows a main clause

Writers frequently place unnecessary commas before *because* and similar subordinate conjunctions that follow a main clause. *Because* isn't a coordinating conjunction, so it shouldn't be set off by a comma unless the comma improves readability.

Incorrect I struggled to complete my essays last year, because I didn't know how to type.

Correct I struggled to complete my essays last year because I didn't know how to type.

But do use a comma after an introductory *because* clause.

Incorrect Because Danny left his hockey stick at home the coach wouldn't let him train.

Correct Because Danny left his hockey stick at home, the coach wouldn't let him train.

Remember: Use a comma after a *because* clause that begins a sentence. Don't use a comma to set off a *because* clause that follows a main clause.

29c Commas with Non-restrictive Modifiers

Imagine that you are sending a friend a group photo that includes your mother. Which sentence is correct?

In the back row the woman wearing the pink scarf is my mother.

In the back row the woman, wearing the pink scarf, is my mother.

Both sentences can be correct depending on what is in the photo. If there are three women standing in the back row and only one is wearing a pink scarf, this piece of information is necessary for identifying your mother. In this case the sentence without commas is correct because it identifies your mother as the woman wearing the pink scarf. Such necessary modifiers are **restrictive** and don't require commas.

If only one woman is standing in the back row, *wearing the pink scarf* is extra information and not necessary to identify your mother. The modifier in this case is **non-restrictive** and is set off by commas.

Distinguish between restrictive and non-restrictive modifiers

You can distinguish between restrictive and non-restrictive modifiers by deleting the modifier and then deciding whether the remaining sentence is changed. For example, delete the modifier *still broadcasting her xenophobic views* from the following sentence:

> Senators from the Greens Party protested against Senator Pauline Hanson, still broadcasting her xenophobic views, by walking out of her maiden speech on September 14, 2016

The result leaves the meaning of the main clause unchanged.

> Senators from the Greens Party protested against Senator Pauline Hanson by walking out of her maiden speech on September 14, 2016.

The modifier is non-restrictive and should be set off by commas.

Pay special attention to appositives

Clauses and phrases can be restrictive or non-restrictive, depending on the context. Often the difference is obvious, but some modifiers require close consideration, especially appositives. An **appositive** is a noun or noun phrase that identifies or adds information to the noun preceding it.

Consider the following pair:

1. Apple's tablet computer the iPad introduced a class of devices between smartphones and laptops.
2. Apple's tablet computer, the iPad, introduced a class of devices between smartphones and laptops.

Which is correct? The appositive *the iPad* is not essential to the meaning of the sentence and offers additional information. Sentence 2 is correct.

Use commas to mark off parenthetical expressions

A **parenthetical expression** provides information or commentary that usually isn't essential to the sentence's meaning.

Incorrect	My mother much to my surprise didn't say anything when she saw my pierced nose.
Correct	My mother, much to my surprise, didn't say anything when she saw my pierced nose.

29d Commas with Items in a Series

In a series of three or more items, place a comma after each item except the last one. Generally, Australian writers do not use a comma before the conjunction (*and, or*) because British and Australian style guides prescribe this convention.

Health officials in Darwin, Townsville and Cairns have all reported new cases of the Ross River fever.

However, American writers tend to add this comma before the conjunction in the serial list because American style guides prescribe it. If writing for an American audience or publication, this is a style variation that might need to be used. In the example above, the nouns in the series are all names of towns and it does not matter to the meaning of the sentence whether a comma is used or is not used.

In some forms of documentation, such as legal writing, a convention called the Oxford comma is required. Consider what would happen if the comma were not used in the following sentence from a legal will document.

Correct	The estate of the late John Smith will be divided, in equal parts, between Peter, John, and Mary. (With the Oxford comma.)
Incorrect	The estate of the late John Smith will be divided, in equal parts, between Peter, John and Mary. (Without the Oxford comma.)

In the second example, Peter might be able to claim 50% of the estate, leaving 25% for each of John and Mary instead of the estate being divided into thirds.

29e Commas with Coordinate Adjectives

Coordinate adjectives are two or more adjectives that modify the same noun independently. Coordinate adjectives that are not linked by *and* must be separated by a comma.

> After Donald Trump was elected as President of the United States, the surprise result was attributed to the swing towards the anti-establishment, protectionist platform in Trump's campaign.

You can recognise coordinate adjectives by reversing their order; if their meaning remains the same, the adjectives are coordinate and must be linked by *and* or separated by a comma.

Commas are not used between **cumulative adjectives**. Cumulative adjectives are two or more adjectives that work together to modify a noun: *deep blue sea, inexpensive mountain bike*. If reversing their order changes the description of the noun (or violates the order of English, such as *mountain inexpensive bike*), the adjectives are cumulative and shouldn't be separated by a comma.

The following example doesn't require a comma in the cumulative adjective series *massive Corinthian.*

> Visitors to Rome's Pantheon pass between the massive Corinthian columns flanking the front door.

We know the adjectives are cumulative because reversing their order to read *Corinthian massive* would alter the way they modify *columns*—in this case, so much so that they no longer make sense.

Commas with Quotations

Properly punctuating quotations with commas can be tricky unless you know a few rules about when and where to use commas. Quotation marks vary between double (" ") and single (' '), depending on which documentation style you are using. While both styles are used in Australia, double quotation marks are more common. Make sure that you check which style your lecturer wants you to use before you start to write. These examples follow Harvard style, which uses single quotation marks.

When to use commas with quotations

Commas set off phrases that attribute quotations to a speaker or writer, such as *he argues, they said* and *she writes.*

'When you come to a fork in the road,' said the guide, 'take it!'

If the attribution follows a quotation that is a complete sentence, replace the full stop that would normally come at the end of the quotation with a comma.

Incorrect 'Simplicity of language is not only reputable but perhaps even sacred.' writes Kurt Vonnegut.

Correct 'Simplicity of language is not only reputable but perhaps even sacred,' writes Kurt Vonnegut.

When an attribution is placed in the middle of a quoted sentence, put the comma preceding the attribution within the quotation mark just before the phrase.

When not to use commas with quotations

Don't replace a question mark or exclamation point with a comma.

Incorrect 'Who's on first,' Costello asked Abbott.

Correct 'Who's on first?' Costello asked Abbott.

Not all phrases that mention the author's name are attributions. When quoting a term or using a quotation within a subordinate clause, don't set off the quotation with commas.

One of the more memorable lines spoken by an Australian prime minister was Malcolm Fraser's admonition that 'life wasn't meant to be easy'.

Commas with Dates, Numbers, Titles and Addresses

Some of the easiest comma rules to remember are the ones we use every day in dates, numbers, personal titles, place names, direct address and brief interjections.

Commas with dates

Use commas to separate the day of the week from the rest of a date.

Monday, 16 November 2011

Commas with numbers

Commas may be used to mark off thousands, millions, billions and so on.

5,000

19,753

16,500,000

Don't use commas in page numbers or street addresses.

page 1542

7602 Dean Street

Commas with personal titles

When a title follows a person's name, set the title off with commas.

Geraldine Doogue, AO

Commas with placenames

In addresses, use commas as shown here:

Write to the society at 123 George Street, Perth, WA, 6000, Australia.

Commas in direct address

When addressing someone directly, set off that person's name in commas.

I was happy to get your letter yesterday, Jamie.

Commas with brief interjections

Use commas to set off brief interjections like *yes* and *no*, as well as short questions that fall at the ends of sentences.

Have another piece of cake, won't you?

29h Commas to Avoid Confusion

Certain sentences can confuse readers if you don't indicate where they should pause within the sentence. Use a comma to guide a reader through these usually compact constructions.

Unclear With supplies low prices of petrol and oil will increase.

This sentence could be read as meaning *With supplies, low prices of petrol and oil will increase.*

Clear	With supplies low, prices of petrol and oil will increase.

29i Unnecessary Commas

Don't place a comma between a subject and the main verb.

Incorrect	Australian children of immigrant parents, often don't speak their parents' native language.
Correct	Australian children of immigrant parents often don't speak their parents' native language.

However, you do use commas to set off modifying phrases that separate subjects from verbs.

Correct	Steven Pinker, author of *The Language Instinct*, argues that the ability to speak and understand language is an evolutionary adaptive trait.

Don't use a comma with a coordinating conjunction unless it joins two main clauses. (See the Common Errors box on page 271.)

Incorrect	Sue thought finishing her first novel was hard, but soon learned that getting a publisher to accept it was much harder.
Correct	Sue thought finishing her first novel was hard but soon learned that getting a publisher to accept it was much harder.
Correct	Sue thought finishing her first novel was hard, but she soon learned that getting a publisher to accept it was much harder.

Don't use a comma after a subordinating conjunction such as *although, despite* or *while.*

Incorrect	Although, baseball is played in Australian schools, it will never be as popular as football or cricket.
Correct	Although baseball is played in Australian schools, it will never be as popular as football or cricket.

Some writers mistakenly use a comma with *than* to try to heighten the contrast in a comparison.

Incorrect Any teacher will tell you that acquiring critical thinking skills is more important, than simply memorising information.

Correct Any teacher will tell you that acquiring critical thinking skills is more important than simply memorising information.

A common mistake is to place a comma after *such as* or *like* before introducing a list.

Incorrect Many hourly workers, such as, waiters, dishwashers and bar staff, don't receive health benefits from their employers.

Correct Many hourly workers, such as waiters, dishwashers and bar staff, don't receive health benefits from their employers.

30 Semicolons and Colons

AT A *GLANCE*

- Use semicolons to link related ideas (see 30a below)
- Use colons correctly in sentences and lists (see 30c and 30d)

30a Semicolons with Closely Related Main Clauses

Why use semicolons? Sometimes we want to join two main clauses to form a complete sentence in order to indicate their close relationship. Such sentences should be used only when there is a close relationship in meaning between the two clauses, and should not be used too often. We can connect the clauses with a comma and a coordinating conjunction such as *or*, *but* or *and*. To create variation in sentence style and avoid wordiness, we can also choose to omit the comma and coordinating conjunction and instead insert a semicolon between the two clauses.

Semicolons can join only clauses that are grammatically equal. In other words, they join main clauses only to other main clauses, not to phrases or subordinate clauses. Look at the following examples:

Incorrect [MAIN CLAUSE: Gloria's new weightlifting program will help her recover from knee surgery]; [PHRASE: doing a series of squats and presses with a physical therapist].

Correct [MAIN CLAUSE: Gloria's new weightlifting program will help her recover from knee surgery]; [MAIN CLAUSE: a physical therapist leads her through a series of squats and presses].

COMMON ERRORS

Semicolons with transitional words and phrases

Closely related main clauses sometimes use a conjunctive adverb (such as *however, therefore, moreover, furthermore, thus, meanwhile, nonetheless, otherwise*) or a transitional phrase (*in fact, for example, that is, for instance, in addition, in other words, on the other hand, even so*) to indicate the relationship between them. When the second clause begins with a conjunctive adverb or a transitional phrase, a semicolon is needed to join the two clauses. This sentence pattern is frequently used; therefore, it pays to learn how to punctuate it correctly.

Incorrect (comma splice)	The police and city councillors want to crack down on drug use at raves, however, their efforts have been unsuccessful so far.
Correct	The police and city councillors want to crack down on drug use at raves; however, their efforts have been unsuccessful so far.

Remember: Main clauses that use a conjunctive adverb or a transitional phrase require a semicolon to join the clauses.

Don't use a semicolon to introduce quotations

Use a comma or colon to introduce quotations.

Incorrect	Robert Frost's poem 'Mending Wall' contains this line; 'Good fences make good neighbours.'
Correct	Robert Frost's poem 'Mending Wall' contains this line: 'Good fences make good neighbours.'

Don't use a semicolon to introduce lists

Incorrect	William Shakespeare wrote four romance plays at the end of his career; *The Tempest, The Winter's Tale, Cymbeline and Pericles*.
Correct	William Shakespeare wrote four romance plays at the end of his career: *The Tempest, The Winter's Tale, Cymbeline and Pericles*.

30b Semicolons Together with Commas

When an item in a series already includes a comma, adding more commas to separate it from the other items will only confuse the reader. Use semicolons instead of commas between items in a series that have internal punctuation.

Confusing The church's design competition drew entries from as far away as Gothenberg, Sweden, London, England, and Athens, Greece.

Clearer The church's design competition drew entries from as far away as Gothenberg, Sweden; London, England; and Athens, Greece.

30c Colons in Sentences

Like semicolons, colons can join two closely related main clauses (complete sentences). Colons indicate that what follows will explain or expand on what comes before the colon. Use a colon in cases where the second main clause interprets or sums up the first.

> Arguably, this highly regulated approach to monitoring and evaluating teaching in Australian universities is paying dividends: a 2015 randomised survey of almost 90,000 students revealed a high degree of student satisfaction.

You may choose to capitalise the first word of the main clause following the colon or leave it lower case. Either is correct as long as you are consistent throughout your text.

Colons linking main clauses with appositives

A colon calls attention to an appositive: a noun or a noun phrase that renames the noun preceding it. If you are not certain whether a colon would be appropriate, put *namely* in its place. If *namely* makes sense when you read the main clause followed by the appositive, you probably need to insert a colon instead of a comma. Remember, the clause that precedes the colon must be a complete sentence.

> I know the perfect person for the job, namely me.

The sentence makes sense with *namely* placed before the appositive. Thus, a colon is appropriate.

I know the perfect person for the job: me.

Never capitalise a word following a colon unless the word starts a complete sentence or is normally capitalised.

Colons joining main clauses with quotations

Use a colon to link a main clause and a quotation that interprets or sums up the clause. Be careful not to use a colon to link a phrase with a quotation.

Incorrect: phrase–colon–quotation

US President Roosevelt's strategy to change the nation's panicky attitude during the Great Depression: 'We have nothing to fear,' he said, 'but fear itself.'

Correct: main clause–colon–quotation

US President Roosevelt's strategy to end the Great Depression was to change the nation's panicky attitude: 'We have nothing to fear,' he said, 'but fear itself.'

The first example is incorrect because there is no main verb in the first part of the sentence and thus it is a phrase rather than a main clause. The second example adds the verb (*was*), making the first part of the sentence a main clause.

Colons with Lists

Use a colon to join a main clause to a list. The main clauses in these cases sometimes include the phrase *the following* or as *follows*. Remember that a colon cannot join a phrase or an incomplete clause to a list.

Incorrect: phrase–colon–list

The structure of a formal speech: tell them what you are going to talk about, tell them it and then tell them what you told them.

Correct: main clause–colon–list

You might use this simple structure for a formal speech: tell them what you are going to talk about, tell them it and then tell them what you told them.

COMMON ERRORS

Colons misused with lists

Some writers think that any time they introduce a list, they should insert a colon. Colons are used correctly only when a complete sentence precedes the colon.

Incorrect Jessica's entire wardrobe for her trip to Hayman Island included: two swimsuits, one pair of shorts, two T-shirts, a party dress and a pair of sandals.

Correct Jessica's entire wardrobe for her trip to Hayman Island included two swimsuits, one pair of shorts, two T-shirts, a party dress and a pair of sandals.

Correct Jessica jotted down what she would need for her trip to Hayman Island: two swimsuits, one pair of shorts, two T-shirts, a party dress and a pair of sandals.

Remember: A colon should be placed only after a clause that can stand by itself as a sentence.

31 Dashes and Parentheses

AT A *GLANCE*

- Use dashed and parentheses rather than commas to set off information (see 31a below)
- Use other punctuation correctly with parentheses (see 31c)

Dashes and Parentheses to Set Off Information

Dashes and parentheses call attention to groups of words. In effect, they tell the reader that a group of words isn't part of the main clause and should be given extra attention. If you want to make an element stand out, especially in the middle of a sentence, use parentheses or dashes instead of commas.

Dashes with final elements

A dash is often used to set off a phrase or subordinate clause at the end of a sentence to offer a significant comment about the main clause. Dashes can also anticipate a shift in tone at the end of a sentence.

> A full-sized four-wheel drive can take you wherever you want to go in style—if your idea of style is a petrol-guzzling tank.

Parentheses with additional information

Parentheses are more often used for identifying information, afterthoughts or asides, examples and clarifications. You can place full sentences, fragments or brief terms within parentheses.

> Some argue that ethanol (the pet solution of politicians for achieving energy independence) costs more energy to manufacture and ship than it produces.

COMMON ERRORS

Don't use dashes as full stops

Don't use dashes to separate two main clauses (clauses that can stand as complete sentences). Use dashes to separate main clauses from subordinate clauses and phrases when you want to emphasise the subordinate clause or phrase.

Incorrect: main clause–dash–main clause

I was one of the few women in my computer science classes—most of the students studying computer science at that time were men.

Correct: main clause–dash–phrase

I was one of the few women in computer science—a field then dominated by men.

Remember: Dashes aren't full stops and shouldn't be used as full stops.

31b Dashes and Parentheses Versus Commas

Like commas, parentheses and dashes enclose material that adds, explains or digresses. However, the three punctuation marks are not interchangeable. The mark you choose depends on how much emphasis you want to place on the material. Dashes indicate the most emphasis. Parentheses offer somewhat less, and commas offer less still.

Commas indicate a moderate level of emphasis

Bill covered the new tattoo on his bicep, a pouncing tiger, because he thought it might upset our mother.

Parentheses lend a greater level of emphasis

I'm afraid to go bungee jumping (though my brother tells me it's less frightening than a roller coaster).

Dashes indicate the highest level of emphasis and, sometimes, surprise and drama

> Christina felt as though she had been punched in the gut; she could hardly believe the stranger at her door was really who he claimed to be—the brother she hadn't seen in twenty years.

COMMON ERRORS

The art of typing a dash

Although dashes and hyphens may look similar, they are actually different marks. The distinction is small but important because dashes and hyphens serve different purposes. A dash is a line much longer than a hyphen. Most word processors will create a dash automatically when you type two hyphens together, or you can type a special character to make a dash. In Microsoft Word™ the command is Insert / Symbol / Special Characters and then choose 'em dash'. An em dash is so called because it is the length of the letter 'm', as opposed to the length of the letter 'n'

Don't leave a space between a dash or a hyphen and the words that come before and after them. Likewise, if you are using two hyphens to indicate a dash, don't leave a space between the hyphens.

Incorrect A well - timed effort at conserving water may prevent long -term damage to drought - stricken farms - - if it's not already too late.

Correct A well-timed effort at conserving water may prevent long-term damage to drought-stricken farms—if it's not already too late.

Remember: Don't put spaces before or after hyphens and dashes.

Other Punctuation with Parentheses

Parentheses around letters or numbers that order a series within a sentence make the list easier to read.

> A well-known strategy to answer reading comprehension questions is to (1) underline the keywords in each question, (2) skim-read the passage looking for these words or synonyms, and (3) scan the area around these words in the passage for the answer.

Abbreviations made from the first letters of words are often used in place of the unwieldy names of institutions, departments, organisations or terms. In order to show the reader what the abbreviation stands for, the writer must state the complete name the first time it appears in a text, followed by the abbreviation in parentheses.

> The Australian Council of Trade Unions (ACTU) was established in 1927 to improve the lives of working people. Over nine decades later, the ACTU is still active in Australian workplaces.

COMMON ERRORS

Using full stops, commas, colons and semicolons with parentheses

When an entire sentence is enclosed in parentheses, place the full stop before the closing parenthesis.

Incorrect Our fear of sharks, heightened by media reports of shark attacks and the need for shark nets, is vastly out of proportion with the minor threat sharks actually pose. (Dying from a dog attack, in fact, is much more likely than dying from a shark attack).

Correct Our fear of sharks, heightened by media reports of shark attacks and the need for shark nets, is vastly out of proportion with the minor threat sharks actually pose. (Dying from a dog attack, in fact, is much more likely than dying from a shark attack.)

When the material in parentheses is part of the sentence and the parentheses fall at the end of the sentence, place the full stop outside the closing parenthesis.

Incorrect Reports of sharks attacking people are rare (much rarer than dog attacks.)

Correct Reports of sharks attacking people are rare (much rarer than dog attacks).

Place commas, colons and semicolons after the closing parenthesis.

Remember: When an entire sentence is enclosed in parentheses, place the full stop inside the closing parenthesis; otherwise, put the punctuation outside the closing parenthesis.

32 Apostrophes

AT A *GLANCE*

- Use apostrophes to show possession (see 32a below)
- Use apostrophes to show omitted letters (see 32b)

32a Possessives

Nouns and indefinite pronouns (for example, *everyone*, *anyone*) indicating possession or ownership are marked by attaching an apostrophe and *-s* or an apostrophe only to the end of the word.

Singular nouns and indefinite pronouns

For singular nouns and indefinite pronouns, add an apostrophe plus *-s*: *-'s*. Even singular nouns that end in *-s* usually follow this principle.

Iris's coat

everyone's favourite

a woman's choice

There are a few exceptions to adding *-'s* for singular nouns:

- Awkward pronunciations: *Herodotus' travels, Jesus' sermons*
- **Official names of certain places, institutions, companies**: *Kings Cross, Sydney Teachers College, Brothers Leagues Club, Woolworths.* Note, however, that many companies do include the apostrophe: *McDonald's, Crazy John's.*

Plural nouns

For plural nouns not ending in *-s*, add an apostrophe plus *-s*: *-'s*.

media's responsibility

children's section

For plural nouns ending in *-s*, add only an apostrophe at the end.

barristers' briefs

the Murdochs' legacy

Compound nouns

For compound nouns, add an apostrophe plus *-s* to the last word of the compound noun: *-'s*.

> mayor of Newcastle's speech

Two or more nouns

For joint possession, add an apostrophe plus *-s* to the final noun: *-'s*.

> Mum and Dad's yard

When people possess or own things separately, add an apostrophe plus *-s* to each noun: *-'s*.

> Robert's and Josh's views are totally opposed.

COMMON ERRORS

Possessive forms of personal pronouns never take the apostrophe

Incorrect	*her's, it's, our's, your's, their's*
	The bird sang in it's cage.
Correct	*hers, its, ours, yours, theirs*
	The bird sang in its cage.

Remember: ***It's = It is***

32b Contractions and Omitted Letters

In speech we often leave out sounds and syllables of familiar words. These omissions are noted with apostrophes.

Contractions

Contractions combine two words into one, using the apostrophe to mark what is left out.

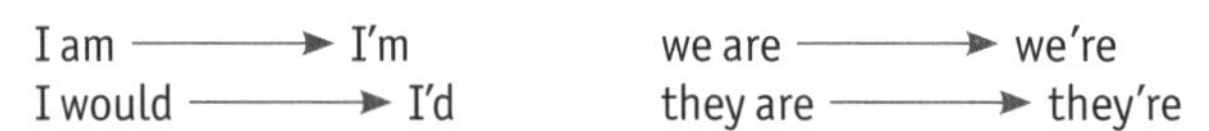
I am → I'm
I would → I'd
we are → we're
they are → they're

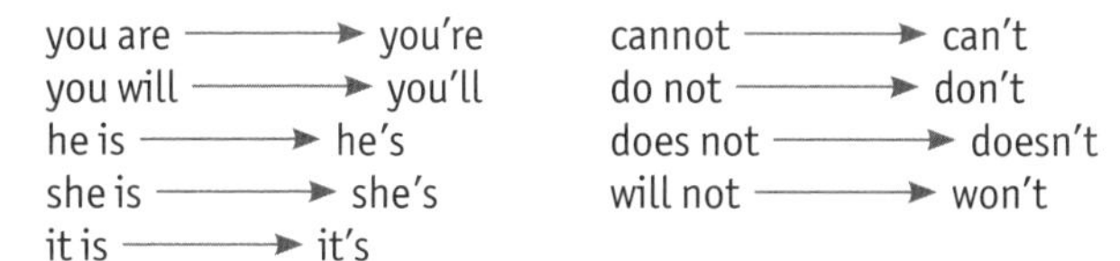

Omissions

Using apostrophes to signal omitted letters is a way of approximating speech in writing. They can make your writing look informal and slangy. Overuse can quickly become annoying.

rock and roll → rock 'n' roll
the 1960s → the '60s
neighbourhood → 'hood

Plurals of Letters, Symbols and Words Referred to as Words

When to use apostrophes to make plurals

Using apostrophes to form plurals of letters, symbols and words referred to as words is no longer common practice. Most readers now prefer *1960s* to the older form, *1960's*. In a few cases adding the apostrophe and *-s* is still used, as in:

> Mind your p's and q's.

Words used as words are italicised. Their plural is formed by adding an -s not in italics, not an apostrophe and *-s*.

> Take a few of the *and*s out of your writing.

Words in quotation marks, however, typically use an apostrophe and *-s*.

> She had too many 'probably's' in her email for me to be confident that the remodelling will be finished on schedule.

When not to use apostrophes to make plurals

Don't use an apostrophe to make family names plural.

Incorrect You've heard of keeping up with the Jones's.

Correct You've heard of keeping up with the Joneses.

COMMON ERRORS

Don't use an apostrophe to make a noun plural

Incorrect The two government's agreed to meet.

Correct The two governments agreed to meet.

Incorrect The video game's of the past were one-dimensional.

Correct The video games of the past were one-dimensional.

Remember: Add only *-s* = plural.
Add apostrophe plus *-s* = possessive

A simple check to see if your possessive apostrophe is correct

Example: **The lecturer(s)** notes can be found...

1 Reverse the order of 'the possessor' and 'the possessed' adding the phrase 'belonging to'

The notes belonging to the lecturer/lecturers.

Add -'s to 'the possessor'

- Therefore, if there is only one lecturer (singular)

  (CHECK: The notes belonging to the lecturer + -'s)

INSERT THE APOSTROPHE INTO THE ORIGINAL TO GIVE:

The lecturer's notes can be found...

- Therefore, if there is more than one lecturer (plural)

  (CHECK: The notes belonging to the lecturers +'(s) ←
  delete the '-s' when written (i.e. do NOT write lecturers's))

INSERT THE APOSTROPHE INTO THE ORIGINAL TO GIVE:

The lecturers' notes can be found...

33 Quotation Marks

AT A *GLANCE*

- Correctly incorporate words from quotations (see 33a below)
- Use quotation marks correctly with other punctuation (see 33d)

33a Direct Quotations

Use quotation marks to enclose direct quotations

Quotation marks vary between double (“ ”) and single (‘ ’) depending on which documentation style you are using. While both styles are used in Australia, double quotation marks are more common. Make sure that you check which style your lecturer wants you to use before you start to write. The samples in this chapter will follow Harvard style, which typically uses single quotation marks.

Enclose direct quotations—someone else’s words repeated verbatim—in quotation marks.

> On the Sydney Futures Exchange the March share price index contract was 67 points higher at 4688. ‘Key drivers today are banks, which are performing strongly, as are the major miners—BHP (Billiton) and Rio Tinto,’ CommSec chief economist Craig James said.

Don’t use quotation marks with indirect quotations

Don’t enclose an indirect quotation—a paraphrase of someone else’s words—in quotation marks. However, do remember that you need to cite your source not only when you quote directly but also when you paraphrase or summarise ideas.

> As Kibler, Valdés and Walqui (2014) state, standards-based reform in settings such as Australia takes as its default monolingual, English-speaking student populations.

Don't use quotation marks with block quotations

When a quotation is long enough to be set off as a block quotation, don't use quotation marks. MLA style defines long quotations as more than four lines of prose or poetry. APA style defines a long quotation as one of more than 40 words. Harvard style defines a long quotation as one of more than 30 words.

In the following example, in Harvard format, notice that the long quotation is indented and single spaced, and quotation marks are omitted. Also notice that the parenthetical citation for a long quotation comes after the full stop.

> The Australian Curriculum advocates explicit teaching of language in the following statement from the overview of the Australian Curriculum for English, Language strand:
>
> > The Australian Curriculum: English provides students with a broad conceptual understanding of what a language is, and its importance in and out of school. Language as a body of knowledge draws largely from historical and linguistic accounts of the English language which draw attention to the ways in which languages change, and to the distinction between language in use and language as system. These accounts acknowledge that students' capability to use grammar will exceed their ability to explicitly reflect on grammar. Young children, for example, will use complex sentences before they can explain how these are structured. These accounts, in describing language, also pay attention to the structure (syntax) and meaning (semantics) at the level of the word, the sentence and the text. (ACARA, 2015)
>
> Setting aside the larger issue of whether grammar should be explicitly taught to students, an aspect of this debate that has not received much attention in the form of empirical studies is what benefits flow from teachers improving their grammatical knowledge?

33b Titles of Short Works

Whereas the titles of longer works such as books, magazines and newspapers are italicised, titles of shorter works should be set off with quotation marks. Use quotation marks with the following kinds of titles:

Short stories	'Big World' by Tim Winton
Magazine articles	'Intelligent Design' by Donald Frazier

Newspaper articles	'Calling home: On the Bali bombing' by Clive James
Short poems	'Performance' by Les Murray
Essays	'The Dreaming' by WEH Stanner

The exception. Don't put the title of your own paper in quotation marks. If the title of another short work appears within the title of your paper, retain the quotation marks around the short work.

33c Other Uses of Quotation Marks

Quotation marks around a term can indicate that the writer is using the term in a novel way, often with scepticism, irony or sarcasm. The quotation marks indicate that the writer is questioning the term's conventional definition.

Italics are usually used to indicate that a word is being used as a word, rather than standing for its conventional meaning. However, quotation marks are correct in these cases as well.

Beginning writers sometimes confuse 'their', 'they're' and 'there'.

33d Other Punctuation with Quotation Marks

The rules for placing punctuation with quotation marks fall into three general categories.

Full stops and commas with quotation marks

Place full stops and commas inside closing quotation marks.

Incorrect	'The smartest people', Dr Geisler pointed out, 'tell themselves the most convincing rationalisations'.
Correct	'The smartest people,' Dr Geisler pointed out, 'tell themselves the most convincing rationalisations.'

Colons and semicolons with quotation marks

Place colons and semicolons outside closing quotation marks.

Incorrect	'From Stettin in the Baltic to Trieste in the Adriatic, an iron curtain has descended across the Continent;' Churchill's statement rang through Cold War politics for the next fifty years.

Correct 'From Stettin in the Baltic to Trieste in the Adriatic, an iron curtain has descended across the Continent'; Churchill's statement rang through Cold War politics for the next fifty years.

Exclamation marks, question marks and dashes with quotation marks

When an exclamation mark, question mark or dash belongs to the original quotation, place it inside the closing quotation mark. When it applies to the entire sentence, place it outside the closing quotation mark.

In the original quotation

'Are we there yet?' came the whine from the back seat.

Applied to the entire sentence

Did the driver in the front seat respond, 'Not even close'?

COMMON ERRORS

Quotations within quotations

The conventions for this vary between documentation styles. Harvard style uses double quotation marks to indicate a quotation within a quotation. In the following example, double quotation marks clarify who is speaking. The rules for placing punctuation with double quotation marks are the same as the rules for placing punctuation with single quotation marks.

Incorrect When he showed the report to Paul Probius, Michener reported that Probius 'took vigorous exception to the sentence 'He wanted to close down the university,' insisting that we add the clarifying phrase 'as it then existed' (Michener 2010, p. 145).

Correct When he showed the report to Paul Probius, Michener reported that Probius 'took vigorous exception to the sentence "He wanted to close down the university", insisting that we add the clarifying phrase "as it then existed"' (Michener 2010, p. 145).

Remember: Double quotation marks are used for quotations within quotations in some documentation styles, such as Harvard style.

33e Misuses of Quotation Marks

It is becoming more and more common to see quotation marks used to emphasise a word or phrase. Resist the temptation in your own writing; it is an incorrect usage. In fact, because quotation marks indicate that a writer is using a term with scepticism or irony, adding quotation marks for emphasis will highlight unintended connotations of the term.

Incorrect 'fresh' seafood

By using quotation marks here, the writer seems to call into question whether the seafood is really fresh.

Correct fresh seafood

Incorrect Enjoy our 'live' music every Saturday night.

Again, the quotation marks unintentionally indicate that the writer is sceptical about whether the music is live.

Correct Enjoy our live music every Saturday night.

You have better ways of creating emphasis using your word processing program: **boldfacing**, underlining, *italicising* and using colour.

34 Other Punctuation Marks

AT A *GLANCE*

- Use full stops, question marks and exclamation marks correctly (see 34a below)
- Use brackets and ellipses correctly (see 34d and 34e)

34a Full Stops

Full stops at the ends of sentences

Place a full stop at the end of a complete sentence if it is not a direct question or an exclamatory statement. As the term suggests, a *direct question* asks a question outright. *Indirect questions*, on the other hand, report the asking of a question.

Full stops with quotation marks and parentheses

When a quotation falls at the end of a sentence, place the full stop outside the closing quotation marks.

> Although he devoted decades to a wide range of artistic and political projects, Allen Ginsberg is best known as the author of the poem 'Howl'.

When a parenthetical phrase falls at the end of a sentence, place the full stop outside the closing parenthesis. When parentheses enclose a whole sentence, place the full stop inside the closing parenthesis.

Full stops with abbreviations

Many abbreviations require full stops; however, there are few set rules. Use a dictionary to check how to punctuate abbreviations on a case-by-case basis. The rules for punctuating two types of abbreviations remain consistent: postal abbreviations for states and most abbreviations for organisations don't require full stops.

Full stops as decimal points

Decimal points are full stops that separate integers from tenths, hundredths and so on.

99.98% pure silver	30.5 °Celsius
on sale for $399.97	2.6 litre engine

Since large numbers with long strings of zeros can be difficult to read accurately, writers sometimes shorten them using decimal points. In this way, 16,600,000 can be written as 16.6 million.

34b Question Marks

Question marks with direct questions

Place a question mark at the end of a direct question. A direct question is one that the questioner puts to someone outright. In contrast, an indirect question merely reports the asking of a question. Question marks give readers a cue to read the end of the sentence with rising intonation. Read the following sentences aloud. Hear how the pitch of your voice rises in the second sentence to convey the direct question.

Indirect question

The journalist asked Malcolm Turnbull whether his government's subsidisation of manufacturing also applied to agriculture.

Direct question

The journalist asked, 'Does your government's subsidisation of manufacturing also apply to agriculture?'

Question marks with quotations

When a quotation falls at the end of a direct question, place the question mark outside the closing quotation mark.

Did he really say 'Australia exports cleaner coal than other coal-producing countries'?

Place the question mark inside the closing quotation when only the quoted material is a direct question.

Increasingly climate scientists are asking the question, 'When will we stop mining fossil fuels?'

When quoting a direct question in the middle of a sentence, place a question mark inside the closing quotation mark and place a full stop at the end of the sentence.

> While some politicians continue to ask 'Is climate change really man-made?' the planet continues to get warmer.

Exclamation Marks

Exclamation mark to convey strong emotion

Exclamation marks conclude sentences and, like question marks, tell the reader how a sentence should sound. They indicate strong emotion. Use exclamation marks sparingly in formal writing; they are rarely appropriate in academic and professional prose.

Exclamation marks with emphatic interjections

Exclamation marks can convey a sense of urgency with brief interjections. Interjections can be incorporated into sentences or stand on their own.

> Stop fracking! It poisons children and pollutes aquifers.

Exclamation marks with quotation marks

In quotations, exclamation marks follow the same rules as question marks. If a quotation falls at the end of an exclamatory statement, place the exclamation mark outside the closing quotation mark.

> The singer forgot the words to 'Advance Australia Fair'!

When quoting an exclamatory statement at the end of a sentence that isn't itself exclamatory, place the exclamation mark inside the closing quotation mark.

> When Hillary Clinton responded that it is a good thing Trump is not in charge of the country's laws, Donald Trump fired back 'Because you'd be in jail!'

34d Brackets

While brackets (sometimes called *square brackets*) look quite similar to parentheses, the two perform different functions. Brackets have a narrow set of uses.

Brackets to provide clarification within quotation marks

Use brackets if you are interjecting a comment of your own or clarifying information within a direct quotation. In the following example the writer quotes a sentence with the pronoun *they*, which refers to a noun in a previous, unquoted sentence. The material in brackets clarifies to whom the pronoun refers.

> The report stated that 'In the last international tests they [Australian Year 4 students] were significantly outperformed by students in 21 countries in mathematics and 17 countries in science.'.

Brackets within parentheses

Since parentheses within parentheses might confuse readers, use brackets to enclose parenthetical information within a parenthetical phrase.

> The Turnbull government's most controversial bills (including the plebiscite on same-sex marriage [Parliament No 45] that the opposition wants to be voted on in parliament) has a slim chance of proceeding.

34e Ellipses

Ellipses let a reader know that a portion of a passage is missing. You can use ellipses to keep quotations concise and direct readers' attention to what is important to the point you are making. An ellipsis is a string of three full stops.

Ellipses to indicate an omission from a quotation

When you quote only a phrase or short clause from a sentence, you usually don't need to use an ellipsis.

> Martin Luther King proclaimed 'I have a dream' in a public speech in 1963.

Indicate omitted words with an ellipsis, except for when the omitted words are at the beginning of a quotation.

The original source

> 'The female praying mantis, so named for the way it holds its front legs together as if in prayer, tears off her male partner's head during mating. Remarkably, the headless male will continue the act of mating. This brutal dance is a stark example of the innate evolutionary drive to pass genes on to offspring; the male praying mantis seems to live and die only for this moment.'

An ellipsis indicates omitted words

> 'The female praying mantis ... tears off her male partner's head during mating.'

When the ellipsis is at the end of a sentence, place the full stop or question mark after the ellipsis and follow with the closing quotation mark.

Words omitted at the end of a sentence

> 'This brutal dance is a stark example of the innate evolutionary drive to pass genes on to offspring ....'

34f Slashes

Slashes to indicate alternative words

Slashes between two words indicate that a choice between them is to be made. When using slashes for this purpose, don't put a space between the slash and words.

Incorrect	Never use the on / off switch to turn off a computer.
Correct	Never use the on/off switch to turn off a computer.

Slashes with fractions

Place a slash between the numerator and the denominator in a fraction. Don't put any spaces around the slash.

Incorrect	3 / 4
Correct	3/4

35 Capitalisation, Italics, Abbreviations and Numbers

AT A *GLANCE*

- Capitalise and italicise words correctly (see 35a below)
- Form abbreviations (see 35c) and acronyms (see 35d) correctly
- How to write numbers (see 35e)

35a Capital Letters

Capitalise the initial letters of proper nouns (nouns that name particular people, places and things). Capitalise the initial letters of proper adjectives (adjectives based on the names of people, places and things).

Aboriginal and Torres Strait Islander art   Boyle's law   Irish music

Don't capitalise the names of seasons, academic disciplines (unless they are languages) or job titles used without a proper noun.

35b Italics

Italicise the titles of entire works (books, magazines, newspapers, films), but place the titles of parts of entire works within quotation marks. Also italicise the names of ships and aircraft.

I am fond of reading *The Age* in the morning.

The exceptions. Don't italicise the names of sacred texts.

The Bible

The Tripitaka

Italicise unfamiliar foreign words

Italicise foreign words that are not part of common English usage. Don't italicise words that have become a common word or phrase in the English vocabulary. How do you decide which words are common? If a word appears in a standard English dictionary, it can be considered as adopted into English.

Use italics to clarify your use of a word, letter or number

In everyday speech, we often use cues—a pause, a louder or different tone—to communicate how we are using a word. In writing, italics help clarify when you use words in a referential manner, or a letter or number as itself.

Abbreviations

Abbreviations are shortened forms of words. Because abbreviations vary widely, you will need to look in the dictionary to determine how to abbreviate words on a case-by-case basis. Nonetheless, there are a few patterns that abbreviations follow.

Abbreviate titles before and degrees after full names

Ms Ella Fitzgerald

Prof. Aggarwal

Diane Broughton, MA

Write out the professional title when it is used with only a last name.

Professor Chin

Doctor Who

Conventions for using abbreviations with years and times

BCE (before the common era) and CE (common era) are now preferred for indicating years, replacing BC (before Christ) and AD (*anno Domini* ['the year of our Lord']). Note that all are now used without full stops.

479 BCE (or BC)

1610 CE (or AD, but AD is placed before the number)

The preferred written conventions for times are am (*ante meridiem*) and pm (*post meridiem*).

9:03 am

3:30 pm

Conventions for using abbreviations in formal writing

Most abbreviations are inappropriate in formal writing except when the reader would be more familiar with the abbreviation than with the words it represents. When your reader is unlikely to be familiar with an abbreviation, spell out the term the first time you use it in a paper, followed by the abbreviation in parentheses. The reader will then understand what the abbreviation refers to, and you may use the abbreviation in subsequent sentences.

> The Australian Council of Trade Unions (ACTU) has been active in Australia for over eight decades. Former prime minister Bob Hawke rose through the ranks of the ACTU.

35d Acronyms

Acronyms are abbreviations formed by capitalising the first letter in each word. Unlike abbreviations, acronyms are pronounced as words.

> AIDS for Acquired Immunodeficiency Syndrome
>
> ASIC for Australian Securities and Investments Commission

A subset of acronyms are initial-letter abbreviations that have become so common that we know the organisation or thing by its initials.

> SARS for severe acute respiratory syndrome
>
> HIV for human immunodeficiency virus
>
> DVD for digital versatile disc

Familiar acronyms and initial-letter abbreviations such as ABC, FBI, IQ and UN are rarely spelled out. Unfamiliar acronyms and abbreviations should always be spelled out. Acronyms and abbreviations frequent in particular fields should be spelled out on first use. For example, MMPI (Minnesota Multiphasic Personality Inventory) is a familiar abbreviation in psychology but is unfamiliar to those outside that discipline. Even when acronyms are generally familiar, few readers will object to your giving the terms from which an acronym derives on the first use.

35e Numbers

In formal writing spell out numbers from zero to nine, as well as any number that appears at the beginning of a sentence. However, you may find it necessary to revise sentences that begin with complicated numbers, such as years.

The exceptions. In scientific reports and some business writing that requires the frequent use of numbers, using numerals more often is appropriate. Most styles don't write out these numbers in words: a year; a date; an address; a page number; the time of day; decimals; sums of money; phone numbers; rates of speed; or the scene and act of a play. Use numerals instead.

> In 2015 only 33% of respondents said they were satisfied with the council's proposals to help the homeless.

> The 17 trials were conducted at temperatures of 12–14°C with results ranging from 2.43 to 2.89 mg/dl.

When one number modifies another number, write one out and express the other in numeral form.

> Only after Meryl had run in twelve 50-kilometre ultramarathons did she finally win first place in her age group.

PART 7
Tips for Success

36 Oral Presentations

AT A *GLANCE*

- Plan all aspects of presentations with care (see 36a below)

36a A Form of Assessment

Oral presentations form part of your university studies and professional life. At university they are a form of assessment like essays or reports. You should approach an oral presentation assignment in the same way you would a written assignment. There are some variations, such as developing a presentation slideshow, poster, cue cards, props, handouts, and perhaps pre-prepared open questions to stimulate discussion.

It is not unusual for some students to be apprehensive about delivering an oral presentation. However, being organised and rehearsing may help you present a calm exterior. For example, it may be useful to prepare some cue cards or a separate page of details or to include information in the notes section of the slide and refer to these during the presentation. When you are prepared, there's less likelihood of stage fright, and this in turn will promote your confidence when delivering future presentations.

36b The Audience

Both your marker and your peers at university are the intended audience for your oral presentation. Therefore, the tone of your delivery should echo the appropriate academic language. Don't be tempted to present a ton of written information on a screen or in handouts. Keep the writing on slides to a minimum, or your audience may be too focused on reading to listen to you.

36c The Structure

Ideally, include a headline or an attention-grabber in the introduction. Obviously, this should be relevant to the topic of your presentation and may take the form of a rhetorical question, a cartoon or a media clip. The introduction should also include an overview of the points you will discuss, definitions if necessary, and an indication of your position on the topic.

The body of your discussion can be signposted by topic sentences, phrases or key words. Elaborate verbally on the points being discussed and remember that these and any evidence should support your argument. Only introduce information contrary to your position in the context of discrediting the counterarguments.

The conclusion, as for an essay, is your opportunity to summarise your key points and demonstrate how these support or confirm your position on the topic. You have a little more creative licence in an oral presentation than in an essay. The aim is to also create a lasting impression on your audience and, importantly, on your marker. Ensure that your presentation is memorable and finishes on a positive note. You may consider ending with a quotation, a joke, a catchy or feel-good anecdote (perhaps a second part to an anecdote where the first was delivered earlier) or some food for thought, perhaps some rhetorical questions that extend beyond the presentation's focus. The conclusion is also a good time to invite follow-up questions from the audience as a way to demonstrate your knowledge of the topic. Listen attentively to understand the audience members' questions and check for clarification if you are not sure of the question.

36d The Delivery

Props

Props are a great way to generate interest and maintain the focus of discussion. However, consider your choice of props carefully, as sometimes they provide too much distraction and can in fact move the discussion off-topic. Props should be relevant to your discussion and appropriate in a tertiary learning environment.

Project your voice

Project your voice so that people at the back of the room are able to hear you clearly. Use intonation and stress words to add meaning and emphasis, rather than speaking in a monotone. You won't maintain everyone's attention if you mumble or talk to the screen at the front of the room. Take care also not to rush your presentation. To make your delivery easy for your audience to follow you should speak in 'thought groups'—complete units of thought, or ideas. After each thought group, provide a short pause for your audience to reflect on what you have said and predict where you are going next. This builds drama and sometimes humour into your presentation, especially when you say something the audience members are not expecting. Try not to focus your attention solely on your friends in the audience. It is important to make eye contact with everyone, to distribute questions evenly and to elicit answers from those who may be reluctant to contribute. Good oral presentations involve more than just speaking to a passive audience. Try preparing questions that will stimulate discussion among the group. Engaging your peers through active participation can mean the difference between achieving a pass grade or a higher grade.

Literary devices

Using literary devices may further enhance your delivery, making it more memorable and engaging. The 'Rule of Three' is based on the idea that three words, phrases, characters and so on are more memorable to an audience than are other numbers. A good example is Barack Obama's presidential victory speech in 2008, where he repeatedly used the catch-phrase 'Yes we can'. President Obama also delivered some of his speech in iambic pentameter—a literary tool often found in poetry that relates to the measure and rhythm of speech. Shakespeare's sonnets and John Milton's *Paradise Lost* are examples of poems written in iambic pentameter. The value of such devices in an oral presentation is that they can reinforce those points central to the critical discussion, and, by effectively varying the pace, the speaker is more likely to sustain the audience's attention. A copy of the transcript and video of Obama's speech can be found at <http://elections.nytimes.com/2008/results/president/speeches/obama-victory-speech.html#>. Skip to 14:59 for the most relevant section.

36e Feedback

After delivering your presentation, there is one important final step to complete—that is, to read and reflect upon the feedback provided by your marker. This feedback provides an indication of the skills you need to improve and those you should capitalise on when presenting your next oral presentation.

37 Feedback

AT A *GLANCE*

- Use formal and informal feedback effectively (see below)

37a An Opportunity for Reflection

Feedback provides you with the opportunity to reflect upon and evaluate your learning. It can be informal verbal feedback from your peers, your tutor or a learning adviser. Alternatively, it may be formal written feedback from the marker including a grade.

37b Informal Feedback

Students may be confused about how to approach or 'unpack' an assignment. They may find it difficult to understand the assignment criteria or they may need some indication that they have interpreted the assignment correctly. If it is difficult to decipher the requirements on you own, form a study group with other students attempting the same assignment. This could be online through discussion boards or Facebook, or face-to-face in a study room in the library or a quiet area on the university grounds. The main aim is to discuss the assignment, analysing the concepts covered in tutorials and how they relate to the assignment. You can also ask your lecturer for the marking rubric, providing the detailed criteria for the assignment in advance. Many lecturers will provide it in advance if they believe in the concept of 'feed forward' in addition to 'feedback'. It doesn't hurt to ask. Following this, it might be worthwhile to confirm your understanding with either a tutor or an academic learning adviser.

Tutors or learning advisers won't edit drafts or help you write your paper. However, they can provide feedback about as the key points you intend to discuss, the overall structure of your assignment, any confusion surrounding referencing styles and the credibility sources. In addition, learning advisers can provide you with guides and links to websites for academic writing techniques. Your tutors and learning advisers are there to support you in your studies; however, it is up to you to seek out their assistance.

37c Formal Feedback

After submitting your assignment, you will most likely receive your mark and feedback within a few weeks. This will usually be in the form of written comments and perhaps a marking rubric. The feedback will identify strengths and weaknesses in your assignment and explain how well you addressed the marking criteria. It's important to read the feedback from your marker so that you can reflect upon how to improve your performance in the future. If, for example, your tutor has identified referencing skills as an area needing improvement, look more closely at referencing guides and engage with online tutorials.

Nobody enjoys failure. However, if you do receive a failing grade, see it as an opportunity to learn about where you went wrong and how you can avoid the problem in the future. A common reason for failing is that the student didn't seek out the kind of informal feedback discussed above and unfortunately misinterpreted the question. A sound writing style will not be enough to achieve a passing grade if the assignment content doesn't address the marking criteria. Whatever the reason for your grade, it's important to follow up with your marker and learning advisers to ensure that you understand the areas in which you need to improve. Their feedback is crucial for you to reflect upon your performance and develop an effective learning plan.

37d Learning Journal

Many students find it worthwhile to begin a learning journal as part of their reflective learning process and may also use it to record their learning plan. Once you have received feedback for a number of assignments, identify those issues that seem to form a common thread throughout. Using a learning journal in this way is particularly useful as it prompts you to find strategies and resources that will help you to address any skill deficits. It also provides a point of reference to evaluate your progress throughout your studies.

Students often place too much focus on their final grade rather than reflecting on and evaluating the formative feedback offered by their peers, tutors and support staff. Reflective practice plays an integral part in developing effective study habits and improving the quality of your assignments.

38 Job Presentation Skills

AT A *GLANCE*

- Writing a résumé or curriculum vitae (see 38b)
- Writing a covering letter (see 38c)
- Doing your best at an interview (see 38d)

38a Applying for a Position

Career centres in Most Australian and New Zealand universities provide information and support for graduate and undergraduate students looking for jobs. Visit the career centre a few months before you start job hunting. Sign up for résumé and interview workshops as well as job fairs and weekly newsletters with useful external links and position vacancies. The staff can give an overview of the job market, help with access to undergraduate and graduate programs and explain the recruitment process of specific employers.

Securing employment may involve applying for positions advertised on external online employment registers such as SEEK www.seek.com.au. Some students may be employed under a traineeship or on a casual contract and in these circumstances may be eligible to apply for positions advertised internally. Regardless of where you learn about a position vacancy, your application should always include a résumé and a covering letter.

38b The Résumé or Curriculum Vitae

Title page

The title page should state your full name and contact details. It's important to design a professional presentation, and your title page needs to create a positive first impression. There are a number of résumé templates available free of charge online and in Word™ with graphic design features already in place. There is no need to include your age, marital status or photo.

Key skills/accomplishments

Highlight those aspects of your résumé that are most relevant to the position you are applying for. Employers receive numerous applications for a position, and this will ensure that their focus is drawn to why you are the most suitable candidate.

Education details

Begin with either your highest qualification or the qualification most relevant to the position you are applying for. Details should include the title of the qualification, the year awarded and the institution.

Employment history

List positions chronologically, leading with the most recent or current position. The details should include the period of employment, the name of the employer, the position title and a brief description of the roles and responsibilities. If you don't have work experience, include volunteer work and relevant extracurricular activities.

Affiliations

List any professional association memberships or affiliations with any organisation that may be relevant to the position you are applying for.

References/Online presence

Most employers will request the contact details of at least two referees. If a referee is employed in the same industry or profession as the advertised position, include the referee's position title. Ask your referees for permission prior to using their names and provide them with background information on the position that they may be contacted about.

Recruiters will check your online presence, so ensure your privacy settings are up to date. Google yourself and remove all images and comments that may make you look unprofessional, including those in which you complain about potential employers or academic work. Some recruiters recommend opening a Twitter handle and/or LinkedIn profile to connect and network with potential employers. Keep those handles professional and use them to learn more about the industry that interests you.

Remember that your online presence is a reference too and gives potential employers an idea of who you are, what you like and how you behave when you interact with others.

The Covering Letter

The covering letter is as important as your résumé. Before you start writing, research the company on their website to learn as much as you can. Then, carefully read the selection criteria specified in the advertisement, and make notes for each of your responses to any selection criteria. Recruitment staff may cull applications that do not address the selection criteria correctly. When you are writing the letter, think about your audience and make sure you are sending clear messages. (Remember that each paragraph should help you establish your credibility.) You will need to write a covering letter for each position you are applying for (there are no one-size-fits-all formats). Ask a friend or fellow student to read the letter and give you feedback. Proofread and edit your letter before sending it to the recruiter.

The Interview

Research the organisation

If offered an interview, research the company's website again, check the annual reports and read the profiles of the company's directors or management. Be prepared to ask and respond to questions based on this information, as this will indicate your genuine commitment to a career with the organisation.

Practise responses

Prepare questions and practise responses prior to the interview. Again, study the selection criteria and look for clues about the types of questions you may be asked. If one criterion stated is 'able to work as part of a team', it is likely that you will be asked for evidence of this ability. If positions you have held did not require you to work as part of a team, relate the answer to group work at university, sports or a voluntary project in the community that you have participated in.

Arrive early

Confirm the time, date and place of the interview and aim to arrive 15 minutes early. It's a good idea to plan your route and refer to public transport timetables; if driving, listen to the traffic reports in the days leading up to the interview date. If you are too nervous to drive and don't have easy access to public transport, book a taxi the day before.

Make eye contact

During the interview, remember to direct your answers initially to the person who asked the question. If you are providing a lengthy answer, however, remember to include and make eye contact with the other members of the selection panel as well. You will probably be given the opportunity to ask questions at the end of the interview, and this is your chance to demonstrate your knowledge of the company. Refer to those questions you have prepared and ask any that have not been covered in the course of the interview. However, it's generally not a good strategy to ask about remuneration during the first interview. Only engage in negotiations after you have been offered the position—you'll be in a much stronger position at that point.

Ask for feedback

Whether you are successful or unsuccessful, it is worthwhile to ask for feedback regarding how you might improve your application and interview performance. You may not be able to contact the interview panel, but human resources personnel are usually able to provide some useful advice regarding your application. Be aware that not all companies are willing to provide feedback to unsuccessful candidates; the policy is usually stated in the notification letter or email, so read it carefully before requesting advice.

SMARTER WRITING

Nathalie Timmins, IT & Technical Recruiter at Amazon Web Services, has five tips to help you succeed in your job search.

1. If you don't have work experience, include in your résumé any volunteer and school project work that you have done.
2. When asked a question in an interview, always try to use a real-life example to demonstrate your skills in leadership, team work, decision making, results orientation and trustworthiness.
3. Be aware of your body language in an interview. Sit up straight, try not to fidget and make eye contact with the interviewer(s).
4. Practise answering interview questions and try not to use the same words all the time—that is, avoid using 'like' or 'obviously' in every sentence.
5. Remember to smile and show enthusiasm. There is no price on enthusiasm.

Glossary of Grammatical Terms and Usage

The glossary gives the definitions of grammatical terms and items of usage. The grammatical terms are shown in blue. Some of the explanations of usage that follow are not rules but guidelines to keep in mind for academic and professional writing. In these formal contexts, the safest course is to avoid words that are described as *non-standard, informal* or *colloquial.*

a/an Use *a* before words that begin with a consonant sound (*a train*, *a house*). Use *an* before words that begin with a vowel sound (*an avocado*, *an hour*).

a lot/alot *A lot* is generally regarded as informal; *alot* is not a word.

accept/except *Accept* is a verb meaning 'receive' or 'approve'. *Except* is sometimes a verb meaning 'leave out', but much more often it is used as a conjunction or preposition meaning 'other than'.

active A clause with a transitive verb in which the subject is the doer of the action (see Section 18a). See also passive.

adjective A modifier that qualifies or describes the qualities of a noun or pronoun (see Sections 27a and 27b).

adjective clause A subordinate clause that modifies a noun or pronoun and is usually introduced by a relative pronoun (see Section 27b). Sometimes called a *relative clause.*

adverb A word that modifies a verb, another modifier or a clause (see Sections 27a and 27c).

adverb clause A subordinate clause that functions as an adverb by modifying a verb, another modifier or a clause (see Section 27c).

advice/advise The noun *advice* means a 'suggestion'; the verb *advise* means to 'recommend' or 'give advice'.

affect/effect Usually, *affect* is a verb (to 'influence') and *effect* is a noun (a 'result'). Less commonly, *affect* is used as a noun and *effect* as a verb.

agreement The number and person of a subject and verb must match—singular subjects with singular verbs, plural subjects with plural verbs (see Chapter 23). Likewise, the number and gender of a pronoun and its antecedent must match (see Section 25b).

all ready/already The adjective phrase *all ready* means 'completely prepared'; the adverb *already* means 'previously'.

all right/alright *All right*, meaning 'acceptable', is the correct spelling. *Alright* is non-standard.

allude/elude *Allude* means 'refer to indirectly'; *elude* means 'evade'.

allusion/illusion An *allusion* is an indirect reference; an *illusion* is a false impression.

among/between *Between* refers to precisely two people or things; *among* refers to three or more.

amount/number Use *amount* with things that cannot be counted; use *number* with things that can be counted.

an See **a/an**.

antecedent The noun (or pronoun) that a pronoun refers to (see Section 25b).

anybody/any body; anyone/any one *Anybody* and *anyone* are indefinite pronouns and have the same meaning. In *any body*, *body* is a noun modified by *any*, and in *any one*, *one* is a pronoun or adjective modified by *any*.

anymore/any more *Anymore* means 'now', while *any more* means 'no more'. Both are used in negative constructions.

anyway/anyways *Anyway* is correct. *Anyways* is non-standard.

articles The words *a*, *an* and *the* (see Section 28b).

as/as if/as though/like Use *as* instead of *like* before dependent clauses (which include a subject and verb). Use *like* before a noun or a pronoun.

assure/ensure/insure *Assure* means 'promise', *ensure* means 'make certain' and *insure* means to 'make certain in either a legal or a financial sense'.

auxiliary verb Forms of *be*, *do* and *have* combine with verbs to indicate tense and mood (see Section 28c). The modal verbs *can*, *could*, *may*, *might*, *must*, *shall*, *should*, *will* and *would* are a subset of auxiliaries.

bad/badly Use *bad* only as an adjective. *Badly* is the adverb.

being as/being that Both constructions are colloquial and awkward substitutes for *because*. Don't use them in formal writing.

beside/besides *Beside* means 'next to'; *besides* means 'in addition to' or 'except'.

between See **among/between**.

bring/take *Bring* describes movement from a more distant location to a nearer one. *Take* describes movement away.

can/may In formal writing, *can* indicates ability or capacity, while *may* indicates permission.

case The form of a noun or pronoun that indicates its function. Nouns change case only to show possession: the dog, the dog's bowl. See **pronoun case** (Section 25a).

censor/censure To *censor* is to edit or ban on moral or political grounds. To *censure* is to reprimand publicly.

cite/sight/site To *cite* is to 'mention specifically'; *sight* as a verb means to 'observe' and as a noun refers to 'vision'; *site* is most commonly used as a noun that means 'location', but it is also used as a verb to mean 'situate'.

clause A group of words with a subject and a predicate. A main or independent clause can stand as a sentence. A subordinate or dependent clause must be attached to a main clause to form a sentence (see Section 20a).

collective noun A noun that refers to a group or a plurality, such as *team*, *army* or *committee* (see Section 23e).

comma splice Two independent clauses joined incorrectly by a comma (see Section 22d).

common noun A noun that names a general group, person, place or thing (see Section 28a). Common nouns are not capitalised unless they begin a sentence.

complement A word or group of words that completes the predicate. See also linking verb.

complement/compliment To *complement* something is to complete it or make it perfect; to *compliment* is to flatter.

complex sentence A sentence that contains at least one subordinate clause attached to a main clause.

compound sentence A sentence that contains at least two main clauses.

compound-complex sentence A sentence that contains at least two main clauses and one subordinate clause.

conjunction See coordinating conjunction and subordinating conjunction.

conjunctive adverb An adverb that often modifies entire clauses and sentences, such as *also*, *consequently*, *however*, *indeed*, *instead*, *moreover*, *nevertheless*, *otherwise*, *similarly* and *therefore* (see Section 27d).

continual/continuous *Continual* refers to a repeated activity; *continuous* refers to an ongoing, unceasing activity.

coordinate A relationship of equal importance, in terms of either grammar or meaning (see Section 20c).

coordinating conjunction A word that links two equivalent grammatical elements, such as *for*, *and*, *nor*, *but*, *or*, *yet* and *so*.

could of Non-standard. See **have/of**.

countable noun A noun that names things that can be counted, such as *block*, *cat* and *toy* (see Section 28a).

dangling modifier A modifier that isn't clearly attached to what it modifies (see Section 27c).

data The plural form of *datum*; it takes plural verb forms.

declarative A sentence that makes a statement.

dependent clause See subordinate clause.

determiners Words that initiate noun phrases, including possessive nouns (*Paul's*); possessive pronouns (*my*, *your*); demonstrative pronouns (*this*, *that*); and indefinite pronouns (*all*, *both*, *many*).

differ from/differ with To *differ from* means to 'be unlike'; to *differ with* means to 'disagree'.

different from/different than Use *different from* where possible.

Dark French roast is different from ordinary coffee.

direct object A noun, pronoun or noun clause that names who or what receives the action of a transitive verb.

discreet/discrete Both are adjectives. *Discreet* means 'prudent' or 'tactful'; *discrete* means 'separate'.

disinterested/uninterested *Disinterested* is often misused to mean *uninterested*. Disinterested means 'impartial'. A judge can be interested in a case but disinterested in the outcome.

double negative The incorrect use of two negatives to signal the same negative meaning.

due to the fact that Avoid this wordy substitute for *because*.

each other/one another Use *each other* for two; use *one another* for more than two.

effect See **affect/effect**.

elicit/illicit The verb *elicit* means to 'draw out'. The adjective *illicit* means 'unlawful'.

emigrate from/immigrate to *Emigrate* means to 'leave one's country'; *immigrate* means to 'settle in another country'.

ensure See **assure/ensure/insure**.

enthused Non-standard in academic and professional writing. Use *enthusiastic* instead.

etc. Avoid this abbreviation for the Latin *et cetera* in formal writing. Either list all the items or use an English phrase such as *and so forth*.

every body/everybody; every one/everyone *Everybody* and *everyone* are indefinite pronouns referring to all people under discussion. *Every one* and *every body* are adjective–noun combinations referring to all members of a group.

except See **accept/except**.

except for the fact that Avoid this wordy substitute for *except that*.

expletive The dummy subjects *it* and *there* used to fill a grammatical slot in a sentence. *It is raining outside. There should be a law against it.*

explicit/implicit Both are adjectives; *explicit* means 'stated outright', while *implicit* means just the opposite, 'unstated'.

farther/further *Farther* refers to physical distance; *further* refers to time or other abstract concepts.

fewer/less Use *fewer* with what can be counted and *less* with what cannot be counted.

flunk In formal writing, avoid this colloquial substitute for *fail.*

fragment A group of words beginning with a capital letter and ending with a full stop that looks like a sentence but lacks a subject or a predicate or both (see Section 22b).

further See **farther/further**.

gerund An *-ing* form of a verb used as a noun, such as *running*, *skiing* or *laughing*.

good/well *Good* is an adjective and is not interchangeable with the adverb *well.* The one exception is health. Both she feels *good* and she feels *well* are correct.

hanged/hung Use *hanged* to refer only to executions; *hung* is used for all other instances.

have/of *Have*, not *of*, follows *should*, *could*, *would*, *may*, *must* and *might*.

he/she; s/he Try to avoid language that appears to exclude either gender (unless this is intended, of course) and awkward compromises such as *he/she* or *s/he*. The best solution is to make pronouns plural (the gender-neutral *they*) wherever possible (see Section 25c).

helping verb See auxiliary verb.

hopefully This adverb is commonly used as a sentence modifier, but many readers object to it.

illusion See **allusion/illusion**.

immigrate See **emigrate from/immigrate to**.

imperative A sentence that expresses a command. Usually the subject is implied rather than stated.

implicit See **explicit/implicit**.

imply/infer *Imply* means to 'suggest'; *infer* means to 'draw a conclusion'.

in regards to Avoid this wordy substitute for *regarding*.

incredible/incredulous *Incredible* means 'unbelievable'; *incredulous* means 'not believing'.

independent clause See main clause.

indirect object A noun, pronoun or noun clause that names who or what is affected by the action of a transitive verb.

infinitive The word *to* plus the base verb form: *to believe*, *to feel*, *to act*. See also split infinitive.

infinitive phrase A phrase that uses the infinitive form of a verb.

interjection A word expressing feeling that is grammatically unconnected to a sentence, such as *cool*, *wow*, *ouch* or *yikes*.

interrogative A sentence that asks a question.

intransitive verb A verb that doesn't take an object, such as *sleep*, *appear* or *laugh* (see Sections 24c and 28c).

irregardless Non-standard for *regardless*.

irregular verb A verb that doesn't use either *-d* or *-ed* to form the past tense and past participle (see Section 24b).

-ise/-wise The suffix *-ise* changes a noun or adjective into a verb (*harmony*, *harmonise*). The suffix *-wise* changes a noun or adjective into an adverb (*clock*, *clockwise*). Some writers are tempted to use these suffixes to convert almost any word into an adverb or verb form. Unless the word appears in a dictionary, don't use it.

it is my opinion that Avoid this wordy substitute for *I believe that*.

its/it's *Its* is the possessive of *it* and doesn't take an apostrophe; *it's* is the contraction for *it is*.

kind of/sort of/type of Avoid using these colloquial expressions if you mean *somewhat* or *rather*. *It's kind of hot* is non-standard. Each is permissible, however, when it refers to a classification of an object. Be sure that it agrees in number with the object it is modifying.

lay/lie *Lay* means 'place' or 'put' and generally takes a direct object (see Section 24c). Its main forms are *lay*, *laid*, *laid*. *Lie* means 'recline' or 'be positioned' and doesn't take an object. Its main forms are *lie*, *lay*, *lain*.

less See **fewer/less**.

lie See **lay/lie**.

linking verb A verb that connects the subject to the complement, such as *appear*, *be*, *feel*, *look*, *seem* or *taste*.

lots/lots of Non-standard in formal writing; use *many* or *much* instead.

main clause A group of words with a subject and a predicate that can stand alone as a sentence. Also called an *independent clause*.

mankind This term offends some readers and is outdated. Use *humans*, *humanity* or *people* instead.

may/can See **can/may**.

may be/maybe *May be* is a verb phrase; *maybe* is an adverb.

media This is the plural form of the noun *medium* and requires a plural verb.

might of See **have/of**.

modal A kind of auxiliary verb that indicates ability, permission, intention, obligation or probability, such as *can*, *could*, *may*, *might*, *must*, *shall*, *should*, *will* or *would*.

modifier A general term for adjectives, adverbs, phrases and clauses that describe other words (see Chapter 27).

must of See **have/of**.

non-restrictive modifier A modifier that isn't essential to the meaning of the word, phrase or clause it modifies and should be set off by commas or other punctuation (see Section 29c).

noun The name of a person, place, thing, concept or action. See also common noun and proper noun (see Section 28a).

noun clause A subordinate clause that functions as a noun.

number See **amount/number**.

object Receiver of the action within the clause or phrase.

OK, okay Informal; avoid using in academic and professional writing. Either spelling is accepted in informal usage.

owing to the fact that Avoid this wordy, colloquial substitute for *because*.

parallelism The principle of putting similar elements or ideas in similar grammatical form (see Section 20c).

participle A form of a verb that uses *-ing* in the present (*laughing*, *playing*) and usually *-ed* or *-en* in the past (*laughed*, *played*). See Section 24a. Participles are either part of the verb phrase (*She had played the game before*) or used as adjectives (*the laughing girl*).

participial phrase A phrase formed either by a present participle (for example, *racing*) or by a past participle (for example, *taken*).

parts of speech The eight classes of words according to their grammatical function: nouns, pronouns, verbs, adjectives, adverbs, prepositions, conjunctions and interjections.

passive A clause with a transitive verb in which the subject is being acted upon (see Section 18a). See also active.

people/persons *People* refers to a general group; *persons* refers to a collection of individuals. Use *people* over *persons* except when you are emphasising the idea of separate persons within the group.

per Try not to use the English equivalent of this Latin word except in technical writing or familiar usages such as *kilometres per litre*.

phenomena This is the plural form of *phenomenon* ('observable fact' or 'unusual event') and takes plural verbs.

phrase A group of words that doesn't contain both a subject and a predicate.

plenty In academic and professional writing, avoid this colloquial substitute for *very*.

plus Don't use *plus* to join clauses or sentences. Use *and*, *also*, *moreover*, *furthermore* or another conjunctive adverb instead.

precede/proceed Both are verbs but they have different meanings: *precede* means 'come before'; *proceed* means 'go ahead' or 'continue'.

predicate The part of the clause that expresses the action or tells something about the subject. The predicate includes the verb and all its complements, objects and modifiers.

prejudice/prejudiced *Prejudice* is a noun; *prejudiced* is an adjective.

preposition A class of words that indicate relationships and qualities.

prepositional phrase A phrase formed by a preposition and its object, including the modifiers of its object.

pronoun A word that stands for other nouns or pronouns. Pronouns have several subclasses, including personal pronouns, possessive pronouns, demonstrative pronouns, indefinite pronouns, relative pronouns, interrogative pronouns, reflexive pronouns and reciprocal pronouns (see Chapter 25).

pronoun case Pronouns that function as the subjects of sentences are in the subjective case (*I*, *you*, *he*, *she*, *it*, *we*, *they*). Pronouns that function as direct or indirect objects are in the objective case (*me*, *you*, *him*, *her*, *it*, *us*, *them*). Pronouns that indicate ownership are in the possessive case (*my*, *your*, *his*, *her*, *its*, *our*, *their*). See Section 25a.

proper noun A noun that names a particular person, place, thing or group (see Section 28a). Proper nouns are capitalised.

question as to whether/question of whether Avoid these wordy substitutes for *whether*.

raise/rise The verb *raise* means 'lift up' and takes a direct object. Its main forms are *raise*, *raised*, *raised*. The verb *rise* means 'get up' and doesn't take a direct object. Its main forms are *rise*, *rose*, *risen*.

real/really Avoid using *real* as if it were an adverb. *Really* is an adverb; *real* is an adjective.

reason is because Omit either *reason is* or *because* when explaining causality.

reason why Avoid using this redundant combination.

relative pronoun A pronoun that initiates clauses, such as *that*, *which*, *what*, *who*, *whom* or *whose*.

restrictive modifier A modifier that is essential to the meaning of the word, phrase or clause it modifies (see Section 29c). Restrictive modifiers are usually not set off by punctuation.

rise/raise See **raise/rise**.

run-on sentence Two main clauses fused together without punctuation or a conjunction, appearing as one sentence (see Section 22c).

sentence A grammatically independent group of words that contains at least one main clause.

sentence fragment See fragment.

set/sit *Set* means 'put' and takes a direct object; its main forms are *set*, *set*, *set*. *Sit* means 'be seated' and doesn't take a direct object; its main forms are *sit*, *sat*, *sat*. *Sit* should not be used as a synonym for *set*.

shall/will *Shall* is used most often in first person questions, while *will* is a future tense helping verb for all persons. British English consistently uses *shall* with first person: *I shall*, *we shall*.

should of See **have/of**.

sit/set See **set/sit**.

some time/sometime/sometimes *Some time* means 'a span of time', *sometime* means 'at some unspecified time' and *sometimes* means 'occasionally'.

somebody/some body; someone/some one *Somebody* and *someone* are indefinite pronouns and have the same meaning. In *some body*, *body* is a noun modified by *some*, and in *some one*, *one* is a pronoun or adjective modified by *some*.

sort of See **kind of/sort of/type of**.

split infinitive An infinitive with a word or words between *to* and the base verb form, such as *to boldly go*, *to better appreciate*.

stationary/stationery *Stationary* means 'motionless'; *stationery* means 'writing paper'.

subject A noun, pronoun or noun phrase that identifies what the clause is about and connects with the predicate.

subject–verb agreement See agreement.

subordinate A relationship of unequal importance, in terms of either grammar or meaning.

subordinate clause A clause that cannot stand alone but must be attached to a main clause (see Section 20a). Also called a *dependent clause*.

subordinating conjunction A word that introduces a subordinate clause. Common subordinating conjunctions are *after*, *although*, *as*, *because*, *before*, *if*, *since*, *that*, *unless*, *until*, *when*, *where* and *while*.

such Avoid using *such* as a synonym for *very*. *Such* should always be followed by *that* and a clause that contains a result.

sure A colloquial term used as an adverb to mean 'certainly'. Avoid using it this way in formal writing.

sure and/sure to; try and/try to *Sure to* and *try to* are correct; don't use *and* after *sure* or *try*.

take See **bring/take**.

that/which *That* introduces a restrictive or essential clause. Restrictive clauses describe an object that must be that particular object and no other. Though some writers occasionally use *which* with restrictive clauses, it is most often used to introduce non-restrictive clauses. These are clauses that contain additional non-essential information about the object (see Section 29c).

transition A word or phrase that notes movement from one unit of writing to another.

transitive verb A verb that takes a direct object (see Section 24c).

type of See **kind of/sort of/type of**.

uncountable noun A noun that names things that cannot be counted, such as *air*, *energy* or *water* (see Section 28a).

verb A word that expresses action or characterises the subject in some way. Verbs can show tense and mood (see Chapter 24 and Section 28c).

verbal A form of a verb used as an adjective, adverb or noun. See also gerund, infinitive, participle.

well/good See **good/well**.

which/that See **that/which**.

who/whom *Who* and *whom* follow the same rules as other pronouns: *who* is the subject pronoun; *whom* is the object pronoun (see Section 25a).

will/shall See **shall/will**.

-wise/-ise See **-ise/-wise**.

would of See **have/of**.

you Avoid indefinite uses of *you*. It should only be used to mean 'you, the reader'.

your/you're The two are not interchangeable. *Your* is the possessive form of 'you'; *you're* is the contraction of 'you are'.

Index

Note: Page numbers in **bold** indicate definition of a key term.

REVISION GUIDE

Commonly used editing and proofreading symbols are listed here, along with references to the relevant chapters and sections of this handbook.

Words, sentences and paragraphs

abbr	Abbreviation problem: 35c
adj	Adjective problem: 27a, 27b
adv	Adverb problem: 27a, 27d
agr	Agreement problem, either subject–verb or pronoun–antecedent: 23, 25b
apos	Apostrophe missing or misused: 32
art	Article is missing or misused: 28b
cap	Capitalisation is needed: 35a
case	Case of a pronoun is incorrect: 25a
coh	Coherence lacking in a paragraph: 3e, 3f, 4b
cs	Comma splice occurs: 22d
dm	Dangling modifier appears: 27c
frag	Fragment instead of complete sentence: 22b
ital	Italics missing or misused: 35b
lc	Lower case needed: 35a
mm	Misplaced modifier: 27b, 27c
num	Number problem: 35e
p	Punctuation problem: 29–34
pass	Passive voice misused: 18a
pl	Plural form misused or needed: 28a
pron	Pronoun problem: 25
ref	Reference of a pronoun unclear: 25d
run-on	Run-on sentence problem: 22c
sexist	Sexist language: 21d
sp	Spelling needs to be checked: 4d
sub	Subordination is faulty: 20a
trans	Transition misused or needed: 4c
vb	Verb problem: 24
w	Wordy: 19
ww	Wrong word: 21
¶	Paragraph break needed: 3f
no ¶	No paragraph break needed: 3f
//	Parallelism needs to be checked: 20c

Punctuation and mechanics

^	Comma needed: 29
ʼ	Apostrophe needed: 32
“ ”	Quotation marks needed: 33
⊙	Full stop needed: 34a
?	Question mark needed: 34b
!	Exclamation mark needed: 34c
—	Dash needed: 31
. . .	Ellipsis needed: 34e
( )	Parentheses needed: 31
[ ]	Brackets needed: 34d
#	Add a space
⁀	Close up a space
~	Delete this
^	Insert something
∽	Transpose (switch the order)